Responsive Web Design
with HTML5 and CSS3
Second Edition

Build responsive and future-proof websites to meet
the demands of modern web users

Ben Frain

[PACKT]
PUBLISHING

BIRMINGHAM - MUMBAI

Responsive Web Design with HTML5 and CSS3
Second Edition

First published: April 2012

Second edition: August 2015

Production reference: 2200815

Published by Packt Publishing Ltd.
Livery Place
35 Livery Street
Birmingham B3 2PB, UK.

ISBN 978-1-78439-893-4

www.packtpub.com

Credits

Author
Ben Frain

Reviewers
Esteban S. Abait
Christopher Scott Hernandez
Mauvis Ledford
Sophie Williams

Commissioning Editor
Edward Gordon

Acquisition Editors
Edward Gordon
Subho Gupta

Content Development Editor
Pooja Nair

Technical Editor
Ankita Thakur

Copy Editors
Rebecca Youé
Sonia Cheema

Project Coordinator
Bijal Patel

Proofreader
Safis Editing

Indexer
Mariammal Chettiyar

Production Coordinator
Nilesh R. Mohite

Cover Work
Nilesh R. Mohite

About the Author

Ben Frain has been a web designer/developer since 1996. He is currently employed as a Senior Front-end Developer at Bet365.

Before the web, he worked as an underrated (and modest) TV actor and technology journalist, having graduated from Salford University with a degree in Media and Performance.

He has written four equally underrated (his opinion) screenplays and still harbors the (fading) belief he might sell one. Outside of work, he enjoys simple pleasures. Playing indoor football while his body and wife still allow it, and wrestling with his two sons.

His other book, *Sass and Compass for Designers* is available now. Visit Ben online at www.benfrain.com and follow him on Twitter at twitter.com/benfrain.

I'd like to thank the technical reviewers of this book for giving up their free time to provide valuable input. Thanks to them, this is a better product.

I'd also like to thank the web community at large for their continued sharing of information. Without them, I wouldn't be able to enjoy my working days as a web developer.

Most importantly, a note of appreciation for my family. Many episodes of sub-standard TV (wife), cups of tea (parents), and piratical sword-fights (sons) were sacrificed for the writing of this book.

About the Reviewers

Esteban S. Abait is a senior software architect and former PhD student. He has experience devising the architecture of complex software products, and planning their development. He has worked both onsite and offshore for clients such as Cisco, Intuit, and Southwest. Throughout his career, he has worked with different technologies such as Java, PHP, Ruby, and Node.js among others. In recent years, his main interests have revolved around web, mobile and REST APIs. He has developed large, maintainable web applications using JavaScript. In addition, he has worked to assess clients on REST best practices. On the other hand, he has worked on high traffic websites, where topics such as replication, sharding, or distributed caches are key to scalability.

Esteban is currently working at Globant as a technical director. In this role, he works to ensure projects' delivery meet their deadlines with the best quality. He also designs software program training, and interviews software developers. In addition, he usually travels to clients to provide consultancy on web technologies.

Globant (http://www.globant.com/) is a new breed of technology service provider, focused on delivering innovative software solutions by leveraging emerging technologies and trends. Globant combines the engineering and technical rigor of IT service providers with the creative and cultural approach of digital agencies. Globant is the place where engineering, design, and innovation meet scale.

Christopher Scott Hernandez is a designer turned developer who has been working on the Web since 1996, when he built the Web's first boat upholstery site for his dad. He's since moved on to bring his expertise to companies small and large, having worked on some of the most visited sites in the world including eBay, LinkedIn, and Apple.

He was also a technical reviewer for *HTML5 Multimedia Development Cookbook, Packt Publishing*. Chris is an avid reader and lover of books. When he's not pushing pixels and writing code, he enjoys spending time with his wife and daughter exploring the parks and trails of the beautiful Austin, Texas.

Mauvis Ledford is a full-stack founder and CTO specializing in the realm of the web, mobile web, and scaling applications on the cloud.

Mauvis has contributed to products at Disney Mobile, Skype, Netflix, and many start-ups in the San Francisco and New York City areas. He is currently CTO at Pathbrite, an EdTech start-up specializing in free, responsive, multimedia e-portfolios and digital resumes for everyone. Create your own at http://www.pathbrite.com.

Mauvis was also a technical reviewer for the first edition of *Responsive Web Design with HTML5 and CSS3, Packt Publishing* and *Building Hybrid Android Apps with Java and JavaScript, O'Reilly Media*.

Sophie Williams is a bit of a perfectionist and has a thing for typography. She has a degree in graphic design and is currently a web/UI designer at www.bet365.com. While she loves designing for the Web, she will always have a special place in her heart for letterpress and print. Outside of work, she makes mean cupcakes, experiments with arts and crafts, and loves to point out (to anyone who will listen) when anything in the real world is misaligned.

You can find Sophie at www.sophiewill.com or follow her on Twitter @sophiewill13.

www.PacktPub.com

Support files, eBooks, discount offers, and more

For support files and downloads related to your book, please visit www.PacktPub.com.

Did you know that Packt offers eBook versions of every book published, with PDF and ePub files available? You can upgrade to the eBook version at www.PacktPub.com and as a print book customer, you are entitled to a discount on the eBook copy. Get in touch with us at service@packtpub.com for more details.

At www.PacktPub.com, you can also read a collection of free technical articles, sign up for a range of free newsletters, and receive exclusive discounts and offers on Packt books and eBooks.

https://www2.packtpub.com/books/subscription/packtlib

Do you need instant solutions to your IT questions? PacktLib is Packt's online digital book library. Here, you can search, access, and read Packt's entire library of books.

Why subscribe?

- Fully searchable across every book published by Packt
- Copy and paste, print, and bookmark content
- On demand and accessible via a web browser

Free access for Packt account holders

If you have an account with Packt at www.PacktPub.com, you can use this to access PacktLib today and view 9 entirely free books. Simply use your login credentials for immediate access.

Table of Contents

Preface ix

Chapter 1: The Essentials of Responsive Web Design 1

Beginning our quest 2
Defining responsive web design 2
Responsive web design in a nutshell 2
Setting browser support levels 3
A brief note on tooling and text editors 5
Our first responsive example 5
Our basic HTML file 6
Taming images 9
Enter media queries 12
Amending the example for a larger screen 13
The shortcomings of our example 17
Summary 17

Chapter 2: Media Queries – Supporting Differing Viewports 19

Why media queries are needed for a responsive web design 20
Basic conditional logic in CSS 21
Media query syntax 21
Media queries in link tags 22
Combining media queries 23
Media queries with @import 24
Media queries in CSS 24
What can media queries test for? 25
Using media queries to alter a design 26
Any CSS can be wrapped in a media query 28
Media queries for HiDPI devices 28
Considerations for organizing and authoring media queries 29
Linking to different CSS files with media queries 29

The practicalities of separating media queries	30
Nesting media queries 'inline'	30
Combine media queries or write them where it suits?	**31**
The viewport meta tag	**33**
Media Queries Level 4	**35**
Scripting media feature	35
Interaction media features	36
The hover media feature	37
Environment media features	38
Summary	**38**
Chapter 3: Fluid Layouts and Responsive Images	**39**
Converting a fixed pixel design to a fluid proportional layout	**40**
Why do we need Flexbox?	45
Inline block and whitespace	45
Floats	45
Table and table-cell	46
Introducing Flexbox	**46**
The bumpy path to Flexbox	47
Browser support for Flexbox	47
Leave prefixing to someone else	47
Getting Flexy	**49**
Perfect vertically centered text	49
Offset items	50
Reverse the order of items	52
How about if we want them laid out vertically instead?	53
Column reverse	53
Different Flexbox layouts inside different media queries	53
Inline-flex	54
Flexbox alignment properties	55
The align-items property	57
The align-self property	58
Possible alignment values	59
The justify-content property	59
The flex property	61
Simple sticky footer	64
Changing source order	65
Wrapping up Flexbox	71
Responsive images	**71**
The intrinsic problem of responsive images	71
Simple resolution switching with srcset	72
Advanced switching with srcset and sizes	73
Did you say the browser 'might' pick one image over another?	74

Art direction with the picture element 74
Facilitate new-fangled image formats 75
Summary **76**
Chapter 4: HTML5 for Responsive Web Designs **77**
HTML5 markup – understood by all modern browsers **78**
Starting an HTML5 page the right way **79**
The doctype 79
The HTML tag and lang attribute 80
Specifying alternate languages 80
Character encoding 81
Easy-going HTML5 **81**
A sensible approach to HTML5 markup 82
All hail the mighty <a> tag 83
New semantic elements in HTML5 **83**
The <main> element 84
The <section> element 85
The <nav> element 85
The <article> element 86
The <aside> element 86
The <figure> and <figcaption> elements 86
The <details> and <summary> elements 87
The <header> element 89
The <footer> element 89
The <address> element 90
A note on h1-h6 elements 90
HTML5 text-level semantics **91**
The <b> element 91
The <em> element 91
The <i> element 91
Obsolete HTML features **92**
Putting HTML5 elements to use **93**
Applying common sense to your element selection 94
WCAG and WAI-ARIA for more accessible web applications **94**
WCAG 94
WAI-ARIA 95
Don't use roles for semantic elements 95
If you only remember one thing 96
Taking ARIA further 96
Embedding media in HTML5 **97**
Adding video and audio the HTML5 way 97
Fallback capability for older browsers 99

Audio and video tags work almost identically   99
Responsive HTML5 video and iFrames   **99**
A note about 'offline first'   **101**
Summary   **102**
Chapter 5: CSS3 – Selectors, Typography, Color Modes,
and New Features   **103**
No one knows it all   **104**
Anatomy of a CSS rule   **104**
Quick and useful CSS tricks   **105**
CSS multi-column layouts for responsive designs   105
Fixed columns, variable width   107
Adding a gap and column divider   107
Word wrapping   **108**
Text ellipsis   109
Creating horizontal scrolling panels   110
Facilitating feature forks in CSS   **112**
Feature queries   112
Combining conditionals   114
Modernizr   114
Feature detection with Modernizr   115
New CSS3 selectors and how to use them   **116**
CSS3 attribute selectors   117
CSS3 substring matching attribute selectors   117
The 'beginning with' substring matching attribute selector   118
The 'contains an instance of' substring matching attribute selector   118
The 'ends with' substring matching attribute selector   119
Gotchas with attribute selection   119
Attribute selectors allow you to select IDs and classes that start
with numbers   120
CSS3 structural pseudo-classes   **121**
The :last-child selector   121
The nth-child selectors   122
Understanding what nth rules do   122
Breaking down the math   123
nth-based selection in responsive web designs   125
The negation (:not) selector   128
The empty (:empty) selector   129
Do something with the :first-line regardless of viewport   130
CSS custom properties and variables   **130**
CSS calc   **131**
CSS Level 4 selectors   **131**
The :has pseudo class   132

Responsive viewport-percentage lengths (vmax, vmin, vh, vw)   132
Web typography   **133**
The @font-face CSS rule   133
Implementing web fonts with @font-face   134
A note about custom @font-face typography and responsive designs   136
New CSS3 color formats and alpha transparency   **137**
RGB color   137
HSL color   138
Alpha channels   139
Color manipulation with CSS Color Module Level 4   140
Summary   **140**
Chapter 6: Stunning Aesthetics with CSS3   **141**
Text shadows with CSS3   **142**
Omitting the blur value when not needed   143
Multiple text shadows   143
Box shadows   **144**
An inset shadow   144
Multiple shadows   145
Understanding spread   145
Background gradients   **146**
The linear-gradient notation   147
Specifying gradient direction   147
Color stops   148
Adding fallback for older browsers   149
Radial background gradients   149
Breakdown of the radial-gradient syntax   150
Handy 'extent' keywords for responsive sizing   150
Repeating gradients   **151**
Background gradient patterns   **152**
Multiple background images   **154**
Background size   155
Background position   155
Background shorthand   156
High-resolution background images   **157**
CSS filters   **158**
Available CSS filters   159
Combining CSS filters   164
A warning on CSS performance   **165**
A note on CSS masks and clipping   166
Summary   **167**

Chapter 7: Using SVGs for Resolution Independence	**169**
A brief history of SVG	**171**
The graphic that is a document	**172**
The root SVG element	173
Namespace	174
The title and desc tags	174
The defs tag	174
The g element	175
SVG shapes	175
SVG paths	175
Creating SVGs with popular image editing packages and services	**176**
Save time with SVG icon services	176
Inserting SVGs into your web pages	**177**
Using an img tag	178
Using an object tag	178
Insert an SVG as a background image	179
A brief aside on data URIs	180
Generating image sprites	181
Inserting an SVG inline	**182**
Re-using graphical objects from symbols	183
Inline SVGs allow different colors in different contexts	185
Make dual-tone icons that inherit the color of their parent	185
Re-using graphical objects from external sources	186
What you can do with each SVG insertion method (inline, object,	
background-image, and img)	**187**
Browser schisms	188
Extra SVG capabilities and oddities	**188**
SMIL animation	188
The end of SMIL	189
Styling an SVG with an external style sheet	190
Styling an SVG with internal styles	191
SVG properties and values within CSS	191
Animate an SVG with CSS	191
Animating SVG with JavaScript	**193**
A simple example of animating an SVG with GreenSock	194
Optimising SVGs	**196**
Using SVGs as filters	**196**
A note on media queries inside SVGs	**199**
Implementation tips	200
Further resources	201
Summary	**201**

Chapter 8: Transitions, Transformations, and Animations   203

What CSS3 transitions are and how we can use them   204
The properties of a transition   206
The transition shorthand property   207
Transition different properties over different periods of time   208
Understanding timing functions   208
Fun transitions for responsive websites   210

CSS3 2D transforms   210
Scale   211
Translate   212
    Using translate to center absolutely positioned elements   212
Rotate   214
Skew   215
Matrix   215
    Matrix transformations for cheats and dunces   216
The transform-origin property   217

CSS3 3D transformations   218
The transform3d property   221
    Use transforms with progressive enhancement   222

Animating with CSS3   225
The animation-fill-mode property   228

Summary   230

Chapter 9: Conquer Forms with HTML5 and CSS3   231

HTML5 forms   232

Understanding the component parts of HTML5 forms   233
placeholder   234
    Styling the placeholder text   234
required   234
autofocus   236
autocomplete   236
List and the associated datalist element   237

HTML5 input types   239
email   239
number   240
    min and max ranges   241
    Changing the step increments   241
url   242
tel   243
search   244
pattern   245
color   246

Date and time inputs   246
    date   247
    month   247
    week   248
    time   249
   range   249
How to polyfill non-supporting browsers   **250**
Styling HTML5 forms with CSS3   **251**
   Indicating required fields   254
   Creating a background fill effect   256
Summary   **257**
Chapter 10: Approaching a Responsive Web Design   **259**
Get designs in the browser as soon as possible   **260**
   Let the design dictate the breakpoints   260
View and use the design on real devices   **261**
Embracing progressive enhancement   **262**
Defining a browser support matrix   **263**
   Functional parity, not aesthetic parity   263
   Choosing the browsers to support   263
Tiering the user experience   **264**
   Practically delivering experience tiers   264
Linking CSS breakpoints to JavaScript   **265**
Avoid CSS frameworks in production   **267**
Coding pragmatic solutions   **268**
   When a link becomes a button   269
Use the simplest code possible   **270**
Hiding, showing, and loading content across viewports   **271**
   Let CSS do the (visual) heavy lifting   272
Validators and linting tools   **272**
Performance   **274**
The next big things   **275**
Summary   **276**
Index   **277**

Preface

A responsive web design provides a single solution that looks great on a phone, desktop, and everything in-between. It will effortlessly respond to the size of the user's screen, providing the best experience possible for both today's and tomorrow's devices.

This book covers every essential aspect of responsive web design. In addition, it extends the responsive design methodology by applying the latest and most useful techniques provided by HTML5 and CSS3, making designs leaner and more maintainable than ever before. It also explains common best practice methods of writing and delivering code, images, and files.

If you can understand HTML and CSS, you can build a responsive web design.

What this book covers

Chapter 1, The Essentials of Responsive Web Design, is a whistle-stop tour of the key ingredients in coding a responsive web design.

Chapter 2, Media Queries – Supporting Differing Viewports, covers everything you need to know about CSS media queries: their capabilities, their syntaxes, and the various ways you can wield them.

Chapter 3, Fluid Layouts and Responsive Images, shows you how to code proportional layouts and responsive images, and provides a thorough exploration of Flexbox layouts.

Chapter 4, HTML5 for Responsive Web Designs, covers all the semantic elements of HTML5, text-level semantics, and considerations of accessibility. We also cover how to insert video and audio into our pages with HTML5.

Chapter 5, CSS3 – Selectors, Typography, Color Modes, and New Features, gets to grips with the endless possibilities of CSS: selectors, HSLA and RGBA colors, web typography, viewport relative units, and a whole lot more.

Chapter 6, Stunning Aesthetics with CSS3, covers CSS filters, box shadows, linear and radial gradients, multiple backgrounds, and how to target background images to high-resolution devices.

Chapter 7, Using SVGs for Resolution Independence, explains everything we need to use SVGs inside documents and as background images, as well as how to interact with them using JavaScript.

Chapter 8, Transitions, Transformations, and Animations, our CSS gets moving as we explore how to make interactions and animations using CSS.

Chapter 9, Conquer Forms with HTML5 and CSS3, web forms have always been tough but the latest HTML5 and CSS3 features make them easier to deal with than ever before.

Chapter 10, Approaching a Responsive Web Design, explores the essential considerations before embarking on a responsive web design and also provides a few last minute nuggets of wisdom to aid you in your responsive quest.

What you need for this book

- A text editor
- An evergreen browser
- A penchant for mediocre jokes

Who this book is for

Are you writing two websites: one for mobile and one for larger displays? Or perhaps you've already implemented your first 'RWD' but are struggling to bring it all together? If so, *Responsive Web Design with HTML5 and CSS3 Second Edition* gives you everything you need to take your websites to the next level.

You'll need some HTML and CSS knowledge to follow along, but everything you need to know about responsive design and making great websites is included in the book!

Conventions

In this book, you will find a number of text styles that distinguish between different kinds of information. Here are some examples of these styles and an explanation of their meaning.

Code words in text, database table names, folder names, filenames, file extensions, pathnames, dummy URLs, user input, and Twitter handles are shown as follows: "We can fix that prior problem easily by adding this snippet in the `<head>`."

A block of code is set as follows:

```
img {
    max-width: 100%;
}
```

New terms and **important words** are shown in bold. Words that you see on the screen, for example, in menus or dialog boxes, appear in the text like this: "At its simplest, you pick a URL and click on **START TEST**."

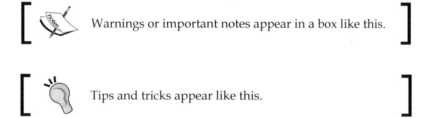

> Warnings or important notes appear in a box like this.

> Tips and tricks appear like this.

Reader feedback

Feedback from our readers is always welcome. Let us know what you think about this book—what you liked or disliked. Reader feedback is important for us as it helps us develop titles that you will really get the most out of.

To send us general feedback, simply e-mail `feedback@packtpub.com`, and mention the book's title in the subject of your message.

If there is a topic that you have expertise in and you are interested in either writing or contributing to a book, see our author guide at `www.packtpub.com/authors`.

Customer support

Now that you are the proud owner of a Packt book, we have a number of things to help you to get the most from your purchase.

Downloading the example code

You can download the example code files from your account at `http://www.packtpub.com` for all the Packt Publishing books you have purchased. If you purchased this book elsewhere, you can visit `http://www.packtpub.com/support` and register to have the files e-mailed directly to you.

Downloading the color images of this book

We also provide you with a PDF file that has color images of the screenshots/ diagrams used in this book. The color images will help you better understand the changes in the output. You can download this file from: `https://www.packtpub.com/sites/default/files/downloads/8934OT_ColorImages.pdf`.

Errata

Although we have taken every care to ensure the accuracy of our content, mistakes do happen. If you find a mistake in one of our books—maybe a mistake in the text or the code—we would be grateful if you could report this to us. By doing so, you can save other readers from frustration and help us improve subsequent versions of this book. If you find any errata, please report them by visiting `http://www.packtpub.com/submit-errata`, selecting your book, clicking on the **Errata Submission Form** link, and entering the details of your errata. Once your errata are verified, your submission will be accepted and the errata will be uploaded to our website or added to any list of existing errata under the Errata section of that title.

To view the previously submitted errata, go to `https://www.packtpub.com/books/content/support` and enter the name of the book in the search field. The required information will appear under the **Errata** section.

Piracy

Piracy of copyrighted material on the Internet is an ongoing problem across all media. At Packt, we take the protection of our copyright and licenses very seriously. If you come across any illegal copies of our works in any form on the Internet, please provide us with the location address or website name immediately so that we can pursue a remedy.

Please contact us at copyright@packtpub.com with a link to the suspected pirated material.

We appreciate your help in protecting our authors and our ability to bring you valuable content.

Questions

If you have a problem with any aspect of this book, you can contact us at questions@packtpub.com, and we will do our best to address the problem.

1
The Essentials of Responsive Web Design

Only a few years ago, websites could be built at a fixed width, with the expectation that all end users would get a fairly consistent experience. This fixed width (typically 960px wide or thereabouts) wasn't too wide for laptop screens, and users with large resolution monitors merely had an abundance of margin either side.

But in 2007, Apple's iPhone ushered in the first truly usable phone browsing experience, and the way people access and interact with the Web changed forever.

In the first edition of this book, it was noted that:

> *"in the 12 months from July 2010 to July 2011, global mobile browser use had risen from 2.86 to 7.02 percent."*

In mid-2015, the same statistics system (`gs.statcounter.com`) reported that this figure had risen to 33.47%. By way of comparison, North America's mobile figure is at 25.86%.

By any metric, mobile device usage is rising ever upwards, while at the other end of the scale, 27 and 30 inch displays are now also commonplace. There is now a greater difference between the smallest and the largest screens browsing the Web than ever before.

Thankfully, there is a solution to this ever-expanding browser and device landscape. A responsive web design, built with HTML5 and CSS3, allows a website to 'just work' across multiple devices and screens. It enables the layout and capabilities of a website to respond to their environment (screen size, input type, device/browser capabilities).

Furthermore, a responsive web design, built with HTML5 and CSS3, can be implemented without the need for server based/back-end solutions.

Beginning our quest

Whether you're new to responsive web design, HTML5, or CSS3, or already well versed, I'm hoping this first chapter will serve one of two purposes.

If you're already using HTML5 and CSS3 in your responsive web designs, this first chapter should serve as a quick and basic refresher. Alternatively, if you're a newcomer, think of it as a 'boot camp' of sorts, covering the essentials so we're all on the same page.

By the end of this first chapter, we will have covered everything you need to author a fully responsive web page.

You might be wondering why the other nine chapters are here. By the end of this chapter, that should be apparent too.

Here's what we will cover in this first chapter:

- Defining responsive web design
- How to set browser support levels
- A brief discussion on tooling and text editors
- Our first responsive example: a simple HTML5 page
- The importance of the viewport `meta` tag
- How to make images scale to their container
- Writing CSS3 media queries to create design breakpoints
- The shortfalls in our basic example
- Why our journey has only just begun

Defining responsive web design

The term, "responsive web design" was coined by Ethan Marcotte in 2010. In his seminal *A List Apart* article (`http://www.alistapart.com/articles/responsive-web-design/`), he consolidated three existing techniques (flexible grid layout, flexible images/media, and media queries) into one unified approach and named it responsive web design.

Responsive web design in a nutshell

Responsive web design is the presentation of web content in the most relevant format for the viewport and device accessing it.

In its infancy, it was typical for a responsive design to be built starting with the 'desktop', fixed-width design. Content was then reflowed, or removed so that the design worked on smaller screens. However, processes evolved and it became apparent that everything from design, to content and development, worked much better when working in the opposite direction; starting with smaller screens and working up.

Before we get into this, there are a couple of subjects I'd like to address before we continue; browser support and text editors/tooling.

Setting browser support levels

The popularity and ubiquity of responsive web design makes it an easier sell to clients and stakeholders than ever before. Most people have some idea what responsive web design is about. The notion of a single codebase that will just work across all devices is a compelling offering.

One question that almost always comes up when starting a responsive design project is that of browser support. With so many browser and device variants, it's not always pragmatic to support every single browser permutation fully. Perhaps time is a limiting factor, perhaps money. Perhaps both.

Typically, the older the browser, the greater the work and code required to gain feature or aesthetic parity with modern browsers. Therefore, it may make more sense to have a leaner, and therefore faster, codebase by tiering the experience and only providing enhanced visuals and capabilities for more capable browsers.

In the previous edition of this book, some time was spent covering how to cater for very old desktop-only browsers. In this edition, we will not.

As I write this in mid-2015, Internet Explorer 6, 7, and 8 are all but gone. Even IE 9 only has a 2.45% worldwide share of the browser market (IE 10 is only 1.94% while IE 11 is rising nicely at 11.68%). If you have no alternative but to develop for Internet Explorer 8 and below, you have my sympathies and I'm afraid I must be upfront and advise you that there won't be a terrific amount you can use in this book.

For everyone else, you owe it to your client/paymaster to explain why developing for ailing browsers might be a mistake and investing development time and resource primarily for modern browsers and platforms makes good fiscal sense in every respect.

Ultimately however, the only statistics that really matter are yours. In all but extreme cases, the sites we build should at least be functional in every common browser. Beyond basic functionality, for any web project it makes sense to decide, in advance, what platforms you want to fully enhance the experience for, and which you are happy to concede visual/functional anomalies to.

You'll also find that practically, starting with the simplest 'base level' experience and enhancing (an approach known as **progressive enhancement**) is easier than coming at the problem from the opposite direction—building the ultimate experience first then attempting to provide fall backs for less capable platforms (an approach known as **graceful degradation**).

To exemplify why knowing this in advance matters, consider that if you were unlucky enough to have 25% of your website visitors using Internet Explorer 9 (for example), you'd need to consider what features that browser supports and tailor your solution accordingly. The same caution would be required if large amounts of your users are visiting with older mobile phone platforms such as Android 2. What you can consider a 'base' experience will vary depending upon the project.

If suitable data isn't available, I apply a simple and crude piece of logic to determine whether I should spend time developing a particular platform/browser version: if the cost of developing and supporting browser X is more than the revenue/benefit created by the users on browser X; don't develop specific solutions for browser X.

It's rarely a question of whether you could 'fix' an older platform/version. It's a question of whether you should.

When considering which platforms and browser versions support which features, if you aren't already, become familiar the http://caniuse.com website. It provides a simple interface for establishing what browser support there is for the features we will be looking at throughout.

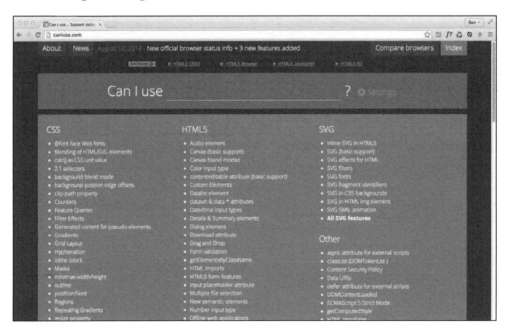

A brief note on tooling and text editors

It makes no difference what text editor or IDE system you use to build your responsive web designs. If the simplest of text editors allows you to write your HTML, CSS, and JavaScript efficiently, that's absolutely fine. Similarly there are no requisite pieces of tooling that are essential to get a responsive web design out of the door. All you actually need is something that enables you to write HTML, CSS, and JavaScript. Whether your preference is Sublime Text, Vim, Coda, Visual Studio, or Notepad - it matters little. Just use what works best for you.

However, be aware that there are more tools available now (often free) to negate many of the manual and time-intensive tasks of building web sites than ever before. For example, CSS processors (Sass, LESS, Stylus, PostCSS) can help with code organization, variables, color manipulations, and arithmetic. Tools like PostCSS can also automate horrible and thankless jobs like CSS vendor prefixing. Furthermore, 'Linting' and validation tools can check your HTML, JavaScript, and CSS code against standards as you work, eliminating many time wasting typos or syntax errors.

New tools come out constantly and they are continually improving. Therefore, whilst some relevant and beneficial tools will be mentioned by name as we go, be aware that something better may be just around the corner. Hence we won't be relying on anything other than standards based HTML and CSS in our examples. You should however, use whatever tools you can to produce your front-end code as quickly and reliably as possible.

Our first responsive example

In the first paragraph I promised that by the end of this chapter you would know all you needed to build a fully responsive web page. So far I've just been talking around the issue at hand. It's time to walk the walk.

Code samples

You can download all the code samples from this book by visiting `rwd.education/download.zip` or via GitHub at `https://github.com/benfrain/rwd`. It's worth knowing that where individual examples are built up throughout a chapter, only the final version of the example is provided in the code download. For example, if you download the code samples for *Chapter 2, Media Queries – Supporting Differing Viewports*, the examples will be in the state they are at by the end of *Chapter 2, Media Queries – Supporting Differing Viewports*. No intermediate states are provided other than in the text.

Our basic HTML file

We will start with a simple HTML5 structure. Don't worry at this point what each of the lines do (especially the content of the <head>, we will cover that in detail in *Chapter 4, HTML5 for Responsive Web Designs*).

For now, simply concentrate on the elements inside the <body> tag. I'm pretty sure nothing there will look too unusual; a few div's, a graphic for a logo, an image (a tasty looking scone), a paragraph or two of text and a list of items.

Here's an abridged version of the code. For brevity I have removed the paragraphs of text in the code below as we only need to concern ourselves with the structure. However, you should know that it's a recipe and description of how to make scones; quintessentially British cakes.

If you want to see the full HTML file, you can download it from the rwd.education website.

```
<!doctype html>
<html class="no-js" lang="en">
    <head>
        <meta charset="utf-8">
        <title>Our first responsive web page with HTML5 and CSS3</
title>
        <meta name="description" content="A basic responsive web page
- an example from Chapter 1">
        <link rel="stylesheet" href="css/styles.css">
    </head>
    <body>
        <div class="Header">
            <a href="/" class="LogoWrapper"><img src="img/SOC-Logo.
png" alt="Scone O'Clock logo" /></a>
            <p class="Strap">Scones: the most resplendent of snacks</
p>
        </div>
        <div class="IntroWrapper">
            <p class="IntroText">Occasionally maligned and
misunderstood; the scone is a quintessentially British classic.</p>
            <div class="MoneyShot">
                <img class="MoneyShotImg" src="img/scones.jpg"
alt="Incredible scones" />
                <p class="ImageCaption">Incredible scones, picture
from Wikipedia</p>
            </div>
        </div>
        <p>Recipe and serving suggestions follow.</p>
        <div class="Ingredients">
```

```
        <h3 class="SubHeader">Ingredients</h3>
        <ul>

        </ul>
    </div>
    <div class="HowToMake">
        <h3 class="SubHeader">Method</h3>
        <ol class="MethodWrapper">

        </ol>
    </div>
</body>
</html>
```

By default, web pages are flexible. If you were to open the example page, even as it is at this point (with no media queries present), and resize the browser window you'll see the text reflows as needed.

What about on different devices? With no CSS whatsoever, this is how that renders on an iPhone:

As you can see, it's rendering like a 'normal' web page would on an iPhone. The reason for that is that iOS renders web pages at 980px wide by default and shrinks them down into the viewport.

The viewable area of a browser is known technically as the **viewport**. The viewport is seldom equivalent to the screen size of a device, especially in instances where a user can resize a browser window.

Therefore, from now on, we will generally use this more accurate term when we are referring to the available space for our web page.

We can fix that prior problem easily by adding this snippet in the `<head>`:

```
<meta name="viewport" content="width=device-width">
```

This viewport `meta` tag is a non-standard (but de facto standard) way of telling the browser how to render the page. In this case, our viewport `meta` tag is effectively saying "make the content render at the width of the device". In fact, it's probably easier to just show you the effect this line has on applicable devices:

Great! The text is now rendering and flowing at a more 'native' size. Let's move on.

We will cover the `meta` tag and its various settings and permutations (and the standards based version of the same functionality) in *Chapter 2, Media Queries – Supporting Differing Viewports*.

Taming images

They say a picture is worth a thousand words. All this writing about scones in our sample page and there's no image of the beauties. I'm going to add in an image of a scone near the top of the page; a sort of 'hero' image to entice users to read the page.

Oh! That nice big image (2000px wide) is forcing our page to render more than a little wonky. We need to fix that. We could add a fixed width to the image via CSS but the problem there is that we want the image to scale to different screen sizes.

For example, our example iPhone is 320px wide so we could set a width of 320px to that image but then what happens if a user rotates the screen? The 320px wide viewport is now 480px wide. Thankfully it's pretty easy to achieve fluid images that will scale to the available width of their container with a single line of CSS.

I'm going to create the `css/styles.css` CSS file now that's linked in the head of the HTML page.

Here is the first thing I'm adding. Ordinarily I'd be setting a few other defaults, and we'll discuss those defaults in later chapters, but for our purposes I'm happy to open with just this:

```
img {
    max-width: 100%;
}
```

Now when the page is refreshed we see something more akin to what we might expect.

All this `max-width` based rule does is stipulate that all images should be a maximum of 100% of their width (in that they should expand to 100% of their size and no more). Where a containing element (such as the `body` or a `div` it sits within) is less than the intrinsic width of the image, it will simply scale up to the maximum available space.

Why not simply width: 100%?

To make images fluid you could also use the more widely used width property. For example, `width: 100%` but this has a different effect. When a property of `width` is used then the image will be displayed at that width, regardless of its own inherent size. The result in our example would be the logo (also an image) stretching to fill 100% of its container. With a container far wider than the image (as is the case with our logo) this leads a massively oversized image.

Excellent. Everything is now laid out as expected. No matter the viewport size, nothing is overflowing the page horizontally.

However, if we look at the page in larger viewports, the basic styles start to get both literally and figuratively stretched. Take a look at the example page at a size around 1400px:

Oh dear! In fact, even around 600px wide it's starting to suffer. Around this point it would be handy if we could rearrange a few things. Maybe resize the image and position it off to one side. Perhaps alter some font sizes and background colors of elements.

Thankfully, we can achieve all this functionality quite easily by employing CSS media queries to bend things to our will.

Enter media queries

As we have established, somewhere beyond the 600px wide point, our current layout starts to look stretched. Let's use CSS3 media queries to adjust the layout depending upon the screen width. Media queries allow us to apply certain CSS rules based upon a number of conditions (screen width and height for example).

Don't set breakpoints to popular device widths

'Breakpoint' is the term used to define the point in which a responsive design should change significantly.

When people first started making use of media queries it was common to see breakpoints in designs built specifically around the popular devices of the day. At the time it was typically iPhone (320px x 480px) and iPad (768px x 1024px) that defined these 'breakpoints'.

That practice was a bad choice then, and it would be an even worse one now. The problem is that by doing that we are catering a design to a specific screen size. We want a responsive design—something that is agnostic of the screen size viewing it; not something that only looks at its best at specific sizes.

Therefore, let the content and the design itself determine where a breakpoint is relevant. Maybe your initial layout starts to look wrong at 500px wide and greater, perhaps 800px. Your own project design should determine when a breakpoint is needed.

We will cover the entire gamut of CSS media queries in *Chapter 2, Media Queries – Supporting Differing Viewports*, inventively titled **Media Queries**.

However, for the purpose of whipping our basic example into shape, we will concentrate on just one type of media query; a minimum width media query. CSS rules within this type of media query only get applied if the viewport is a minimum defined width. The exact minimum width can be specified using a raft of different length units including percent, em, rem, and px. In CSS, a minimum width media query is written like this:

```
@media screen and (min-width: 50em) {
    /* styles */
}
```

The `@media` directive tells the browser we are starting a media query, the `screen` part (declaring 'screen' is technically not needed in this situation but we will deal with that in detail in the next chapter) tells the browser these rules should be applied to all screen types and the `and (min-width: 50em)` tells the browser that the rules should be limited to all viewports above 50em of size.

I believe it was Bryan Rieger (http://www.slideshare.net/bryanrieger/rethinking-the-mobile-web-by-yiibu) who first wrote that:

> "*The absence of support for media queries is in fact the first media query.*"

What he meant by that is that the first rules we write, outside of a media query should be our 'base' rules which we then enhance for more capable devices.

For now, simply be aware that this approach re-enforces our smallest screen first mentality and allows us to progressively layer on detail as and when the design necessitates it.

Amending the example for a larger screen

We've already established that our design is starting to suffer at around 600px/37.5rem width.

Therefore, let's mix things up a little by way of a simple example of how we can lay things out differently at different viewport sizes.

Almost all browsers have a default text size of 16px so you can easily convert widths to rems by dividing the px value by 16. We will discuss why you might want to do this in *Chapter 2, Media Queries – Supporting Differing Viewports*.

First off, we will stop that main 'hero' image getting too big and keep it over on the right. Then the intro text can sit to the left.

We will then have the main portion of text, the 'method' that describes how to make the scones, on the left below with a small boxed out section detailing the ingredients over on the right.

All these changes can be achieved relatively simply by encapsulating these specific styles within a media query. Here's what things look like with the relevant styles added:

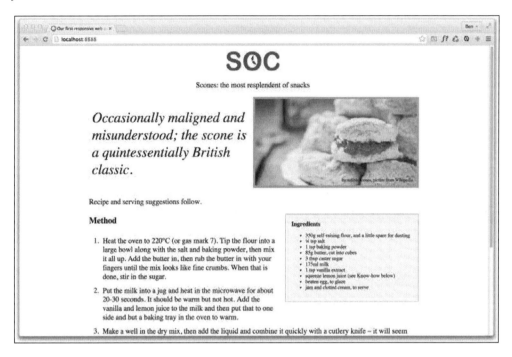

It still looks essentially the same as it did before on smaller screens but adjusts to the new layout as soon as the viewport is 50rem or wider.

Here are the layout styles that were added:

```
@media screen and (min-width: 50rem) {
    .IntroWrapper {
        display: table;
        table-layout: fixed;
        width: 100%;
    }

    .MoneyShot,
    .IntroText {
        display: table-cell;
        width: 50%;
        vertical-align: middle;
        text-align: center;
    }
```

```
.IntroText {
    padding: .5rem;
    font-size: 2.5rem;
    text-align: left;
}

.Ingredients {
    font-size: .9rem;
    float: right;
    padding: 1rem;
    margin: 0 0 .5rem 1rem;
    border-radius: 3px;
    background-color: #ffffdf;
    border: 2px solid #e8cfa9;
}

.Ingredients h3 {
    margin: 0;
}
}
```

That wasn't too bad was it? With only minimal code we have built a page that responds to the viewport size and offers a preferable layout as needed. By adding just a few more styles things look even easier on the eye. With those in place, our basic responsive page now looks like this on an iPhone:

And like this above 50rem width:

SOC

Scones: the most resplendent of snacks

Occasionally maligned and misunderstood; the scone is a quintessentially British classic.

Incredible scones, picture from Wikipedia

Recipe and serving suggestions follow.

Method

1. Heat the oven to 220°C (or gas mark 7). Tip the flour into a large bowl along with the salt and baking powder, then mix it all up. Add the butter in, then rub the butter in with your fingers until the mix looks like fine crumbs. When that is done, stir in the sugar.

Ingredients

- 350g self-raising flour, and a little spare for dusting
- ¼ tsp salt
- 1 tsp baking powder
- 85g butter, cut into cubes
- 3 tbsp caster sugar
- 175ml milk
- 1 tsp vanilla extract
- squeeze lemon juice (see Know-how below)
- beaten egg, to glaze
- jam and clotted cream, to serve

2. Put the milk into a jug and heat in the microwave for about 20-30 seconds. It should be warm but not hot. Add the vanilla and lemon juice to the milk and then put that to one side and but a baking tray in the oven to warm.

These further visual embellishments don't add to the understanding of what's happening responsively, hence I have omitted them here but if you'd like to view the relevant code, download the chapter code at `http://rwd.education` or `https://github.com/benfrain/rwd`.

This has been a very basic example but it has encapsulated the essential methodology of building out a responsive web design.

To reiterate the essential things we have covered; start with 'base' styles, styles that can work on any device. Then layer enhancements on progressively as the viewport size and/or capabilities increase.

You can find the full specifications for CSS Media Queries (Level 3) here: `http://www.w3.org/TR/css3-mediaqueries/`

There is also a working draft for CSS Media Queries (Level 4) here: `http://dev.w3.org/csswg/mediaqueries-4/`

The shortcomings of our example

In this chapter we've covered all the essential component parts of a basic responsive HTML5 and CSS3 powered web page.

But you and I both know that this basic responsive example is rarely the limit of what we're tasked with building. Nor should it reflect the limit of what we are capable of building.

What about if we want our page to respond to different light conditions? What about changing the size of links when people use different pointing devices (a finger rather than a mouse for example)? What about being able to animate and move visual elements simply, using nothing but CSS?

Then there's the markup. How do go about marking up pages with more semantic elements; article, section, menu, and the like, or make forms with built in validation (no JavaScript needed)? And what if we want to change the visual order of elements at different viewports?

Let's not forget images. We have fluid images in this example but if people visit this page on a mobile phone, they will need to download a large graphic (2000px wide no less) that will only be shown on their phone at a fraction of that size. That will make the page considerably slower to load than needed. Surely there's a better way?

And what about logos and icons? We've used a PNG in this example, but we could easily use **scalable vector graphics** (**SVGs**) to enjoy graphics with resolution independence. That way they will look pin-sharp, regardless of the resolution of the viewing screen.

Hopefully you have time to stick around, as these are the very questions we will answer in the coming chapters.

Summary

Well done, you now know and understand the essential elements needed to create a fully responsive web page. However, as we have just discovered, there are plenty of places where things could be improved.

But that's fine. We don't just want the ability to make competent responsive web designs, we want to be able to create 'best of breed' experiences. So let's press on.

First up, we will wrap our heads around all that Level 3 and Level 4 CSS Media Queries have to offer. We have already seen how a web page can respond to viewport width but there's so much more we can do right now — and a lot more fun stuff coming to your browser soon. Let's go and take a look.

2
Media Queries – Supporting Differing Viewports

In the previous chapter, we had a brief look at the essential components for a responsive web page: a fluid layout, fluid images, and media queries.

This chapter will look in detail at media queries, hopefully providing all that's needed to fully understand their capability, syntax, and future development.

In this chapter, we shall:

- Learn why media queries are needed for a responsive web design
- Understand the media query syntax
- Learn how to use media queries in `link` tags, with CSS `@import` statements and within CSS files themselves
- Understand what device features we can test for
- Use media queries to facilitate visual changes dependent upon available screen space
- Consider whether media queries should be grouped together or written as and where needed
- Understand the `meta` viewport tag, to allow media queries to work as intended on iOS and Android devices
- Consider the capabilities being proposed for future media queries specifications

The CSS3 specification is made up of a number of modules. Media Queries (Level 3) are just one of these modules. Media queries allow us to target specific CSS styles depending upon the capabilities of a device. For example, with just a few lines of CSS we can change the way content is displayed, dependent upon things such as viewport width, screen aspect ratio, orientation (landscape or portrait), and so on.

Media queries are widely implemented. Pretty much everything other than ancient versions of Internet Explorer (8 and below) support them. In short, there's absolutely no good reason not to be using them!

Specifications at the W3C go through a ratification process. If you have a spare day, knock yourself out with the official explanation of the process at http://www.w3.org/2005/10/ Process-20051014/tr. The simpler version is that specifications go from **Working Draft (WD)**, to **Candidate Recommendation (CR)**, to **Proposed Recommendation (PR)** before finally arriving, many years later, at W3C Recommendation (REC). Modules at a greater maturity level than others are generally safer to use. For example, CSS Transforms Module Level 3 (http://www.w3.org/TR/css3-3d-transforms/) has been at WD status since March 2009 and browser support for it is far poorer than CR modules such as media queries.

Why media queries are needed for a responsive web design

CSS3 media queries enable us to target particular CSS styles to particular device capabilities or situations. If you head over to the W3C specification of the CSS3 media query module (http://www.w3.org/TR/css3-mediaqueries/), you'll see that this is their official introduction to what media queries are all about:

> *"A media query consists of a media type and zero or more expressions that check for the conditions of particular media features. Among the media features that can be used in media queries are 'width', 'height', and 'color'. By using media queries, presentations can be tailored to a specific range of output devices without changing the content itself."*

Without media queries we would be unable to substantially alter the visuals of a website using CSS alone. They facilitate us writing defensive CSS rules that pre-empt such eventualities as portrait screen orientation, small or large viewport dimensions, and more.

Whilst a fluid layout can carry a design a substantial distance, given the gamut of screen sizes we hope to cover, there are times when we need to revise the layout more fully. Media queries make this possible. Think of them as basic conditional logic for CSS.

Basic conditional logic in CSS

True programming languages all have some facility in which one of two or more possible situations are catered for. This usually takes the form of conditional logic, typified by an `if/else` statement.

If programming vernacular makes your eyes itch, fear not; it's a very simple concept. You probably dictate conditional logic every time you ask a friend to order for you when visiting a cafe, "If they've got triple chocolate muffins I'll have one of those, if not, I'll have a slice of carrot cake". It's a simple conditional statement with two possible (and equally fine, in this case) results.

At the time of writing, CSS does not facilitate true conditional logic or programmatic features. Loops, functions, iteration, and complex math are still firmly in the domain of CSS processors (did I mention a fine book on the subject of the Sass pre-processor, called *Sass and Compass for Designers*?). However, media queries are one mechanism in CSS that allows us to author basic conditional logic. By using a media query the styles within are scoped depending upon whether certain conditions are met.

Programming features on their way

The popularity of CSS pre-processors has made the people working on CSS specifications take note. Right now there is a WD specification for CSS variables: `http://www.w3.org/TR/css-variables/`

However, browser support is currently limited to Firefox so it's really not something to consider using in the wild at present.

Media query syntax

So what does a CSS media query look like and more importantly, how does it work?

Enter the following code at the bottom of any CSS file and preview the related web page. Alternatively, you can open `example_02-01`:

```css
body {
  background-color: grey;
}
```

```
@media screen and (min-width: 320px) {
  body {
    background-color: green;
  }
}
@media screen and (min-width: 550px) {
  body {
    background-color: yellow;
  }
}
@media screen and (min-width: 768px) {
  body {
    background-color: orange;
  }
}
@media screen and (min-width: 960px) {
  body {
    background-color: red;
  }
}
```

Now, preview the file in a browser and resize the window. The background color of the page will vary depending upon the current viewport size. We'll cover how the syntax works in more detail shortly. First, it's important to know how and where you can use media queries.

Media queries in link tags

Those that have been working with CSS since version 2 will know it's possible to specify the type of device (for example, `screen` or `print`) applicable to a style sheet with the media attribute of the `<link>` tag. Consider this example (which you'd place in the `<head>` tags of your markup):

```
<link rel="style sheet" type="text/css" media="screen" href="screen-styles.css">
```

Media queries add the ability to target styles based upon the capability or features of a device, rather than merely the type of device. Think of it as a question to the browser. If the browser's answer is "true", the enclosed styles are applied. If the answer is "false", they are not. Rather than just asking the browser "Are you a screen?"—as much as we could effectively ask with just CSS2—media queries ask a little more. Instead, a media query might ask, "Are you a screen and are you in portrait orientation?" Let's look at that as an example:

```
<link rel="stylesheet" media="screen and (orientation: portrait)" href="portrait-screen.css" />
```

First, the media query expression asks the type (are you a screen?), and then the feature (is your screen in portrait orientation?). The `portrait-screen.css` style sheet will be applied for any screen device with a portrait screen orientation and ignored for any others. It's possible to reverse the logic of any media query expression by adding not to the beginning of the media query. For example, the following code would negate the result in our prior example, applying the file for anything that wasn't a screen with a portrait orientation:

```
<link rel="stylesheet" media="not screen and (orientation: portrait)"
href="portrait-screen.css" />
```

Combining media queries

It's also possible to string multiple expressions together. For example, let's extend one of our prior examples and also limit the file to devices that have a viewport greater than 800 pixels.

```
<link rel="stylesheet" media="screen and (orientation: portrait) and
(min-width: 800px)" href="800wide-portrait-screen.css" />
```

Further still, we could have a list of media queries. If any of the listed queries are true, the file will be applied. If none are true, it won't. Here is an example:

```
<link rel="stylesheet" media="screen and (orientation: portrait) and
(min-width: 800px), projection" href="800wide-portrait-screen.css" />
```

There are two points to note here. Firstly, a comma separates each media query. Secondly, you'll notice that after projection, there is no trailing and/or feature/value combination in parentheses. That's because in the absence of these values, the media query is applied to all media types. In our example, the styles will apply to all projectors.

> You should be aware that you can use any CSS length unit to specify media queries with. **Pixels (px)** are the most commonly used but **ems (em)** and **rems (rem)** are equally appropriate. For some further info on the merits of each, I wrote a little more on the subject here: `http://benfrain.com/just-use-pixels`
>
> Therefore, if you want a break point at 800px (but specified in em units) simply divide the number of pixels by 16. For example, 800px could also be specified as 50em (800 / 16 = 50).

Media queries with @import

We can also use the `@import` feature of CSS to conditionally load style sheets into our existing style sheet. For example, the following code would import the style sheet called `phone.css`, providing the device was screen based and had a maximum viewport of 360 pixels:

```
@import url("phone.css") screen and (max-width:360px);
```

Remember that using the `@import` feature of CSS, adds to HTTP requests (which impacts load speed) so use this method sparingly.

Media queries in CSS

So far, we have included them as links to CSS files that we would place within the `<head></head>` section of our HTML and as `@import` statements. However, it's more likely we will want to use media queries within CSS style sheets themselves. For example, if we add the following code into a style sheet, it will make all `h1` elements green, providing the device has a screen width of 400 pixels or less:

```
@media screen and (max-device-width: 400px) {
   h1 { color: green }
}
```

First we specify we want a media query with the `@media` at-rule, then we specify the type we want to match. In the preceding example, we want to apply the rules enclosed only to screens (and not, for example, `print`). Then, inside parenthesis we enter the specifics of the query. Then like any CSS rule, we open the braces and write the required styles.

At this point it's probably prudent of me to point out that in most situations, you don't actually need to specify `screen`. Here's the key point in the specification:

> *"A shorthand syntax is offered for media queries that apply to all media types; the keyword 'all' can be left out (along with the trailing 'and'). I.e. if the media type is not explicitly given it is 'all'."*

Therefore, unless you want to target styles to particular media types, just leave the `screen and` part out. That's the way we will be writing media queries in the example files from this point on.

What can media queries test for?

When building responsive designs, the media queries that get used most, usually relate to a device's viewport width (`width`). In my own experience, I have found little need (with the occasional exception of resolution and viewport height) to employ the other capabilities. However, just in case the need arises, here is a list of all capabilities that Media Queries Level 3 can test for. Hopefully some will pique your interest:

- `width`: The viewport width.
- `height`: The viewport height.
- `device-width`: The rendering surface's width (for our purposes, this is typically the screen width of a device).
- `device-height`: The rendering surface's height (for our purposes, this is typically the screen height of a device).
- `orientation`: This capability checks whether a device is portrait or landscape in orientation.
- `aspect-ratio`: The ratio of width to height based upon the viewport width and height. A 16:9 widescreen display can be written as `aspect-ratio: 16/9`.
- `device-aspect-ratio`: This capability is similar to `aspect-ratio` but is based upon the width and height of the device rendering surface, rather than viewport.
- `color`: The number of bits per color component. For example, `min-color: 16` will check that the device has 16-bit color.
- `color-index`: The number of entries in the color lookup table of the device. Values must be numbers and cannot be negative.
- `monochrome`: This capability tests how many bits per pixel are in a monochrome frame buffer. The value would be a number (integer), for example, `monochrome: 2`, and cannot be negative.
- `resolution`: This capability can be used to test screen or print resolution; for example, `min-resolution: 300dpi`. It can also accept measurements in dots per centimeter; for example, `min-resolution: 118dpcm`.
- `scan`: This can be either progressive or interlace features largely particular to TVs. For example, a 720p HD TV (the p part of 720p indicates "progressive") could be targeted with `scan: progressive` while a 1080i HD TV (the i part of 1080i indicates "interlaced") could be targeted with `scan: interlace`.
- `grid`: This capability indicates whether or not the device is grid or bitmap based.

All the preceding features, with the exception of `scan` and `grid`, can be prefixed with `min` or `max` to create ranges. For example, consider the following code snippet:

```
@import url("tiny.css") screen and (min-width:200px) and (max-width:360px);
```

Here, a minimum (`min`) and maximum (`max`) have been applied to width to set a range. The tiny.css file will only be imported for screen devices with a minimum viewport width of 200 pixels and a maximum viewport width of 360 pixels.

> **Features deprecated in CSS Media Queries Level 4**
>
> It's worth being aware that the draft specification for Media Queries Level 4 deprecates the use of a few features (`http://dev.w3.org/csswg/mediaqueries-4/#mf-deprecated`); most notably `device-height`, `device-width`, and `device-aspect-ratio`. Support for those queries will remain in browsers but it's recommended you refrain from writing any new style sheets that use them.

Using media queries to alter a design

By their very nature, styles further down a **cascading style sheet** (CSS file to you and me) override equivalent styles higher up (unless styles higher up are more specific). We can therefore set base styles at the beginning of a style sheet, applicable to all versions of our design (or at least providing our 'base' experience), and then override relevant sections with media queries further on in the document. For example, we might choose to set navigation links as text alone in limited viewports (or perhaps just smaller text) and then overwrite those styles with a media query to give us both text and icons at larger viewports where more space is available.

Let's have a look at how this might look in practice (`example_02-02`). First the markup:

```
<a href="#" class="CardLink CardLink_Hearts">Hearts</a>
<a href="#" class="CardLink CardLink_Clubs">Clubs</a>
<a href="#" class="CardLink CardLink_Spades">Spades</a>
<a href="#" class="CardLink CardLink_Diamonds">Diamonds</a>
```

Now the CSS:

```
.CardLink {
    display: block;
    color: #666;
    text-shadow: 0 2px 0 #efefef;
    text-decoration: none;
    height: 2.75rem;
    line-height: 2.75rem;
```

```
        border-bottom: 1px solid #bbb;
        position: relative;
}

@media (min-width: 300px) {
    .CardLink {
        padding-left: 1.8rem;
        font-size: 1.6rem;
    }
}

.CardLink:before {
    display: none;
    position: absolute;
    top: 50%;
    transform: translateY(-50%);
    left: 0;
}

.CardLink_Hearts:before {
    content: "♥";
}

.CardLink_Clubs:before {
    content: "♣";
}

.CardLink_Spades:before {
    content: "♠";
}

.CardLink_Diamonds:before {
    content: "♦";
}

@media (min-width: 300px) {
    .CardLink:before {
        display: block;
    }
}
```

Downloading the example code

You can download the example code files for all Packt books you have purchased from your account at http://www.packtpub.com. If you purchased this book elsewhere, you can visit http://www.packtpub.com/support and register to have the files e-mailed directly to you.

Here's a screen grab of the links in a small viewport:

And here's a grab of them at a larger viewport:

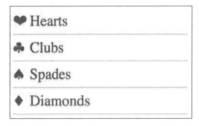

Any CSS can be wrapped in a media query

It's important to remember that anything you would normally write in CSS can also be enclosed inside a media query. As such, it's possible to entirely change the layout and look of a site in different situations (usually for differing viewport sizes) with media queries.

Media queries for HiDPI devices

Another common use case for media queries is to change styles when the site is viewed on a high-resolution device. Consider this:

```
@media (min-resolution: 2dppx) {
   /* styles */
}
```

Here our media query is specifying that we only want the enclosed styles to apply where the screen resolution is 2 dots per pixel unit (2dppx). This would apply to devices like the iPhone 4 (Apple's HiDPI devices are given the 'Retina' moniker) and a whole raft of Android devices. You could change that media query to apply to a wider range of devices by reducing the dppx value.

For the broadest possible support, when writing min-resolution media queries, ensure you have a prefixing tool running to provide relevant vendor prefixes. Don't worry if the term vendor prefixes doesn't make much sense right now as we deal with the subject in more detail in the next chapter.

Considerations for organizing and authoring media queries

We will take a brief tangent at this point to consider some of the different approaches that authors can take when writing and organizing their media queries. Each approach offers some benefits and some tradeoffs so it's worth at least knowing about these factors, even if you decide they are largely irrelevant for your needs.

Linking to different CSS files with media queries

From a browser perspective, CSS is considered to be a 'render blocking' asset. The browser needs to fetch and parse a linked CSS file before rendering of the page can complete.

However, modern browsers are smart enough to discern which style sheets (linked with media queries in the head) need to be analyzed immediately and which can be deferred until after the initial page rendering.

For these browsers, CSS files linked to with non-applicable media queries (for example if the screen is too small for the media query to apply) can be 'deferred' until after the initial page load, providing some performance advantage.

There's more on this topic over on Google's developer pages: `https://developers.google.com/web/fundamentals/performance/critical-rendering-path/render-blocking-css`

However, I would like to draw your attention to this part in particular:

> *"...note that "render blocking" only refers to whether the browser will have to hold the initial rendering of the page on that resource. In either case, the CSS asset is still downloaded by the browser, albeit with a lower priority for non-blocking resources."*

To reiterate, all the linked files will still be downloaded, the browser just won't hold up rendering of the page if they don't immediately apply.

Therefore, a modern browser loading a responsive web page (take a look at `example_02-03`) with four different style sheets linked with different media queries (to apply different styles for different viewport ranges) will download all four CSS files but probably only parse the applicable one initially before rendering the page.

The practicalities of separating media queries

Although we have just learned that the process of splitting media queries potentially offers some benefit, there is not always a large tangible advantage (apart from personal preference and/or compartmentalization of code) in separating different media query styles into separate files.

After all, using separate files increases the number of HTTP requests needed to render a page, which in turn can make the pages slower in certain other situations. Nothing is ever easy on the Web! It's therefore really a question of evaluating the entire performance of your site and testing each scenario on different devices.

My default stance on this is that, unless the project has considerable time available for performance optimizations, this is one of the last places I would look to make performance gains. Only once I am certain that:

- All images are compressed
- All scripts are concatenated and minified
- All assets are being served gzipped
- All static content is being cached via CDNs
- All surplus CSS rules have been removed

Perhaps then I would start looking to split up media queries into separate files for performance gains.

 gzip is a compression and decompression file format. Any good server should allow gzip for files such as CSS and this greatly decreases the size of the file as it travels from server to device (at which point it is decompressed to its native format). You can find a good summary of gzip on Wikipedia: `http://en.wikipedia.org/wiki/Gzip`

Nesting media queries 'inline'

In all but extreme circumstances, I recommend adding media queries within an existing style sheet alongside the 'normal' rules.

If you are happy to do the same, it leads to one further consideration: should media queries be declared underneath the associated selector? Or split off into a separate block of code at the end for all identical media queries? I'm glad you asked.

Combine media queries or write them where it suits?

I'm a fan of writing media queries underneath the original 'normal' definition. For example, let's say I want to change the width of a couple of elements, at different places in the style sheet, depending upon the viewport width I would do this:

```
.thing {
    width: 50%;
}

@media screen and (min-width: 30rem) {
    .thing {
        width: 75%;
    }
}

/* A few more styles would go between them */

.thing2 {
    width: 65%;
}

@media screen and (min-width: 30rem) {
    .thing2 {
        width: 75%;
    }
}
```

This seems like lunacy at first. We have two media queries that both relate to when the screen has a minimum width of 30rem. Surely repeating the same @media declaration is overly verbose and wasteful? Shouldn't I be advocating grouping all the identical media queries into a single block like this:

```
.thing {
    width: 50%;
}

.thing2 {
    width: 65%;
```

```
}

@media screen and (min-width: 30rem) {
    .thing {
        width: 75%;
    }
    .thing2 {
        width: 75%;
    }
}
```

That is certainly one way to do it. However, from a maintenance point of view I find this more difficult. There is no 'right' way to do this but my preference is to define a rule for an individual selector once and have any variations of that rule (such as changes within media queries) defined immediately after. That way I don't have to search for separate blocks of code to find the declaration that is relevant to a particular selector.

> With CSS pre and post processors, this can be even more convenient as the media query 'variant' of a rule can be nested directly within the rule set. There's a whole section on that in my other book *Sass and Compass for Designers*.

It would seem fair to argue against the former technique on the grounds of verbosity. Surely file size alone should be enough reason not to write media queries in this manner? After all, no one wants a big bloated CSS file to serve their users. However, the simple fact is that gzip compression (which should be compressing all the possible assets on your server) reduces the difference to a completely inconsequential amount. I've done various tests on this in the past so if it's something you would like to read more about, head over to: `http://benfrain.com/inline-or-combined-media-queries-in-sass-fight/`. The bottom line is, I don't believe you should concern yourself with file size if you would rather write media queries directly after the standard styles.

> If you want to author your media queries directly after the original rule but have all identical media queries definitions merged into one, there are a number of build tools (at the time of writing, Grunt and Gulp both have relevant plugins) that facilitate this.

The viewport meta tag

To get the most out of media queries, you will want smaller screen devices to display web pages at their native size (and not render them in a 980px window that you then have to zoom in and out of).

When Apple released the iPhone in 2007, they introduced a proprietary `meta` tag called the viewport `meta` tag which Android and a growing number of other platforms now also support. The purpose of the viewport `meta` tag is to provide a way for web pages to communicate to mobile browsers how they would like the web browser to render the page.

For the foreseeable future, any web page you want to be responsive, and render well across small screen devices, will need to make use of this `meta` tag.

Testing responsive designs on emulators and simulators

Although there is no substitute for testing your development work on real devices, there are emulators for Android and a simulator for iOS.

For the pedantic, a simulator merely simulates the relevant device whereas an emulator actually attempts to interpret the original device code.

The Android emulator for Windows, Linux, and Mac is available for free by downloading and installing the Android **Software Development Kit (SDK)** at http://developer.android.com/sdk/.

The iOS simulator is only available to Mac OS X users and comes as part of the Xcode package (free from the Mac App Store).

Browsers themselves are also including ever improving tools for emulating mobile devices in their development tools. Both Firefox and Chrome currently have specific settings to emulate different mobile devices/viewports.

The viewport `<meta>` tag is added within the `<head>` tags of the HTML. It can be set to a specific width (which we could specify in pixels, for example) or as a scale, for example `2.0` (twice the actual size). Here's an example of the viewport `meta` tag set to show the browser at twice (200 percent) the actual size:

```
<meta name="viewport" content="initial-scale=2.0,width=device-width"
/>
```

Let's break down the preceding `<meta>` tag so we can understand what's going on. The `name="viewport"` attribute is obvious enough. The `content="initial-scale=2.0` section is then saying, "scale the content to twice the size" (where 0.5 would be half the size, 3.0 would be three times the size, and so on) while the `width=device-width` part tells the browser that the width of the page should be equal to device-width.

The `<meta>` tag can also be used to control the amount a user can zoom in and out of the page. This example allows users to go as large as three times the device width and as small as half the device width:

```
<meta name="viewport" content="width=device-width, maximum-scale=3,
minimum-scale=0.5" />
```

You could also disable users from zooming at all, although as zooming is an important accessibility tool, it's rare that it would be appropriate in practice:

```
<meta name="viewport" content="initial-scale=1.0, user-scalable=no" />
```

The `user-scalable=no` being the relevant part.

Right, we'll change the scale to `1.0`, which means that the mobile browser will render the page at 100 percent of its viewport. Setting it to the device's width means that our page should render at 100 percent of the width of all supported mobile browsers. For the majority of cases, this `<meta>` tag would be appropriate:

```
<meta name="viewport" content="width=device-width,initial-scale=1.0"
/>
```

 Noticing that the viewport `meta` element is seeing increasing use, the W3C is making attempts to bring the same capability into CSS. Head over to `http://dev.w3.org/csswg/css-device-adapt/` and read all about the new `@viewport` declaration. The idea is that rather than writing a `<meta>` tag in the `<head>` section of your markup, you could write `@viewport { width: 320px; }` in the CSS instead. This would set the browser width to 320 pixels. However, browser support is scant, although to cover all bases and be as future proof as possible you could use a combination of `meta` tag and the `@viewport` declaration.

At this point, you should have a solid grasp of media queries and how they work. However, before we move on to a different topic entirely, I think it's nice to consider what may be possible in the near future with the next version of media queries. Let's take a sneak peak!

Media Queries Level 4

At the time of writing, while CSS Media Queries Level 4 enjoy a draft specification (`http://dev.w3.org/csswg/mediaqueries-4/`), the features in the draft don't enjoy many browser implementations. This means that while we will take a brief look at the highlights of this specification, it's highly volatile. Ensure you check browser support and double-check for syntax changes before using any of these features.

For now, while there are other features in the level 4 specification, we will concern ourselves only with scripting, pointer and hover, and luminosity.

Scripting media feature

It's a common practice to set a class on the HTML tag to indicate that no JavaScript is present by default and then replace that class with a different class when JavaScript runs. This provides a simple ability to fork code (including CSS) based upon that new HTML class. Specifically, using this practice you can then write rules specific to users that have JavaScript enabled.

That's potentially confusing so let's consider some example code. By default, this would be the tag as authored in the HTML:

```
<html class="no-js">
```

When JavaScript was run on the page, one of its first tasks would be to replace that `no-js` class:

```
<html class="js">
```

Once this is done, we can then write specific CSS rules that will only apply when JavaScript is present. For example, `.js .header { display: block; }`.

However, the scripting media feature of CSS Media Queries Level 4 aims to provide a more standardized manner to do this directly in the CSS:

```
@media (scripting: none) {
    /* styles for when JavaScript not working */
}
```

And when JavaScript is present:

```
@media (scripting: enabled) {
    /* styles for when JavaScript is working */
}
```

Finally, it also aims to provide the ability to ascertain when JavaScript is present but only initially. One example given in the W3C specification is that of a printed page that could be laid out initially but does not have JavaScript available after that. In such an eventuality, you should be able to do this:

```
@media (scripting: initial-only) {
    /* styles for when JavaScript works initially */
}
```

The current Editor's draft of this feature can be read here: `http://dev.w3.org/ csswg/mediaqueries-4/#mf-scripting`

Interaction media features

Here is the W3C introduction to the pointer media feature:

> *"The pointer media feature is used to query about the presence and accuracy of a pointing device such as a mouse. If a device has multiple input mechanisms, the pointer media feature must reflect the characteristics of the "primary" input mechanism, as determined by the user agent."*

There are three possible states for the pointer features: `none`, `coarse`, and `fine`.

A `coarse` pointer device would be a finger on a touch screen device. However, it could equally be a cursor from a games console that doesn't have the fine grained control of something like a mouse.

```
@media (pointer: coarse) {
    /* styles for when coarse pointer is present */
}
```

A `fine` pointer device would be a mouse but could also be a stylus pen or any future fine grained pointer mechanism.

```
@media (pointer: fine) {
    /* styles for when fine pointer is present */
}
```

As far as I'm concerned, the sooner browsers implement these pointer features, the better. At present it's notoriously difficult to know whether or not a user has mouse, touch input, or both. And which one they are using at any one time.

The safest bet is always to assume users are using touch-based input and size user interface elements accordingly. That way, even if they are using a mouse they will have no difficulty using the interface with ease. If however you assume mouse input, and can't reliably detect touch to amend the interface, it might make for a difficult experience.

For a great overview of the challenges of developing for both touch and pointer, I recommend this set of slides called *Getting touchy* from Patrick H. Lauke: `https://patrickhlauke.github.io/getting-touchy-presentation/`

Read the Editor's draft of this feature here: `http://dev.w3.org/csswg/mediaqueries-4/#mf-interaction`

The hover media feature

As you might imagine, the hover media feature tests the users' ability to hover over elements on the screen. If the user has multiple inputs at their disposal (touch and mouse for example), characteristics of the primary input are used. Here are the possible values and example code:

For users that have no ability to hover, we can target styles for them with a value of `none`.

```
@media (hover: none) {
    /* styles for when the user cannot hover */
}
```

For users that can hover but have to perform a significant action to initiate it, `on-demand` can be used.

```
@media (hover: on-demand) {
    /* styles for when the user can hover but doing so requires
significant effort */
}
```

For users that can hover, `hover` alone can be used.

```
@media (hover) {
    /* styles for when the user can hover */
}
```

Be aware that there are also `any-pointer` or `any-hover` media features. They are like the preceding hover and pointer but test the capabilities of any of the possible input devices.

Environment media features

Wouldn't it be nice if we had the ability to alter our designs based upon environmental features such as ambient light level? That way if a user was in a darker room, we could dim the lightness of the colors used. Or conversely, increase contrast in brighter sunlight. The environment media features aim to solve these very problems. Consider these examples:

```
@media (light-level: normal) {
    /* styles for standard light conditions */
}
@media (light-level: dim) {
    /* styles for dim light conditions */
}
@media (light-level: washed) {
    /* styles for bright light conditions */
}
```

Remember there are few implementations of these Level 4 Media Queries in the wild. It's also probable that the specifications will change before we can safely use them. It is however useful to have some feel for what new capabilities are on the way for us in the next few years.

Read the Editor's draft of this feature here: `http://dev.w3.org/csswg/mediaqueries-4/#mf-environment`

Summary

In this chapter, we've learned what CSS3 media queries are, how to include them in our CSS files, and how they can help our quest to create a responsive web design. We've also learned how to use the `meta` tag to make modern mobile browsers render pages as we'd like.

However, we've also learned that media queries alone can only provide an adaptable web design, one that snaps from one layout to another. Not a truly responsive one that smoothly transitions from one layout to another. To achieve our ultimate goal we will also need to utilize fluid layouts. They will allow our designs to flex between the break points that the media queries handle. Creating fluid layouts to smooth the transition between our media query break points is what we'll be covering in the next chapter.

3
Fluid Layouts and Responsive Images

Eons ago, in the mists of time (well the late 1990s), websites were typically built with their widths defined as percentages. These percentage-based widths fluidly adjusted to the screen viewing them and became known as fluid layouts.

In the years shortly after, in the mid to late 2000s, there was an intervening fixation on fixed width designs (I blame those pesky print designers and their obsession with pixel perfect precision). Nowadays, as we build responsive web designs we need to look back to fluid layouts and remember all the benefits they offer.

In *Chapter 2, Media Queries – Supporting Differing Viewports*, we ultimately conceded that while media queries allowed our design to adapt to changing viewport sizes, by snapping from one set of styles to another, we needed some ability to flex our design between the 'break points' that media queries provided. By coding a 'fluid' layout, we can facilitate this need perfectly; it will effortlessly stretch to fill the gaps between our media query break points.

In 2015, we have better means to build responsive web sites than ever. There is a new CSS layout module called **Flexible Box** (or **Flexbox** as it is more commonly known) that now has enough browser support to make it viable for everyday use.

It can do more than merely provide a fluid layout mechanism. Want to be able to easily center content, change the source order of markup, and generally create amazing layouts with relevant ease? Flexbox is the layout mechanism for you. The majority of this chapter deals with Flexbox, covering all the incredible capabilities it has to offer.

There is another key area to responsive web design we can address better now than ever before and that's responsive images. There are now specified methods and syntax for sending devices the most relevant version of an image for their viewport. We will spend the last section of this chapter understanding how responsive images work and how we can make them work for us.

In this chapter we will cover:

- How to convert fixed pixel sizes to proportional sizes
- Consider existing CSS layout mechanisms and their shortfalls
- Understand the Flexible Box Layout Module and the benefits it offers
- Learn the correct syntax for resolution switching and art direction with responsive images

Converting a fixed pixel design to a fluid proportional layout

Graphic composites made in a program like Photoshop, Illustrator, Fireworks (RIP), or Sketch all have fixed pixel dimensions. At some point, the designs need to be converted to proportional dimensions by a developer when recreating the design as a fluid layout in a browser.

There is a beautifully simple formula for making this conversion that the father of responsive web design, Ethan Marcotte, set down in his 2009 article, *Fluid Grids* (`http://alistapart.com/article/FLUIDGRIDS`):

target / context = result

If anything resembling math makes you quiver, think of it this way: divide the units of the thing you want, by the thing it lives in. Let's put that into practice as understanding it will enable you to convert any fixed dimension layouts into responsive/fluid equivalents.

Consider a very basic page layout intended for desktop. In an ideal world we would always be moving to a desktop layout from a smaller screen layout, but for the sake of illustrating the proportions we will look at the two situations back to front.

Here's an image of the layout:

The layout is 960px wide. Both header and footer are the full width of layout. The left hand side area is 200px wide, the right hand area is 100px wide. Even with my mathematically challenged brain I can tell you the middle section will be 660px wide. We need to convert the middle and side sections to proportional dimensions.

First up, the left hand side. It's 200 units wide (target). Divide that size by 960 units (the context) and we have a result: .208333333. Now, whenever we get our result with that formula we need to shift the decimal point two to the right. That would give us 20.8333333%. That's 200px described as a percentage of 960px.

OK, what about the middle section? 660 (target) divided by 960 (context) gives us .6875. Move the decimal two points to the right and we have 68.75%. Finally, the right hand section. 100 (target) divided by 960 (context) gives us .104166667. Move the decimal point and we have 10.4166667%. That's as difficult as it gets. Say it with me: target, divided by context, equals result.

To prove the point, let's quickly build that basic layout as blocks in the browser. You can view the layout as `example_03-01`. Here is the HTML:

```
<div class="Wrap">
    <div class="Header"></div>
    <div class="WrapMiddle">
        <div class="Left"></div>
        <div class="Middle"></div>
        <div class="Right"></div>
    </div>
    <div class="Footer"></div>
</div>
```

And here is the CSS:

```
html,
body {
    margin: 0;
    padding: 0;
}

.Wrap {
    max-width: 1400px;
    margin: 0 auto;
}

.Header {
    width: 100%;
    height: 130px;
    background-color: #038C5A;
}

.WrapMiddle {
    width: 100%;
    font-size: 0;
}

.Left {
    height: 625px;
    width: 20.8333333%;
    background-color: #03A66A;
    display: inline-block;
}

.Middle {
```

```
        height: 625px;
        width: 68.75%;
        background-color: #bbbf90;
        display: inline-block;
    }

    .Right {
        height: 625px;
        width: 10.4166667%;
        background-color: #03A66A;
        display: inline-block;
    }

    .Footer {
        height: 200px;
        width: 100%;
        background-color: #025059;
    }
```

If you open the example code in a browser and resize the page you will see the dimensions of the middle sections remain proportional to one another. You can also play around with the max-width of the .Wrap values to make the bounding dimensions for the layout bigger or smaller (it's set in the example to `1400px`).

 If you're looking at the markup and wondering why I haven't used semantic elements like `header`, `footer`, and `aside`, then worry not. *Chapter 4, HTML5 for Responsive Web Designs*, deals with those semantic HTML5 elements in detail.

Now, let's consider how we would have the same content on a smaller screen that flexes to a point and then changes to the layout we have already seen. You can view the final code of this layout in `example_03-02`.

The idea is that for smaller screens we will have a single 'tube' of content. The left hand side area will only be viewable as an 'off canvas' area; typically an area for a menu area or similar, that sits off the viewable screen area and slides in when a menu button is pressed. The main content sits below the header, then the right hand section below that, and finally the footer area. In our example, we can expose the left hand menu area by clicking anywhere on the header. Typically, when making this kind of design pattern for real, a menu button would be used to activate the side menu.

To switch the class on the body of the document, I've employed a little JavaScript. This isn't 'production ready' though as we are using 'click' as the event handler in JavaScript, when ideally we would have some provision for touch (to remove the 300ms delay still present on iOS devices).

As you would expect, when combining this with our newly mastered media query skills we can adjust the viewport and the design just 'responds'—effortlessly moving from one layout to another and stretching between the two.

I'm not going to list out all the CSS here, it's all in example_03-02. However, here's an example—the left hand section:

```
.Left {
    height: 625px;
    background-color: #03A66A;
    display: inline-block;
    position: absolute;
    left: -200px;
    width: 200px;
    font-size: .9rem;
    transition: transform .3s;
}

@media (min-width: 40rem) {
    .Left {
        width: 20.8333333%;
        left: 0;
        position: relative;
    }
}
```

You can see that up first, without a media query, is the small screen layout. Then, at larger screen sizes, the width becomes proportional, the positioning relative and the left value is set to zero. We don't need to re-write properties such as the height, display, or background-color as we aren't changing them.

This is progress. We have combined two of the core responsive web design techniques we have covered; converting fixed dimensions to proportions and using media queries to target CSS rules relevant to the viewport size.

There are two important things to note in our prior example. Firstly, you may be wondering if it's strictly necessary to include all the digits after the decimal point. While the widths themselves will ultimately be converted to pixels by the browser, their values are retained for future calculations (for example, more accurately computing the width of nested elements). Subsequently, I always recommend leaving the numbers after the decimals in.

Secondly, in a real project we should be making some provision for if JavaScript isn't available and we need to view the content of the menu. We deal with this scenario in detail in *Chapter 8, Transitions, Transformations, and Animations*.

Why do we need Flexbox?

We are now going to get into the detail of using CSS Flexible Box Layouts, or Flexbox as it is more commonly known.

However, before we do that, I think it will be prudent to first consider the shortfalls of existing layout techniques such as inline-block, floats and tables.

Inline block and whitespace

The biggest issue with using inline-block as a layout mechanism is that it renders space in-between HTML elements. This is not a bug (although most developers would welcome a sane way to remove the space) but it does mean a few hacks to remove the space when it's unwanted, which for me is about 95% of the time. There are a bunch of ways to do this, in the previous example we used the 'font-size zero' approach; an approach not without its own problems and limitations. However, rather than list each possible workaround for removing the whitespace when using inline-block, check out this article by the irrepressible Chris Coyier: `http://css-tricks.com/fighting-the-space-between-inline-block-elements/`.

It's also worth pointing out that there no simple way to vertically center content within an inline-block. Using inline-blocks, there is also no way of having two sibling elements where one has a fixed width and another fluidly fills the remaining space.

Floats

I hate floats. There I said it. In their favor they work everywhere fairly consistently. However, there are two major irritations.

Firstly, when specifying the width of floated elements in percentages, their computed widths don't get rounded consistently across browsers (some browsers round up, some down). This means that sometimes sections will drop down below others when it isn't intended and other times they can leave an irritating gap at one side.

Secondly you usually have to 'clear' the floats so that parent boxes/elements don't collapse. It's easy enough to do this but it's a constant reminder that floats were never intended to be used as a robust layout mechanism.

Table and table-cell

Don't confuse `display: table` and `display: table-cell` with the equivalent HTML elements. These CSS properties merely mimic the layout of their HTML based brethren. They in no way affect the structure of the HTML.

I've found enormous utility in using CSS table layouts. For one, they enable consistent and robust vertical centring of elements within one another. Also, elements set to be `display: table-cell` inside an element set as `display: table` space themselves perfectly; they don't suffer rounding issues like floated elements. You also get support all the way back to Internet Explorer 7!

However, there are limitations. Generally, it's necessary to wrap an extra element around items (to get the joys of perfect vertical centring, a table-cell must live inside an element set as a table). It's also not possible to wrap items set as `display: table-cell` onto multiple lines.

In conclusion, all of the existing layout methods have severe limitations. Thankfully, there is a new CSS layout method that addresses these issues and much more. Cue the trumpets, roll out the red carpet. Here comes Flexbox.

Introducing Flexbox

Flexbox addresses the shortfalls in each of the aforementioned display mechanisms. Here's a brief overview of its super powers:

- It can easily vertically center contents
- It can change the visual order of elements
- It can automatically space and align elements within a box, automatically assigning available space between them
- It can make you look 10 years younger (probably not, but in low numbers of empirical tests (me) it has been proven to reduce stress)

The bumpy path to Flexbox

Flexbox has been through a few major iterations before arriving at the relatively stable version we have today. For example, consider the changes from the 2009 version (`http://www.w3.org/TR/2009/WD-css3-flexbox-20090723/`), the 2011 version (`http://www.w3.org/TR/2011/WD-css3-flexbox-20111129/`), and the 2014 version we are basing our examples on (`http://www.w3.org/TR/css-flexbox-1/`). The syntax differences are marked.

These differing specifications mean there are three major implementation versions. How many of these you need to concern yourself with depends on the level of browser support you need.

Browser support for Flexbox

Let's get this out of the way up front: there is no Flexbox support in Internet Explorer 9, 8, or below.

For everything else you'd likely want to support (and virtually all mobile browsers), there is a way to enjoy most (if not all) of Flexbox's features. You can check the support information at `http://caniuse.com/`.

Before we get stuck into Flexbox, we need to take a brief but essential tangent.

Leave prefixing to someone else

It's my hope that once you have seen a few examples of Flexbox, you will appreciate its utility and feel empowered to use it. However, manually writing all the necessary code to support each of the different Flexbox specifications is a tough task. Here's an example. I'm going to set three Flexbox related properties and values. Consider this:

```
.flex {
    display: flex;
    flex: 1;
    justify-content: space-between;
}
```

That's how the properties and values would look in the most recent syntax. However, if we want support for Android browsers (v4 and below) and IE 10, here is what would actually be needed:

```
.flex {
    display: -webkit-box;
    display: -webkit-flex;
    display: -ms-flexbox;
```

```
    display: flex;
    -webkit-box-flex: 1;
    -webkit-flex: 1;
        -ms-flex: 1;
            flex: 1;
    -webkit-box-pack: justify;
    -webkit-justify-content: space-between;
        -ms-flex-pack: justify;
            justify-content: space-between;
}
```

It's necessary to write all that because in the last few years, as browsers made experimental versions of new functionality available, they did so with a 'vendor prefix'. Each vendor had their own prefix. For example -ms- for Microsoft, -webkit- for WebKit, -moz- for Mozilla, and so on. For every new feature this meant it was necessary to write multiple versions of the same property; the vendor prefixed versions first, and the official W3C version at the bottom.

The result of this spell in web history is CSS that looks like the previous example. It's the only way to get the feature working across the widest number of devices. Nowadays, vendors rarely add prefixes but for the foreseeable future we must live with the reality of many existing browsers still requiring prefixes to enable certain features. This brings us back to Flexbox, an extreme example of vendor prefixing thanks to not just multiple vendor versions but also different specifications of the feature. And understanding and remembering everything you need to write in the current format and each previous format is not a whole lot of fun.

I don't know about you, but I'd rather spend my time doing something more productive than writing out that little lot each time! In short, if you intend to use Flexbox in anger, take the time to setup an auto-prefixing solution.

Choosing your auto-prefixing solution

For the sake of your sanity, to accurately and easily add vendor-prefixes to CSS, use some form of automatic prefixing solution. Right now, I favor Autoprefixer (https://github.com/postcss/autoprefixer). It's fast, easy to setup and very accurate.

There are versions of Autoprefixer for most setups; you don't necessarily need a command line based build tool (for example, Gulp or Grunt). For example, if you use Sublime Text, there is a version that will work straight from the command palette: https://github.com/sindresorhus/sublime-autoprefixer. There are also versions of Autoprefixer for Atom, Brackets, and Visual Studio.

From this point on, unless essential to illustrate a point, there will be no more vendor prefixes in the code samples.

Getting Flexy

Flexbox has four key characteristics: **direction**, **alignment**, **ordering**, and **flexibility**. We'll cover all these characteristics and how they relate by way of a few examples.

The examples are deliberately simplistic; just moving some boxes and their content around so we can understand the principals of how Flexbox works.

Perfect vertically centered text

Note that this first Flexbox example is `example_03-03`:

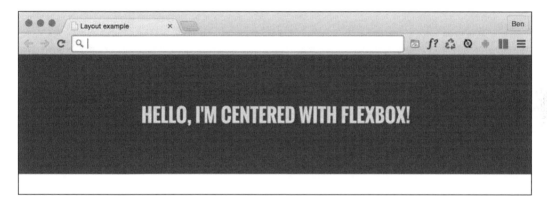

Here's the markup:

```
<div class="CenterMe">
    Hello, I'm centered with Flexbox!
</div>
```

Here is the entire CSS rule that's styling that markup:

```
.CenterMe {
    background-color: indigo;
    color: #ebebeb;
    font-family: 'Oswald', sans-serif;
    font-size: 2rem;
    text-transform: uppercase;
    height: 200px;
    display: flex;
    align-items: center;
    justify-content: center;
}
```

The majority of the property/value pairs in that rule are merely setting colors and font sizing. The three properties we are interested in are:

```
.CenterMe {
    /* other properties */
    display: flex;
    align-items: center;
    justify-content: center;
}
```

If you have not used Flexbox or any of the properties in the related Box Alignment specification (`http://www.w3.org/TR/css3-align/`) these properties probably seem a little alien. Let's consider what each one does:

- `display: flex`: This is the bread and butter of Flexbox. This merely sets the item to be a Flexbox (as opposed to a block, inline-block, and so on).
- `align-items`: This aligns the items within a Flexbox in the cross axis (vertically centering the text in our example).
- `justify-content`: This sets the main axis centring of the content. With a Flexbox row, you can think of it like the button in a word processor that sets the text to the left, right, or center (although there are additional `justify-content` values we will look at shortly).

OK, before we get further into the properties of Flexbox, we will consider a few more examples.

 In some of these examples I'm making use of the Google hosted font 'Oswald' (with a fallback to a sans-serif font). In *Chapter 5, CSS3 – Selectors, Typography, Color Modes, and New Features*, we will look at how we can use the `@font-face` rule to link to custom font files.

Offset items

How about a simple list of navigation items, but with one offset to one side?

Here's what it looks like:

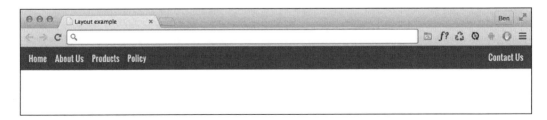

Here's the markup:

```
<div class="MenuWrap">
    <a href="#" class="ListItem">Home</a>
    <a href="#" class="ListItem">About Us</a>
    <a href="#" class="ListItem">Products</a>
    <a href="#" class="ListItem">Policy</a>
    <a href="#" class="LastItem">Contact Us</a>
</div>
```

And here is the CSS:

```
.MenuWrap {
    background-color: indigo;
    font-family: 'Oswald', sans-serif;
    font-size: 1rem;
    min-height: 2.75rem;
    display: flex;
    align-items: center;
    padding: 0 1rem;
}

.ListItem,
.LastItem {
    color: #ebebeb;
    text-decoration: none;
}

.ListItem {
    margin-right: 1rem;
}

.LastItem {
    margin-left: auto;
}
```

How about that—not a single float, inline-block, or table-cell needed! When you set display: flex; on a wrapping element, the children of that element become flex-items which then get laid out using the flex layout model. The magic property here is margin-left: auto which makes that item use all available margin on that side.

Reverse the order of items

Want to reverse the order of the items?

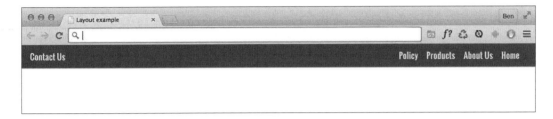

It's as easy as adding `flex-direction: row-reverse;` to the wrapping element and changing `margin-left: auto` to `margin-right: auto` on the offset item:

```
.MenuWrap {
    background-color: indigo;
    font-family: 'Oswald', sans-serif;
    font-size: 1rem;
    min-height: 2.75rem;
    display: flex;
    flex-direction: row-reverse;
    align-items: center;
    padding: 0 1rem;
}

.ListItem,
.LastItem {
    color: #ebebeb;
    text-decoration: none;
}

.ListItem {
    margin-right: 1rem;
}

.LastItem {
    margin-right: auto;
}
```

How about if we want them laid out vertically instead?

Simple. Change to `flex-direction: column;` on the wrapping element and remove the auto margin:

```css
.MenuWrap {
    background-color: indigo;
    font-family: 'Oswald', sans-serif;
    font-size: 1rem;
    min-height: 2.75rem;
    display: flex;
    flex-direction: column;
    align-items: center;
    padding: 0 1rem;
}

.ListItem,
.LastItem {
    color: #ebebeb;
    text-decoration: none;
}
```

Column reverse

Want them stacked in the opposite direction? Just change to `flex-direction: column-reverse;` and you're done.

 You should be aware that there is a `flex-flow` property that is shorthand for setting `flex-direction` and `flex-wrap` in one. For example, `flex-flow: row wrap;` would set the direction to a row and set wrapping on. However, at least initially, I find it easier to specify the two settings separately. The `flex-wrap` property is also absent from the oldest Flexbox implementations so can render the whole declaration void in certain browsers.

Different Flexbox layouts inside different media queries

As the name suggests, Flexbox is inherently flexible so how about we go for a column list of items at smaller viewports and a row style layout when space allows. It's a piece of cake with Flexbox:

```css
.MenuWrap {
    background-color: indigo;
```

```
        font-family: 'Oswald', sans-serif;
        font-size: 1rem;
        min-height: 2.75rem;
        display: flex;
        flex-direction: column;
        align-items: center;
        padding: 0 1rem;
    }

    @media (min-width: 31.25em) {
        .MenuWrap {
            flex-direction: row;
        }
    }

    .ListItem,
    .LastItem {
        color: #ebebeb;
        text-decoration: none;
    }

    @media (min-width: 31.25em) {
        .ListItem {
            margin-right: 1rem;
        }
        .LastItem {
            margin-left: auto;
        }
    }
```

You can view that as `example_03-05`. Be sure to resize the browser window to see the different layouts.

Inline-flex

Flexbox has an inline variant to complement inline-block and inline-table. As you might have guessed it is `display: inline-flex;`. Thanks to its beautiful centering abilities you can do some wacky things with very little effort.

Here's the markup:

```
<p>Here is a sentence with a <a href="http://www.w3.org/TR/css-
flexbox-1/#flex-containers" class="InlineFlex">inline-flex link</a>.</
p>
```

And here is the CSS for that:

```
.InlineFlex {
    display: inline-flex;
    align-items: center;
    height: 120px;
    padding: 0 4px;
    background-color: indigo;
    text-decoration: none;
    border-radius: 3px;
    color: #ddd;
}
```

When items are set as `inline-flex` anonymously (for example, their parent element is not set to `display: flex;`) then they retain whitespace between elements, just like inline-block or inline-table do. However, if they are within a flex container, then whitespace is removed, much as it is with table-cell items within a table.

Of course, you don't always have to center items within a Flexbox. There are a number of different options. Let's look at those now.

Flexbox alignment properties

If you want to play with this example, you can find it at `example_03-07`. Remember the example code you download will be at the point where we finish this section so if you want to 'work along' you may prefer to delete the CSS in the example file and start again.

The important thing to understand with Flexbox alignment is the concept of axis. There are two axis to consider, the 'main axis' and the 'cross axis'. What each of these represents depends upon the direction the Flexbox is heading. For example, if the direction of your Flexbox is set to `row`, the main axis will be the horizontal axis and the cross axis will be the vertical axis.

Conversely, if your Flexbox direction is set to `column`, the main axis will be the vertical axis and the cross axis will be the horizontal.

The specification (http://www.w3.org/TR/css-flexbox-1/#justify-content-property) provides the following illustration to aid authors:

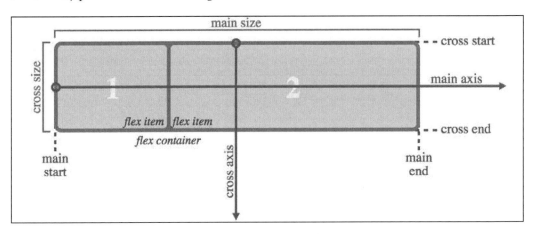

Here's the basic markup of our example:

```
<div class="FlexWrapper">
    <div class="FlexInner">I am content in the inner Flexbox.</div>
</div>
```

Let's set basic Flexbox related styles:

```
.FlexWrapper {
    background-color: indigo;
    display: flex;
    height: 200px;
    width: 400px;
}

.FlexInner {
    background-color: #34005B;
    display: flex;
    height: 100px;
    width: 200px;
}
```

In the browser, that produces this:

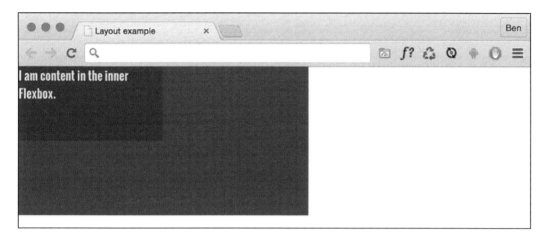

Right, let's test drive the effects of some of these properties.

The align-items property

The `align-items` property positions items in the cross axis. If we apply this property to our wrapping element like so:

```
.FlexWrapper {
    background-color: indigo;
    display: flex;
    height: 200px;
    width: 400px;
    align-items: center;
}
```

As you would imagine, the item within that box gets centered vertically:

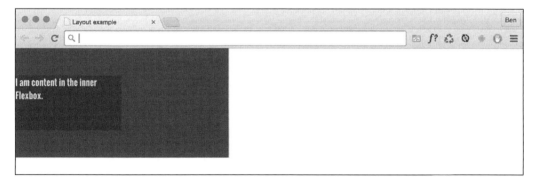

The same effect would be applied to any number of children within.

The align-self property

Sometimes, you may want to pull just one item into a different alignment. Individual flex items can use the `align-self` property to align themselves. At this point, I'll remove the previous alignment properties, add another two items into the markup (they have been given the `.FlexInner` HTML class), and on the middle one I'll add another HTML class (`.AlignSelf`) and use it to add the `align-self` property. Viewing the CSS at this point may be more illustrative:

```css
.FlexWrapper {
    background-color: indigo;
    display: flex;
    height: 200px;
    width: 400px;
}
.FlexInner {
    background-color: #34005B;
    display: flex;
    height: 100px;
    width: 200px;
}

.AlignSelf {
    align-self: flex-end;
}
```

Here is the effect in the browser:

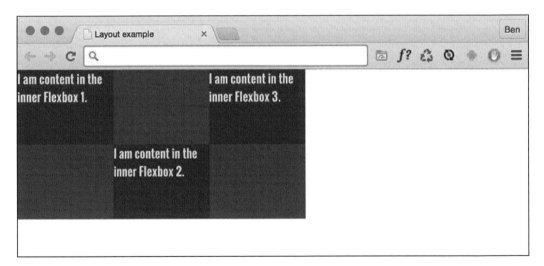

Wow! Flexbox really makes these kinds of changes trivial. In that example the value of `align-self` was set to `flex-end`. Let's consider the possible values we could use on the cross axis before looking at alignment in the main axis.

Possible alignment values

For cross axis alignment, Flexbox has the following possible values:

- `flex-start`: Setting an element to `flex-start` would make it begin at the 'starting' edge of its flex container

- `flex-end`: Setting to `flex-end` would align the element at the end of the flex container

- `center`: Puts it in the middle of the flex container

- `baseline`: Sets all flex items in the container so that their baselines align

- `stretch`: Makes the items stretch to the size of their flex container (in the cross axis)

 There are some particulars inherent to using these properties, so if something isn't playing happily, always refer to the specification for any edge case scenarios: `http://www.w3.org/TR/css-flexbox-1/`.

The justify-content property

Alignment in the main axis is controlled with `justify-content` (for non Flexbox/block-level items, the `justify-self` property has also been proposed (`http://www.w3.org/TR/css3-align/`). Possible values for `justify-content` are:

- `flex-start`
- `flex-end`
- `center`
- `space-between`
- `space-around`

The first three do exactly what you would now expect. However, let's take a look what `space-between` and `space-around` do. Consider this markup:

```
<div class="FlexWrapper">
    <div class="FlexInner">I am content in the inner Flexbox 1.</div>
    <div class="FlexInner">I am content in the inner Flexbox 2.</div>
    <div class="FlexInner">I am content in the inner Flexbox 3.</div>
</div>
```

And then consider this CSS. We are setting the three flex-items (`FlexInner`) to each be 25% width, wrapped by a flex container (`FlexWrapper`) set to be 100% width.

```css
.FlexWrapper {
    background-color: indigo;
    display: flex;
    justify-content: space-between;
    height: 200px;
    width: 100%;
}
.FlexItems {
    background-color: #34005B;
    display: flex;
    height: 100px;
    width: 25%;
}
```

As the three items will only take up 75% of the available space, `justify-content` explains what we would like the browser to do with the remaining space. A value of `space-between` puts equal amount of space between the items and `space-around` puts it around. Perhaps a screenshot here will help: This is `space-between`.

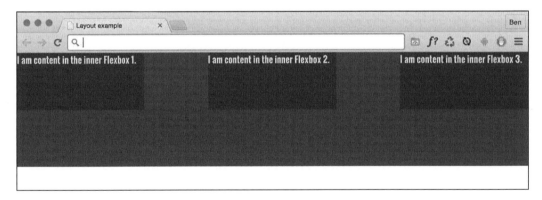

And here is what happens if we switch to `space-around`.

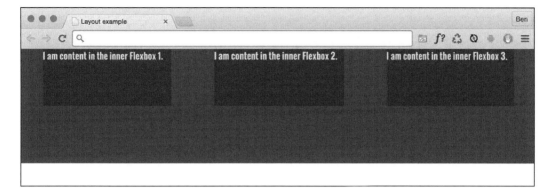

Those two values are pretty handy I think you will agree.

The various alignment properties of Flexbox are currently being specified into the CSS Box Alignment Module Level 3. This should give the same fundamental alignment powers to other display properties, such as `display: block;` and `display: table;`. The specification is still being worked upon so check the status at `http://www.w3.org/TR/css3-align/`.

The flex property

We've used the `width` property on those flex-items but it's also possible to define the width, or 'flexiness' if you will, with the `flex` property. To illustrate, consider another example; same markup, but amended CSS for the items:

```
.FlexItems {
    border: 1px solid #ebebeb;
    background-color: #34005B;
    display: flex;
    height: 100px;
    flex: 1;
}
```

The `flex` property is actually a shorthand way of specifying three separate properties: `flex-grow`, `flex-shrink`, and `flex-basis`. The specification covers these individual properties in more detail at `http://www.w3.org/TR/css-flexbox-1/`. However, the specification recommends that authors use the `flex` shorthand property, so that's what we're rolling with here, capiche?

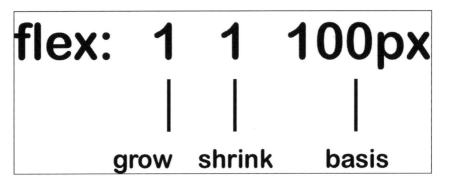

For flex-items, if a `flex` property is present (and the browser supports it), it is used to size the item rather than a width or height value (if present). Even if the width or height value is specified after the `flex` property, it will still have no effect. Let's look at what each of these values do.

- `flex-grow` (the first value you can pass to flex) is the amount, relevant to the other flex items, the flex-item can grow when free space is available

- `flex-shrink` is the amount the flex-item can shrink relevant to the other flex-items when there is not enough space available

- `flex-basis` (the final value you can pass to Flex) is the basis size the flex-item is sized to

Although it's possible to just write `flex: 1`, I recommend writing all the values into a `flex` property. I think it's clearer what you intend to happen. For example: `flex: 1 1 auto` means that the item will grow into 1 part of the available space, it will also shrink 1 part when space is lacking and the basis size for the flexing is the intrinsic width of the content (the size the content would be if flex wasn't involved).

Let's try another: `flex: 0 0 50px` means this item will neither grow nor shrink and it's basis is 50px (so it will be 50px regardless of any free space). How about flex: 2 0 50% — that's going to take two 'lots' of available space, it won't shrink and its basis size is 50%. Hopefully, these brief examples have demystified the flex property a little.

[If you set the `flex-shrink` value to zero, then the flex basis effectively behaves like a minimum width.]

You can think of the `flex` property as a way to set ratios. With each flex-item set to 1, they each take an equal amount of space:

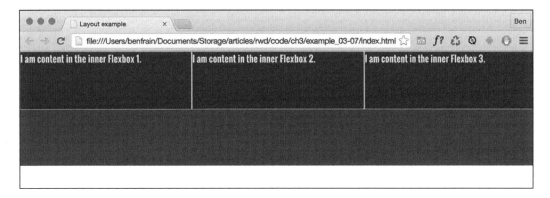

Right, so to test the theory, let's amend the HTML classes in the markup:

```
<div class="FlexWrapper">
    <div class="FlexItems FlexOne">I am content in the inner Flexbox
1.</div>
    <div class="FlexItems FlexTwo">I am content in the inner Flexbox
2.</div>
    <div class="FlexItems FlexThree">I am content in the inner Flexbox
3.</div>
</div>
```

And then here is the amended CSS:

```
.FlexItems {
    border: 1px solid #ebebeb;
    background-color: #34005B;
    display: flex;
    height: 100px;
}

.FlexOne {
    flex: 1.5 0 auto;
}

.FlexTwo,
.FlexThree {
    flex: 1 0 auto;
}
```

In this instance, `FlexOne` takes up 1.5 the amount of space that `FlexTwo` and `FlexThree` take up.

This shorthand syntax really becomes useful for quickly bashing out relationships between items. For example, if the request comes in, "that needs to be 1.8 times wider than the others", you could easily facilitate that request with the flex property.

Hopefully, the incredibly powerful flex property is starting to make a little sense now?

I could write chapters and chapters on Flexbox! There are so many examples we could look at. However, before we move on to the other main topic of this chapter (responsive images) there are just two more things I would like to share with you.

Simple sticky footer

Suppose you want a footer to sit at the bottom of the viewport when there is not enough content to push it there. This has always been a pain to achieve but with Flexbox it's simple. Consider this markup (which can be viewed in `example_03-08`):

```
<body>
    <div class="MainContent">
        Here is a bunch of text up at the top. But there isn't enough
content to push the footer to the bottom of the page.
    </div>
    <div class="Footer">
        However, thanks to flexbox, I've been put in my place.
    </div>
</body>
```

And here's the CSS:

```
html,
body {
    margin: 0;
    padding: 0;
}

html {
    height: 100%;
}

body {
    font-family: 'Oswald', sans-serif;
    color: #ebebeb;
    display: flex;
```

```
    flex-direction: column;
    min-height: 100%;
}

.MainContent {
    flex: 1;
    color: #333;
    padding: .5rem;
}

.Footer {
    background-color: violet;
    padding: .5rem;
}
```

Take a look at that in the browser and test adding more content into .MainContentdiv. You'll see that when there is not enough content, the footer is stuck to the bottom of the viewport. When there is, it sits below the content.

This works because our flex property is set to grow where space is available. As our body is a flex container of 100% minimum height, the main content can grow into all that available space. Beautiful.

Changing source order

Since the dawn of CSS, there has only been one way to switch the visual ordering of HTML elements in a web page. That was achieved by wrapping elements in something set to display: table and then switching the display property on the items within, between display: table-caption (puts it on top), display: table-footer-group (sends it to the bottom), and display: table-header-group (sends it to just below the item set to display: table-caption). However, as robust as this technique is, it was a happy accident, rather than the true intention of these settings.

However, Flexbox has visual source re-ordering built in. Let's have a look at how it works.

Consider this markup:

```
<div class="FlexWrapper">
    <div class="FlexItems FlexHeader">I am content in the Header.</
div>
    <div class="FlexItems FlexSideOne">I am content in the SideOne.</
div>
    <div class="FlexItems FlexContent">I am content in the Content.</
div>
```

```
    <div class="FlexItems FlexSideTwo">I am content in the SideTwo.</
div>
    <div class="FlexItems FlexFooter">I am content in the Footer.</
div>
</div>
```

You can see here that the third item within the wrapper has a HTML class of `FlexContent` — imagine that this `div` is going to hold the main content for the page.

OK, let's keep things simple. We will add some simple colors to more easily differentiate the sections and just get these items one under another in the same order they appear in the markup.

```
.FlexWrapper {
    background-color: indigo;
    display: flex;
    flex-direction: column;
}

.FlexItems {
    display: flex;
    align-items: center;
    min-height: 6.25rem;
    padding: 1rem;
}

.FlexHeader {
    background-color: #105B63;
}

.FlexContent {
    background-color: #FFFAD5;
}

.FlexSideOne {
    background-color: #FFD34E;
}

.FlexSideTwo {
    background-color: #DB9E36;
}

.FlexFooter {
    background-color: #BD4932;
}
```

That renders in the browser like this:

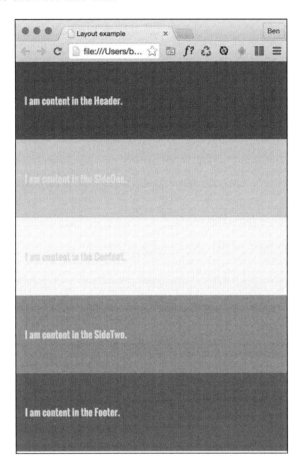

Now, suppose we want to switch the order of `.FlexContent` to be the first item, without touching the markup. With Flexbox it's as simple as adding a single property/value pair:

```
.FlexContent {
    background-color: #FFFAD5;
    order: -1;
}
```

The `order` property lets us revise the order of items within a Flexbox simply and sanely. In this example, a value of `-1` means that we want it to be before all the others.

If you want to switch items around quite a bit, I'd recommend being a little more declarative and add an order number for each. This makes things a little easier to understand when you combine them with media queries.

Let's combine our new source order changing powers with some media queries to produce not just a different layout at different sizes but different ordering.

Note: you can view this finished example at example_03-09.

As it's generally considered wise to have your main content at the beginning of a document, let's revise our markup to this:

```
<div class="FlexWrapper">
    <div class="FlexItems FlexContent">I am content in the Content.</
div>
    <div class="FlexItems FlexSideOne">I am content in the SideOne.</
div>
    <div class="FlexItems FlexSideTwo">I am content in the SideTwo.</
div>
    <div class="FlexItems FlexHeader">I am content in the Header.</
div>
    <div class="FlexItems FlexFooter">I am content in the Footer.</
div>
</div>
```

First the page content, then our two sidebar areas, then the header and finally the footer. As I'll be using Flexbox, we can structure the HTML in the order that makes sense for the document, regardless of how things need to be laid out visually.

For the smallest screens (outside of any media query), I'll go with this ordering:

```
.FlexHeader {
    background-color: #105B63;
    order: 1;
}

.FlexContent {
    background-color: #FFFAD5;
    order: 2;
}

.FlexSideOne {
```

```
    background-color: #FFD34E;
    order: 3;
}

.FlexSideTwo {
    background-color: #DB9E36;
    order: 4;
}

.FlexFooter {
    background-color: #BD4932;
    order: 5;
}
```

Which gives us this in the browser:

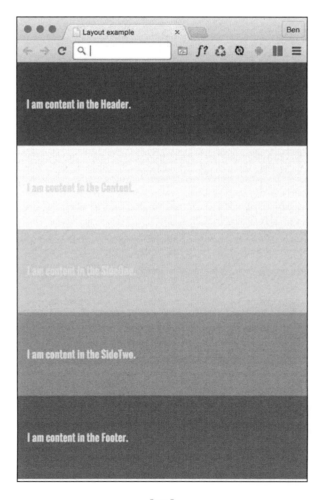

And then, at a breakpoint, I'm switching to this:

```
@media (min-width: 30rem) {
    .FlexWrapper {
        flex-flow: row wrap;
    }
    .FlexHeader {
        width: 100%;
    }
    .FlexContent {
        flex: 1;
        order: 3;
    }
    .FlexSideOne {
        width: 150px;
        order: 2;
    }
    .FlexSideTwo {
        width: 150px;
        order: 4;
    }
    .FlexFooter {
        width: 100%;
    }
}
```

Which gives us this in the browser:

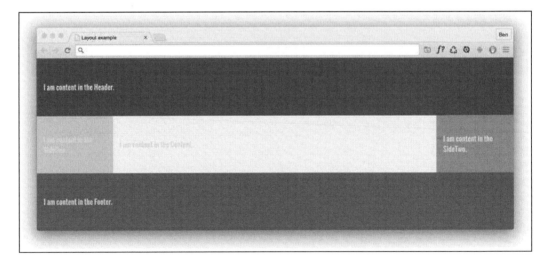

In that example, the shortcut `flex-flow: row wrap` has been used. That allows the flex items to wrap onto multiple lines. It's one of the poorer supported properties, so depending upon how far back support is needed, it might be necessary to wrap the content and two side bars in another element.

Wrapping up Flexbox

There are near endless possibilities when using the Flexbox layout system and due to its inherent 'flexiness', it's a perfect match for responsive design. If you've never built anything with Flexbox before, all the new properties and values can seem a little odd and it's sometimes disconcertingly easy to achieve layouts that have previously taken far more work. To double-check implementation details against the latest version of the specification, make sure you check out `http://www.w3.org/TR/css-flexbox-1/`.

I think you'll love building things with Flexbox.

Hot on the heels of the Flexible Box Layout Module is the Grid Layout Module Level 1: `http://www.w3.org/TR/css3-grid-layout/`.

It's relatively immature compared to Flexbox (much like the early history of Flexbox, grid layout has already been through some major changes) and as such we aren't looking at it in detail here. However, it's definitely one to keep an eye on as it promises us even more layout powers.

Responsive images

Serving the appropriate image to users based upon the particulars of their device and environment has always been a tricky problem. This problem was highlighted with the advent of responsive web design, the very nature of which is to serve a single code base to each and every device.

The intrinsic problem of responsive images

As an author, you cannot know or plan for every possible device that may visit your site now or in the future. Only a browser knows the particulars of the device using it (screen size and device capabilities for example) at the moment it serves up and renders the content.

Conversely only the author (you and I) know what versions of an image we have at our disposal. For example, we may have three versions of the same image. A small, medium, and large: each with increasing dimensions to cover off a host of screen size and density eventualities. The browser does not know this. We have to tell it.

To summarize the conundrum, we have halve of the solution in that we know what images we have, and the browser has the other halve of the solution in that the browser knows what device is visiting the site and what the most appropriate image dimensions and resolution would be.

How can we tell the browser what images we have at our disposal so that it may chose the most appropriate one for the user?

In the first few years of responsive web design, there was no specified way. Thankfully, now we have the Embedded Content specification: `https://html.spec.whatwg.org/multipage/embedded-content.html`.

The Embedded Content specification describes ways to deal with the simple resolution switching of images (to facilitate a user on a higher resolution screen receiving a higher resolution version of images) and 'art direction' situations, for when authors want users to see a totally different image, depending upon a number of device characteristics (think media queries).

Demonstrating responsive image examples is tricky. It's not possible to appreciate on a single screen the different images that could be loaded with a particular syntax or technique. Therefore, the examples that follow will be mainly code and you'll just have to trust me that's it's going to produce the result you need in supporting browsers.

Let's look at the two most common scenarios you likely need responsive images for. These are switching an image when a different resolution is needed, and changing an image entirely depending upon the available viewport space.

Simple resolution switching with srcset

Let's suppose you have three versions of an image. They all look the same except one is a smaller size or resolution intended for smaller viewports, another caters for medium size viewports, and finally a larger version covers off every other viewport. Here is how we can let the browser know we have these three versions available.

```
<img src="scones_small.jpg" srcset="scones_medium.jpg 1.5x, scones_large.jpg 2x" alt="Scones taste amazing">
```

This is about as simple as things get with responsive images, so let's ensure that syntax makes perfect sense.

First of all, the `src` attribute, which you will already be familiar with, has a dual role here; it's specifying the small 1x version of the image and it also acts as a fallback image if the browser doesn't support the `srcset` attribute. That's why we are using it for the small image. This way, older browsers that will ignore the `srcset` information will get the smallest and best performing image possible.

For browsers that understand `srcset`, with that attribute, we provide a comma-separated list of images that the browser can choose from. After the image name (such as `scones_medium.jpg`) we issue a simple resolution hint. In this example 1.5x and 2x have been used but any integer would be valid. For example, 3x or 4x would work too (providing you can find a suitably high resolution screen).

However, there is an issue here; a device with a 1440px wide, 1x screen will get the same image as a 480px wide, 3x screen. That may or may not be the desired effect.

Advanced switching with srcset and sizes

Let's consider another situation. In a responsive web design, it wouldn't be uncommon for an image to be the full viewport width on smaller viewports, but only half the width of the viewport at larger sizes. The main example in *Chapter 1, The Essentials of Responsive Web Design*, was a typical example of this. Here's how we can communicate these intentions to the browser:

```
<img srcset="scones-small.jpg 450w, scones-medium.jpg 900w"
sizes="(min-width: 17em) 100vw, (min-width: 40em) 50vw" src="scones-
small.jpg" alt="Scones">
```

Inside the image tag we are utilizing `srcset` again. However, this time, after specifying the images we are adding a value with a w suffix. This tells the browser how wide the image is. In our example we have a 450px wide image (called `scones-small.jpg`) and a 900px wide image (called `scones-medium.jpg`). It's important to note this w suffixed value isn't a 'real' size. It's merely an indication to the browser, roughly equivalent to the width in 'CSS pixels'.

 What exactly defines a pixel in CSS? I wondered that myself. Then I found the explanation at `http://www.w3.org/TR/css3-values/` and wished I hadn't wondered.

This w suffixed value makes more sense when we factor in the `sizes` attribute. The `sizes` attribute allows us to communicate the intentions for our images to the browser. In our preceding example, the first value is equivalent to, "for devices that are at least 17em wide, I intend the image to be shown around 100vw wide".

If some of the units used, such as vh (where 1vh is equal to 1% of the viewport height) and vw (where 1vw is equal to 1% of the viewport width) don't make sense, be sure to read *Chapter 5*, *CSS3 – Selectors, Typography, Color Modes, and New Features*.

The second part is effectively, "Hi browser, for devices that are at least 40em wide, I only intend the image to be shown at 50vw". That may seem a little redundant until you factor in DPI (or DPR for Device Pixel Ratio). For example, on a 320px wide device with a 2x resolution (effectively requiring a 640px wide image if shown at full width) the browser might decide the 900px wide image is actually a better match as it's the first option it has for an image that would be big enough to fulfill the required size.

Did you say the browser 'might' pick one image over another?

An important thing to remember is that the `sizes` attributes are merely hints to the browser. That doesn't necessarily ensure that the browser will always obey. This is a good thing. Trust me, it really is. It means that in future, if there is a reliable way for browsers to ascertain network conditions, it may choose to serve one image over another because it knows things at that point that we can't possibly know at this point as the author. Perhaps a user has a setting on their device to 'only download 1x images' or 'only download 2x images'; in these scenarios the browser can make the best call.

The alternative to the browser deciding is to use the `picture` element. Using this element ensures that the browser serves up the exact image you asked for. Let's take a look at how it works.

Art direction with the picture element

The final scenario you may find yourself in is one in which you have different images that are applicable at different viewport sizes. For example, consider our cake based example again from *Chapter 1*, *The Essentials of Responsive Web Design*. Maybe on the smallest screens we would like a close up of the scone with a generous helping of jam and cream on top. For larger screens, perhaps we have a wider image we would like to use. Perhaps it's a wide shot of a table loaded up with all manner of cakes. Finally, for larger viewports still, perhaps we want to see the exterior of a cake shop on a village street with people sat outside eating cakes and drinking tea (I know, sounds like nirvana, right?). We need three different images that are most appropriate at different viewport ranges. Here is how we could solve this with `picture`:

```
<picture>
    <source media="(min-width: 30em)" srcset="cake-table.jpg">
```

```
    <source media="(min-width: 60em)" srcset="cake-shop.jpg">
    <img src="scones.jpg" alt="One way or another, you WILL get
cake.">
</picture>
```

First of all, be aware that when you use the `picture` element, it is merely a wrapper to facilitate other images making their way to the `img` tag within. If you want to style the images in any way, it's the `img` that should get your attention.

Secondly, the `srcset` attribute here works exactly the same as the previous example.

Thirdly, the `img` tag provides your fallback image and also the image that will be displayed if a browser understands picture but none of the media definitions match. Just to be crystal clear; do not omit the `img` tag from within a `picture` element or things won't end well.

The key difference with picture is that we have a `source` tag. Here we can use media query style expressions to explicitly tell the browser which asset to use in a matching situation. For example, our first one in the preceding example is telling the browser, "Hey you, if the screen is at least 30em wide, load in the `cake-table.jpg` image instead". As long as conditions match, the browser will dutifully obey.

Facilitate new-fangled image formats

As a bonus, `picture` also facilitates us providing alternate formats of an image. 'WebP' (more info at `https://developers.google.com/speed/webp/`) is a newer format that plenty of browsers lack support for (`http://caniuse.com/`). For those that do, we can offer a file in that format and a more common format for those that don't:

```
<picture>
    <source type="image/webp" srcset="scones-baby-yeah.webp">
    <img src="scones-baby-yeah.jpg" alt="Again, you WILL eat cake.">
</picture>
```

Hopefully this is now a little more straightforward. Instead of the `media` attribute, we are using `type` (we will do more with the type attribute in *Chapter 4*, *HTML5 for Responsive Web Designs*), which, although more typically used to specify video sources (possible video source types can be found at `https://html.spec.whatwg.org/multipage/embedded-content.html`), allows us here to define WebP as the preferred image format. If the browser can display it, it will, otherwise it will grab the default one in the `img` tag.

There are plenty of older browsers that will never be able to make use of the official W3C responsive images. Unless there is a specific reason not to, my advice would be to allow the built-in fallback capabilities do their thing. Use a sensibly sized fallback image to provide them with a good experience and allow more capable devices to enjoy an enhanced experience.

Summary

We've covered a lot of ground in this chapter. We have spent considerable time getting acquainted with Flexbox, the most recent, powerful, and now well-supported layout technique. We have also covered how we can serve up any number of alternative images to our users depending upon the problems we need to solve. By making use of `srcset`, `sizes`, and `picture`, our users should always get the most appropriate image for their needs, both now and in the future.

So far we've looked at lots of CSS and some of its emerging possibilities and capabilities, but only with responsive images have we looked at more modern markup. Let's address that issue next.

The next chapter is going to be all about HTML5. What it offers, what's changed from the previous version, and for the most part, how we can make best use of its new semantic elements to create cleaner, more meaningful HTML documents.

4
HTML5 for Responsive Web Designs

If you are looking for guidance on using the HTML5 **application programming interfaces** (**APIs**), I'm going to paraphrase a line from a great Western movie and say, "I'm not your Huckleberry".

What I would like to look at with you is the 'vocabulary' part of HTML5; its semantics. More succinctly, the way we can use the new elements of HTML5 to describe the content we place in markup. The majority of content in this chapter is not specific to a responsive web design. However, HTML is the very foundation upon which all web-based designs and applications are built. Who doesn't want to build upon the strongest possible foundation?

You might be wondering 'what is HTML5 anyway?' In which case I would tell you that HTML5 is simply the description given to the latest version of HTML, the language of tags we use to build web pages. HTML itself is a constantly evolving standard, with the prior major version being 4.01.

For a little more background on the versions and timeline of HTML's evolution, you can read the Wikipedia entry at `http://en.wikipedia.org/wiki/HTML#HTML_versions_timeline`.

 HTML5 is now a recommendation from the W3C. You can read the specification at `http://www.w3.org/TR/html5/`.

The topics we will cover in this chapter are:

- How well supported is HTML5?
- Starting an HTML5 page the right way
- Easy-going HTML5
- New semantic elements
- Text-level semantics
- Obsolete features
- Putting the new elements to use
- **Web Content Accessibility Guidelines (WCAG)** accessibility conformance and **Web Accessibility Initiative-Accessible Rich Internet Applications (WAI-ARIA)** for more accessible web applications
- Embedding media
- Responsive video and iFrames
- A note about 'offline first'

 HTML5 also provides specific tools for handling forms and user input. This set of features takes much of the burden away from more resource heavy technologies like JavaScript for things like form validation. However, we're going to look at HTML5 forms separately in *Chapter 9, Conquer Forms with HTML5 and CSS3*.

HTML5 markup – understood by all modern browsers

Nowadays, the majority of websites I see (and all of those I make myself) are written using HTML5, rather than the older HTML 4.01 standard.

All modern browsers understand the new semantic elements of HTML5 (the new structural elements, video, and audio tags) and even older versions of Internet Explorer (versions before Internet Explorer 9) can be served a tiny 'polyfill' to allow it to render these new elements.

What is a polyfill?

The term **polyfill** was originated by Remy Sharp as an allusion to filling the cracks in older browsers with Polyfilla (known as **Spackling Paste** in the US). Therefore, a polyfill is a JavaScript 'shim' to effectively replicate newer features in older browsers. However, it's important to be aware that polyfills add extra flab to your code. Therefore, even if you could add 15 polyfill scripts to make Internet Explorer 6 render a site identically to every other browser, it doesn't mean you necessarily should.

If you need to enable HTML5 structural elements, I'd look at Remy Sharp's original script (`http://remysharp.com/2009/01/07/html5-enabling-script/`) or create a custom build of Modernizr (`http://modernizr.com`). If Modernizr is a tool you've not come across or used, there is a whole section on it in the next chapter.

With that in mind, let's consider the start of an HTML5 page. Let's get a handle on all the opening tags and what they do.

Starting an HTML5 page the right way

Let's start right at the beginning of an HTML5 document. Screw this part up and you could spend a long time wondering why your page doesn't behave as it should. The first few lines should look something like this:

```
<!DOCTYPE html>
<html lang="en">
<head>
<meta charset=utf-8>
```

Let's go through these tags one by one. Generally, they will be the same every time you create a web page but trust me, it's worth understanding what they do.

The doctype

The `doctype` is a means of communicating to the browser the type of document we have. Otherwise, it wouldn't necessarily know how to use the content within it.

We opened our document with the HTML5 `doctype` declaration:

```
<!DOCTYPE html>
```

If you're a fan of lowercase, then `<!doctype html>` is just as good. It makes no difference.

This is a welcome change from HTML 4.01 pages. They used to start something like this:

```
<!DOCTYPE html PUBLIC "-//W3C//DTD XHTML 1.0 Transitional//EN"
"http://www.w3.org/TR/xhtml1/DTD/xhtml1-transitional.dtd">
```

What an enormous pain in the pimply rear! No wonder I used to copy and paste it!

The HTML5 `doctype` on the other hand is nice and short, just `<!DOCTYPE html>`. Interesting fact (to me anyway): it actually ended up this way as it was determined that this was the shortest method of telling a browser to render the page in "standards mode".

 Want a history lesson in what 'quirks' and 'standards' mode were? Wikipedia has you covered: `http://en.wikipedia.org/wiki/Quirks_mode`

The HTML tag and lang attribute

After the `doctype` declaration, we open the `html` tag; the root tag for our document. We also use the `lang` attribute to specify the language for the document, and then we open the `<head>` section:

```
<html lang="en">
<head>
```

Specifying alternate languages

According to the W3C specifications (`http://www.w3.org/TR/html5/dom.html#the-lang-and-xml:lang-attributes`), the `lang` attribute specifies the primary language for the element's contents and for any of the element's attributes that contain text. If you're not writing pages in English, you'd best specify the correct language code. For example, for Japanese, the HTML tag would be `<html lang="ja">`. For a full list of languages take a look at `http://www.iana.org/assignments/language-subtag-registry`.

Character encoding

Finally, we specify the character encoding. As it's a void element (cannot contain anything) it doesn't require a closing tag:

```
<meta charset="utf-8">
```

Unless you have a good reason to specify otherwise, the value for the charset is almost always utf-8. For the curious, more information on the subject can be found at http://www.w3.org/International/questions/qa-html-encoding-declarations#html5charset.

Easy-going HTML5

I remember, back in school, every so often our super-mean (but actually very good) math teacher would be away. The class would breathe a collective sigh of relief as, rather than "Mr. Mean" (names have been changed to protect the innocent), the replacement teacher was usually an easy-going and amiable man. He sat quietly and left us to get on without shouting or constant needling. He didn't insist on silence whilst we worked, he didn't much care if we adhered to the way he worked out problems, all that mattered was the answers and that we could articulate how we came to them. If HTML5 were a math teacher, it would be that easy-going supply teacher. I'll now qualify this bizarre analogy.

If you pay attention to how you write code, you'll typically use lower-case for the most part, wrap attribute values in quotation marks, and declare a "type" for scripts and style sheets. For example, perhaps you link to a style sheet like this:

```
<link href="CSS/main.css" rel="stylesheet" type="text/css" />
```

HTML5 doesn't require such precision, it's just as happy to see this:

```
<link href=CSS/main.css rel=stylesheet >
```

Did you notice that? There's no end tag/slash, there are no quotation marks around the attribute values, and there is no type declaration. However, easy going HTML5 doesn't care. The second example is just as valid as the first.

This more lax syntax applies across the whole document, not just linked assets. For example, specify a div like this if you like:

```
<div id=wrapper>
```

That's perfectly valid HTML5. The same goes for inserting an image:

```
<img SRC=frontCarousel.png aLt=frontCarousel>
```

That's also valid HTML5. No end tag/slash, no quotes, and a mix of capitalization and lower case characters. You can even omit things such as the opening `<head>` tag and the page still validates. What would XHTML 1.0 say about this?

Want a short-cut to great HTML5 code? Consider the HTML5 Boilerplate (`http://html5boilerplate.com/`). It's a pre-made "best practice" HTML5 file, including essential styles, polyfills, and optional tools such as Modernizr. You can pick up lots of great tips just by viewing the code and it's also possible to custom build the template to match your specific needs. Highly recommended!

A sensible approach to HTML5 markup

Personally, I like writing my markup 'XHTML' style. That means closing tags, quoting attribute values, and adhering to a consistent letter case. One could argue that ditching some of these practices would save a few bytes of data but that's what tools are for (any needless characters/data could be stripped if needed). I want my markup to be as legible as possible and I would encourage others to do the same. I'm of the opinion that clarity in code should trump brevity.

When writing HTML5 documents therefore, I think you can write clean and legible code while still embracing the economies afforded by HTML5. To exemplify, for a CSS link, I'd go with the following:

```
<link href="CSS/main.css" rel="stylesheet"/>
```

I've kept the closing tag and the quotation marks but omitted the `type` attribute. The point to make here is that you can find a level you're happy with yourself. HTML5 won't be shouting at you, flagging up your markup in front of the class and standing you in a corner with a dunces hat on for not validating (was it just my school that did that?). However you want to write your markup is just fine.

Who am I kidding? I want you to know right now that if you're writing your code without quoting attribute values and closing your tags, I am silently judging you.

Despite HTML5's looser syntax, it's always worth checking whether your markup is valid. Valid markup is more accessible markup. The W3C validator was created for just this reason: `http://validator.w3.org/`

Enough of me berating writers of 'hipster' style markup. Let's look at some more benefits of HTML5.

All hail the mighty <a> tag

A huge economy in HTML5 is that we can now wrap multiple elements in an <a> tag (woohoo! About time, right?). Previously, if you wanted your markup to validate, it was necessary to wrap each element in its own <a> tag. For example, look at the following HTML 4.01 code:

```
<h2><a href="index.html">The home page</a></h2>
<p><a href="index.html">This paragraph also links to the home page</a></p>
<a href="index.html"><img src="home-image.png" alt="home-slice" /></a>
```

With HTML5, we can ditch all the individual <a> tags and instead wrap the group with one:

```
<a href="index.html">
  <h2>The home page</h2>
  <p>This paragraph also links to the home page</p>
  <img src="home-image.png" alt="home-slice" />
</a>
```

The only limitations to keep in mind are that, understandably, you can't wrap one <a> tag within another <a> tag (because, like, duh) or another interactive element such as a button (because like, double duh!) and you can't wrap a form in an <a> tag either (because like, oh, you get the idea).

New semantic elements in HTML5

If I check the definition of the word 'semantics' in the dictionary of OS X, it is defined as:

"the branch of linguistics and logic concerned with meaning".

For our purposes, semantics is the process of giving our markup meaning. Why is this important? Glad you asked.

Most websites follow fairly standard structural conventions; typical areas include a header, a footer, a sidebar, a navigation bar, and so on. As web authors we will often name the divs we use to more clearly designate these areas (for example, class="Header"). However, as far as the code itself goes, any user agent (web browser, screen reader, search engine crawler, and so on) looking at it couldn't say for sure what the purpose of each of these div elements is. Users of assistive technology would also find it difficult to differentiate one div from another. HTML5 aims to solve that problem with new semantic elements.

For the full list of HTML5 elements, get yourself (very) comfy and point your browser at http://www.w3.org/TR/html5/semantics.html#semantics.

We won't cover every one of the new elements here, merely those I feel are the most beneficial or interesting in day-to-day responsive web design use. Let's dig in.

The <main> element

For a long time, HTML5 had no element to demarcate the main content of a page. Within the body of a web page, this would be the element that contains the main block of content.

At first, it was argued that the content that wasn't inside one of the other new semantic HTML5 elements would, by negation, be the main content. Thankfully, the spec changed and we now have a more declarative way to group the main content; the aptly named <main> tag.

Whether you're wrapping the main content of a page or the main section of a web-based application, the main element is what you should be grouping it all with. Here's a particularly useful line from the specification:

> *"The main content area of a document includes content that is unique to that document and excludes content that is repeated across a set of documents such as site navigation links, copyright information, site logos and banners and search forms (unless the document or applications main function is that of a search form)."*

It's also worth noting that there shouldn't be more than one main on each page (after all, you can't have two main pieces of content) and it shouldn't be used as a descendent as some of the other semantic HTML5 elements such as article, aside, header, footer, nav, or header. They can live within a main element however.

 Read the official line on the main element at: http://www.w3.org/TR/html5/grouping-content.html#the-main-element

The <section> element

The `<section>` element is used to define a generic section of a document or application. For example, you may choose to create sections round your content; one section for contact information, another section for news feeds, and so on. It's important to understand that it isn't intended for styling purposes. If you need to wrap an element merely to style it, you should continue to use a `div` as you would have before.

When working on web-based applications I tend to use `section` as the wrapping element for visual components. It provides a simple way to see the beginning and end of components in the markup.

You can also qualify for yourself whether you should be using a section based upon whether the content you are sectioning has a natural heading within it (for example an `h1`). If it doesn't, it's likely you'd be better off opting for a `div`.

> To find out what the W3C HTML5 specification says about `<section>` go to the following URL:
>
> `http://www.w3.org/TR/html5/sections.html#the-section-element`

The <nav> element

The `<nav>` element is used to wrap major navigational links to other pages or parts within the same page. It isn't strictly intended for use in footers (although it can be) and the like, where groups of links to other pages are common.

If you usually markup your navigational elements with an un-ordered list (`<ul>`) and a bunch of list tags (`li`), you may be better served with a `nav` and a number of nested `a` tags instead.

> To find out what the W3C HTML5 specification says about `<nav>` go to the following URL:
>
> `http://www.w3.org/TR/html5/sections.html#the-nav-element`

The <article> element

The <article> element, alongside <section> can easily lead to confusion. I certainly had to read and re-read the specifications of each before it sank in. Here's my re-iteration of the specification. The <article> element is used to wrap a self-contained piece of content. When structuring a page, ask whether the content you're intending to use within a <article> tag could be taken as a whole lump and pasted onto a different site and still make complete sense? Another way to think about it is, would the content that you are considering wrapping in an <article> actually constitute a separate article in a RSS feed? Obvious examples of content that should be wrapped with an <article> element would be blog posts or news stories. Be aware that if nesting <article> elements, it is presumed that the nested <article> elements are principally related to the outer article.

To see what the W3C HTML5 specification says about <article> visit http://www.w3.org/TR/html5/sections.html#the-article-element.

The <aside> element

The <aside> element is used for content that is tangentially related to the content around it. In practical terms, I often use it for sidebars (when it contains suitable content). It's also considered suitable for pull quotes, advertising, and groups of navigation elements. Basically anything not directly related to the main content would work well in an aside. If it was an e-commerce site, I'd consider areas like 'customers who bought this also bought' as prime candidates for an <aside>.

For more on what the W3C HTML5 specification says about <aside> visit http://www.w3.org/TR/html5/sections.html#the-aside-element.

The <figure> and <figcaption> elements

The specification relates that the figure element:

"...can thus be used to annotate illustrations, diagrams, photos, code listings, etc."

Here's how we could use it to revise a portion of markup from the first chapter:

```
<figure class="MoneyShot">
  <img class="MoneyShotImg" src="img/scones.jpg" alt="Incredible
scones" />
  <figcaption class="ImageCaption">Incredible scones, picture from
Wikipedia</figcaption>
</figure>
```

You can see that the `<figure>` element is used to wrap this little self-contained block. Inside, the `<figcaption>` is used to provide a caption for the parent `<figure>` element.

It's perfect when images or code need a little caption alongside (that wouldn't be suitable in the main text of the content).

> The specification for the `figure` element can be found at `http://www.w3.org/TR/html5/grouping-content.html#the-figure-element`.
>
> The specification for the `figcaption` is at `http://www.w3.org/TR/html5/grouping-content.html#the-figcaption-element`.

The <details> and <summary> elements

How many times have you wanted to create a simple open and close 'widget' on your page? A piece of summary text that when clicked, opens a panel with additional information. HTML5 facilitates this pattern with the `details` and `summary` elements. Consider this markup (you can open `example3.html` from this chapter's code to play with it for yourself):

```
<details>
    <summary>I ate 15 scones in one day</summary>
    <p>Of course I didn't. It would probably kill me if I did. What a
way to go. Mmmmmm, scones!</p>
</details>
```

Opening this in Chrome, with no added styling, shows only the summary text by default:

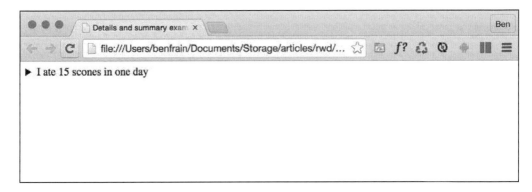

Clicking anywhere on the summary text opens the panel. Clicking it again toggles it shut. If you want the panel open by default you can add the open attribute to the details element:

```
<details open>
    <summary>I ate 15 scones in one day</summary>
    <p>Of course I didn't. It would probably kill me if I did. What a
way to go. Mmmmmm, scones!</p>
</details>
```

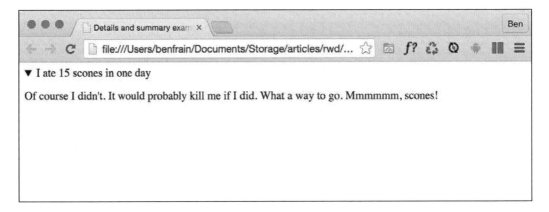

Supporting browsers typically add some default styling to indicate the panel can be opened. Here in Chrome (and also Safari) that's a dark disclosure triangle. To disable this, you need to use a WebKit specific proprietary pseudo selector:

```
summary::-webkit-details-marker {
   display: none;
}
```

You can of course use that same selector to style the marker differently.

Currently, there is no way of animating the open and close. Neither is there a (non JavaScript) way of toggling other details panels closed (at the same level) when a different one is open. I'm not sure either of these desires will (or should) ever be addressed. You should think of it more as a way to facilitate what you would have done with a `display: none;` toggle with the help of JavaScript.

Sadly, as I write this (mid 2015), there is no support for this element in Firefox or Internet Explorer (they just render the two elements as inline elements). Polyfills exist (`https://mathiasbynens.be/notes/html5-details-jquery`) and hopefully will be fully implemented soon.

The <header> element

Practically, the `<header>` element can be used for the "masthead" area of a site's header. It can also be used as an introduction to other content such as a section within an `<article>` element. You can use it as many times on the same page as needed (you could have a `<header>` inside every `<section>` on your page for example).

This is what the W3C HTML5 specification says about `<header>`:
`http://www.w3.org/TR/html5/sections.html#the-header-element`

The <footer> element

The `<footer>` element should be used to contain information about the section it sits within. It might contain links to other documents or copyright information for example. Like the `<header>` it can be used multiple times within a page if needed. For example, it could be used for the footer of a blog but also a `footer` section within a blog post article. However, the specification explains that contact information for the author of a blog post should instead be wrapped by an `<address>` element.

See what the W3C HTML5 specification says about `<footer>`:
`http://www.w3.org/TR/html5/sections.html#the-footer-element`

The <address> element

The <address> element is to be used explicitly for marking up contact information for its nearest <article> or <body> ancestor. To confuse matters, keep in mind that it isn't to be used for postal addresses and the like (unless they are indeed the contact addresses for the content in question). Instead postal addresses and other arbitrary contact information should be wrapped in good ol' <p> tags.

I'm not a fan of the <address> element as in my experience it would be far more useful to markup a physical address in its own element, but that's a personal gripe. Hopefully it makes more sense to you.

> For more on what the W3C HTML5 specification says about <address> check out:
>
> http://www.w3.org/TR/html5/sections.html#the-address-element

A note on h1-h6 elements

Something that I hadn't realized until very recently is that using h1-h6 tags to markup headings and sub-headings is discouraged. I'm talking about this kind of thing:

```
<h1>Scones:</h1>
<h2>The most resplendent of snacks</h2>
```

Here's a quote from the HTML5 specification:

h1–h6 elements must not be used to markup subheadings, subtitles, alternative titles and taglines unless intended to be the heading for a new section or subsection.

That's certainly one of the less ambiguous sentences in the specification! Ooops!

So, how should we author such eventualities? The specification actually has a whole section, (http://www.w3.org/TR/html5/common-idioms.html#common-idioms) dedicated to this. Personally, I preferred the old <hgroup> element but sadly that ship has sailed (more information in the *Obsolete HTML features* section). So, to follow the advice of the specification, our prior example could be rewritten as:

```
<h1>Scones:</h1>
<p>The most resplendent of snacks</p>
```

HTML5 text-level semantics

Besides the structural and grouping elements we've looked at, HTML5 also revises a few tags that used to be referred to as inline elements. The HTML5 specification now refers to these tags as text-level semantics (`http://www.w3.org/TR/html5/text-level-semantics.html#text-level-semantics`). Let's take a look at a few common examples.

The <b> element

Historically, the `<b>` element meant "make this bold" (`http://www.w3.org/TR/html4/present/graphics.html#edef-B`). This was from back in the day when stylistic choices were part of the markup. However, you can now officially use it merely as a styling hook in CSS as the HTML5 specification now declares that `<b>` is:

> *"The b element represents a span of text to which attention is being drawn for utilitarian purposes without conveying any extra importance and with no implication of an alternate voice or mood, such as key words in a document abstract, product names in a review, actionable words in interactive text-driven software, or an article lede."*

Although no specific meaning is now attached to it, as it's text level, it's not intended to be used to surround large groups of markup, use a `div` for that. You should also be aware that because it was historically used to bold text, you'll typically have to reset the font-weight in CSS if you want content within a `<b>` tag to not appear bold.

The <em> element

OK, hands up, I've often used `<em>` merely as a styling hook too. I need to mend my ways, as in HTML5:

The `em` element represents stress emphasis of its contents.

Therefore, unless you actually want the enclosed contents to be emphasized, consider using a `<b>` tag or, where relevant, an `<i>` tag instead.

The <i> element

The HTML5 specification describes the `<i>` as:

> *"...a span of text in an alternate voice or mood, or otherwise offset from the normal prose in a manner indicating a different quality of text."*

Suffice it to say, it's not to be used to merely italicize something. For example, we could use it to markup the odd name in this line of text:

```
<p>However, discussion on the hgroup element is now frustraneous as
it's now gone the way of the <i>Raphus cucullatus</i>.</p>
```

There are plenty of other text-level semantic tags in HTML5. For the full run down, take a look at the relevant section of the specification at the following URL:

`http://www.w3.org/TR/html5/text-level-semantics.html#text-level-semantics`

Obsolete HTML features

Besides things such as the language attributes in script links, there are some further parts of HTML you may be used to using that are now considered "obsolete" in HTML5. It's important to be aware that there are two camps of obsolete features in HTML5—conforming and non-conforming. Conforming features will still work but will generate warnings in validators. Realistically, avoid them if you can but they aren't going to make the sky fall down if you do use them. Non-conforming features might still render in certain browsers but if you use them, you are considered very, very naughty and you might not get a treat at the weekend!

In terms of obsolete and non-conforming features, there is quite a raft. I'll confess that many I have never used (some I've never even seen!). It's possible you may experience a similar reaction. However, if you're curious, you can find the full list of obsolete and non-conforming features at `http://www.w3.org/TR/html5/obsolete.html`. Notable obsolete and non-conforming features are `strike`, `center`, `font`, `acronym`, `frame`, and `frameset`.

There are also features that were present in earlier drafts of HTML5 which have now been dropped. `hgroup` is one such example. The tag was originally proposed to wrap groups of headings; an `h1` for a title and a `h2` for a sub-title might have been wrapped in a `hgroup` element. However, discussion on the `hgroup` element is now frustraneous as it's now gone the way of the Raphus cucullatus (go on, Google it, you know you want to).

Putting HTML5 elements to use

It's time to practice using some of the elements we have just looked at. Let's revisit the example from *Chapter 1, The Essentials of Responsive Web Design*. If we compare the markup below to the original markup in *Chapter 1, The Essentials of Responsive Web Design*, (remember, you can download all the examples from the `http://rwd.education` website, or from the GitHub repo) you can see where the new elements we've looked at have been employed below.

```
<article>
  <header class="Header">
    <a href="/" class="LogoWrapper"><img src="img/SOC-Logo.png"
alt="Scone O'Clock logo" /></a>
    <h1 class="Strap">Scones: the most resplendent of snacks</h1>
  </header>
  <section class="IntroWrapper">
    <p class="IntroText">Occasionally maligned and misunderstood; the
scone is a quintessentially British classic.</p>
    <figure class="MoneyShot">
      <img class="MoneyShotImg" src="img/scones.jpg" alt="Incredible
scones" />
      <figcaption class="ImageCaption">Incredible scones, picture from
Wikipedia</figcaption>
    </figure>
  </section>
  <p>Recipe and serving suggestions follow.</p>
  <section class="Ingredients">
    <h3 class="SubHeader">Ingredients</h3>
  </section>
  <section class="HowToMake">
    <h3 class="SubHeader">Method</h3>
  </section>
  <footer>
    Made for the book, <a href="http://rwd.education">'Resonsive
web design with HTML5 and CSS3'</a> by <address><a href="http://
benfrain">Ben Frain</a></address>
  </footer>
</article>
```

Applying common sense to your element selection

I've removed a good portion of the inner content so we can concentrate on the structure. Hopefully you will agree that it's easy to discern different sections of markup from one another. However, at this point I'd also like to offer some pragmatic advice; it isn't the end of the world if you don't always pick the correct element for every single given situation. For example, whether or not I used a `<section>` or `<div>` in the preceding example is of little real consequence. If we use an `<em>` when we should actually be using an `<i>`, I certainly don't feel it's a crime against humanity; the folks at the W3C won't hunt you down and feather and tar you for making the wrong choice. Just apply a little common sense. That said, if you can use elements like the `<header>` and `<footer>` when relevant, there are inherent accessibility benefits in doing so.

WCAG and WAI-ARIA for more accessible web applications

Even since writing the first edition of this book from 2011 to 2012, the W3C has made strides in making it easier for authors to write more accessible web pages.

WCAG

The WCAG exists to provide:

> *"a single shared standard for web content accessibility that meets the needs of individuals, organizations, and governments internationally."*

When it comes to more pedestrian web pages (as opposed to single page web applications and the like) it makes sense to concentrate on the WCAG guidelines. They offer a number of (mostly common sense) guidelines for how to ensure your web content is accessible. Each recommendation is rated as a conformance level: A, AA, or AAA. For more on these conformance levels look at http://www.w3.org/TR/UNDERSTANDING-WCAG20/conformance.html#uc-levels-head.

You'll probably find that you are already adhering to many of the guidelines, like providing alternative text for images for example. However, you can get a brief run-down of the guidelines at http://www.w3.org/WAI/WCAG20/glance/Overview.html and then build your own custom quick reference list of checks at http://www.w3.org/WAI/WCAG20/quickref/.

I'd encourage everyone to spend an hour or two looking down the list. Many of the guidelines are simple to implement and offer real benefits to users.

WAI-ARIA

The aim of WAI-ARIA is principally to solve the problem of making dynamic content on a web page accessible. It provides a means of describing roles, states, and properties for custom widgets (dynamic sections in web applications) so that they are recognizable and usable by assistive technology users.

For example, if an on-screen widget displays a constantly updating stock price, how would a blind user accessing the page know that? WAI-ARIA attempts to solve these very problems.

Don't use roles for semantic elements

It used to be advisable to add 'landmark' roles to headers and footers like this:

```
<header role="banner">A header with ARIA landmark banner role</header>
```

However, this is now considered surplus to requirements. If you look at the specifications for any of the elements listed earlier there is a dedicated *Allowed ARIA role attributes* section. Here is the relevant explanation from the section element as an example:

> "*Allowed ARIA role attribute values:*
>
> *region role (default - do not set), alert, alertdialog, application, contentinfo, dialog, document, log, main, marquee, presentation, search or status.*"

The key part there being 'role (default - do not set)'. This means that explicitly adding an ARIA role to the element is pointless as it is implied by the element itself. A note in the specification now makes this clear:

> "*In the majority of cases setting an ARIA role and/or aria-* attribute that matches the default implicit ARIA semantics is unnecessary and not recommended as these properties are already set by the browser.*"

If you only remember one thing

The easiest thing you can do to aid assistive technologies is to use the correct elements where possible. A `header` element is going to be far more useful than `div class="Header"`. Similarly, if you have a button on your page, use the `<button>` element (rather than a `span` or other element styled to look like a `button`). I accept that the `button` element doesn't always allow exact styling (it doesn't like being set to `display: table-cell` or `display: flex` for example) and in those instances at least choose the next best thing; usually an `<a>` tag.

Taking ARIA further

ARIA isn't limited to landmark roles only. To take things further, a full list of the roles and a succinct description of their usage suitability is available at `http://www.w3.org/TR/wai-aria/roles`.

For a lighter take on the subject, I'd also recommend Heydon Pickering's book, *Apps For All: Coding Accessible Web Applications* (available at `https://shop.smashingmagazine.com/products/apps-for-all-coding-accessible-web-applications`).

Test your designs for free with non-visual desktop access (NVDA)

If you develop on the Windows platform and you'd like to test your ARIA enhanced designs on a screen reader, you can do so for free with NVDA. You can get it at the following URL:

`http://www.nvda-project.org/`

Google now also ships the free 'Accessibility Developer Tools' for the Chrome browser (available cross-platform); well worth checking out.

There's also a growing number of tools that help quickly test your own designs against things like color blindness. For example, `https://michelf.ca/projects/sim-daltonism/` is a Mac app that lets you switch color blindness types and see a preview in a floating palette.

Finally, OS X also includes VoiceOver utility for testing your web pages.

Hopefully, this brief introduction to WAI-ARIA and WCAG has given you enough information to think a little more about how to approach supporting assistive technologies. Perhaps adding assistive technology support to your next HTML5 project will be easier than you think.

As a final resource for all things accessibility, there are handy links and advice galore on the A11Y project home page at `http://a11yproject.com/`.

Embedding media in HTML5

For many, HTML5 first entered their vocabulary when Apple refused to add support for Flash in their iOS devices. Flash had gained market dominance (some would argue market stranglehold) as the plugin of choice to serve up video through a web browser. However, rather than using Adobe's proprietary technology, Apple decided to rely on HTML5 instead to handle rich media rendering. While HTML5 was making good headway in this area anyway, Apple's public support of HTML5 gave it a major leg up and helped its media tools gain greater traction in the wider community.

As you might imagine, Internet Explorer 8 and lower versions don't support HTML5 video and audio. Most other modern browsers (Firefox 3.5+, Chrome 4+, Safari 4, Opera 10.5+, Internet Explorer 9+, iOS 3.2+, Opera Mobile 11+, Android 2.3+) handle it just fine.

Adding video and audio the HTML5 way

Video and audio in HTML5 is easy. The only real difficulty with HTML5 media used to be listing out alternate source formats for media (as different browsers supported different file formats). Nowadays, MP4 is ubiquitous across desktop and mobile platforms, making the inclusion of media in your web pages via HTML5 a breeze. Here's a 'simple as can be' example of how to link to a video file in your page:

```
<video src="myVideo.mp4"></video>
```

HTML5 allows a single `<video></video>` tag (or `<audio></audio>` for audio) to do all the heavy lifting. It's also possible to insert text between the opening and closing tag to inform users when there is a problem. There are also additional attributes you'd ordinarily want to add, such as the `height` and `width`. Let's add these in:

```
<video src="myVideo.mp4" width="640" height="480">What, do you mean
you don't understand HTML5?</video>
```

Now, if we add the preceding code snippet into our page and look at it in Safari, it will appear but there will be no controls for playback. To get the default playback controls we need to add the `controls` attribute. We could also add the `autoplay` attribute (not recommended—it's common knowledge that everyone hates videos that auto-play). This is demonstrated in the following code snippet:

```
<video src="myVideo.mp4" width="640" height="480" controls autoplay>
What, do you mean you don't understand HTML5?</video>
```

The result of the preceding code snippet is shown in the following screenshot:

Further attributes include `preload` to control pre-loading of media (early HTML5 adopters should note that preload replaces autobuffer), `loop` to repeat the video, and `poster` to define a poster frame for the video. This is useful if there's likely to be a delay in the video playing (or buffering is likely to take some time). To use an attribute, simply add it to the tag. Here's an example including all these attributes:

```
<video src="myVideo.mp4" width="640" height="480" controls autoplay
preload="auto" loop poster="myVideoPoster.png">What, do you mean you
don't understand HTML5?</video>
```

Fallback capability for older browsers

The `<source>` tag enables us to provide fallbacks, as needed. For example, alongside providing an MP4 version of the video, if we wanted to ensure a suitable fallback for Internet Explorer 8 and lower versions, we could add a Flash fallback. Further still, if the user didn't have any suitable playback technology in the browser, we could provide download links to the files themselves. Here's an example:

```
<video width="640" height="480" controls preload="auto" loop
poster="myVideoPoster.png">
    <source src="video/myVideo.mp4" type="video/mp4">
    <object width="640" height="480" type="application/x-shockwave-
flash" data="myFlashVideo.SWF">
        <param name="movie" value="myFlashVideo.swf" />
        <param name="flashvars" value="controlbar=over&amp;image=myVideo
Poster.jpg&amp;file=myVideo.mp4" />
        <img src="myVideoPoster.png" width="640" height="480" alt="__
TITLE__"
            title="No video playback capabilities, please download the
video below" />
    </object>
    <p><b>Download Video:</b>
  MP4 Format:  <a href="myVideo.mp4">"MP4"</a>
    </p>
</video>
```

That code example and the sample video file (me appearing in the UK soap Coronation Street, back when I had hair and hopes of staring alongside DeNiro) in MP4 format are in `example2.html` of the chapter code.

Audio and video tags work almost identically

The `<audio>` tag works on the same principles with the same attributes (excluding `width`, `height`, and `poster`). The main difference between the two being the fact that `<audio>` has no playback area for visible content.

Responsive HTML5 video and iFrames

We have seen that, as ever, supporting older browsers leads to code bloat. What began with the `<video>` tag being one or two lines ended up being 10 or more lines (and an extra Flash file) just to make older versions of Internet Explorer happy! For my own part, I'm usually happy to forego the Flash fallback in pursuit of a smaller code footprint but each use-case differs.

Now, the only problem with our lovely HTML5 video implementation is it's not responsive. That's right, an example in a responsive web design with HTML5 and CSS3 book that doesn't 'respond'.

Thankfully, for HTML5 embedded video, the fix is easy. Simply remove any height and width attributes in the markup (for example, remove `width="640"` `height="480"`) and add the following in the CSS:

```
video { max-width: 100%; height: auto; }
```

However, while that works fine for files that we might be hosting locally, it doesn't solve the problem of videos embedded within an iFrame (take a bow YouTube, Vimeo, and others). The following code will add a film trailer for Midnight Run from YouTube:

```
<iframe width="960" height="720" src="https://www.youtube.com/
watch?v=B1_N28DA3gY" frameborder="0" allowfullscreen></iframe>
```

However, if you add that to a page as is, even if adding that earlier CSS rule, if the viewport is less than 960px wide, things will start to get clipped.

The easiest way to solve this problem is with a little CSS trick pioneered by Gallic CSS maestro Thierry Koblentz; essentially creating a box of the correct aspect ratio for the video it contains. I won't spoil the magician's own explanation, go take a read at `http://alistapart.com/article/creating-intrinsic-ratios-for-video`.

If you're feeling lazy, you don't even need to work out the aspect ratio and plug it in yourself, there's an online service that can do it for you. Just head to `http://embedresponsively.com/` and paste your iFrame URL in. It will spit you out a simple chunk of code you can paste into your page. For example, our Midnight Run trailer results in this:

```
<style>.embed-container { position: relative; padding-bottom: 56.25%;
height: 0; overflow: hidden; max-width: 100%; height: auto; } .embed-
container iframe, .embed-container object, .embed-container embed {
position: absolute; top: 0; left: 0; width: 100%; height: 100%; }</
style><div class='embed-container'><iframe src='http://www.youtube.
com/embed/B1_N28DA3gY' frameborder='0' allowfullscreen></iframe></div>
```

That's all there is to it, simply add to your page and you're done: we now have a fully responsive YouTube video (note: kids, don't pay any attention to Mr. DeNiro; smoking is bad)!

A note about 'offline first'

I believe that the ideal way to build responsive web pages and web-based applications is 'offline first'. This approach means that websites and applications will continue to work and load, even without an Internet connection.

HTML5 offline web applications (`http://www.w3.org/TR/2011/WD-html5-20110525/offline.html`) were specified to meet this aim.

Although support for offline web applications is good (`http://caniuse.com/#feat=offline-apps`), sadly, it's an imperfect solution. Although it's relatively simple to set up, there are a number of limitations and pitfalls. Documenting them all here is beyond the scope of this book. Instead I would recommend reading the humorous and thorough post by Jake Archibald on the subject at `http://alistapart.com/article/application-cache-is-a-douchebag`.

I'm therefore of the opinion that while it's possible to achieve offline first experiences using offline web applications (a good tutorial of how to do so is at `http://diveintohtml5.info/offline.html`) and LocalStorage (or some combination of the two), a better solution will be with us before too long. I'm pinning my hopes on 'Service Workers' (`http://www.w3.org/TR/service-workers/`).

At the time of writing, Service Workers is still a relatively new specification but for a good overview I'd encourage you to watch this 15-minute introduction: `https://www.youtube.com/watch?v=4uQM17mFB6g`. Read this introduction `http://www.html5rocks.com/en/tutorials/service-worker/introduction/` and check for support at `https://jakearchibald.github.io/isserviceworkerready/`

I'm hopeful that if and when I come to write a third edition of this book, we will be able to consider a full overview and implementation of this technique. Fingers crossed.

Summary

We've covered a lot in this chapter. Everything from the basics of creating a page that validates as HTML5, through to embedding rich media (video) into our markup and ensuring it behaves responsively.

Although not specific to responsive designs, we've also covered how we can write semantically rich and meaningful code and considered how we might ensure pages are meaningful and usable for users that are relying on assistive technology.

By necessity, it's been a very markup heavy chapter so let's change tack now. In the next couple of chapters we're going to embrace the power and flexibility of CSS. First up, let's look at the power of CSS level 3 and 4 selectors, new viewport relative CSS units, and capabilities such as calc and HSL color. They will all enable us to create faster, more capable, and maintainable responsive designs.

5
CSS3 – Selectors, Typography, Color Modes, and New Features

In the last few years, CSS has enjoyed a raft of new features. Some enable us to animate and transform elements, others allow us to create background images, gradients, mask and filter effects, and others still allow us to bring SVG elements to life.

We will get to all those capabilities in the next few chapters. Firstly I think it will be useful to look at some of the fundamentals that have changed in CSS in the last few years: how we select elements on the page, the units we can use to style and size our elements, and how existing (and future) pseudo-classes and pseudo-elements make CSS ever more powerful. We will also look at how we can create forks in our CSS code to facilitate the features supported in different browsers.

In this chapter, we will learn the following:

- The anatomy of a CSS rule (what defines a rule, declaration and property, and value pairs)
- Quick and handy CSS tricks for responsive designs (multiple columns, word wraps, truncation/text ellipsis, scrolling areas)
- Facilitating feature forks in CSS (how to have some rules apply to some browsers and other rules apply to others)
- How to use sub-string attribute selectors to select HTML elements
- What nth-based selectors are and how we can use them
- What pseudo classes and pseudo elements are (`:empty`, `::before`, `::after`, `:target`, `:scope`)

- The new selectors in CSS Level 4 Selectors module (`:has`)
- What CSS variables and custom properties are and how to write them
- What the CSS `calc` function is and how to use it
- Making use of viewport related units (`vh`, `vw`, `vmin`, and `vmax`)
- How to make use of web typography with `@font-face`
- RGB and HSL color modes with Alpha transparency

No one knows it all

No one can know everything. I've been working with CSS for over a decade and on a weekly basis I still discover something new in CSS (or rediscover something I'd forgotten). As such, I don't feel that trying to know every possible CSS property and value permutation is actually a worthy pursuit. Instead, I think it's more sensible to develop a good grasp of what's possible.

As such, we are going to concentrate in this chapter on some of the techniques, units, and selectors I have found most useful when building responsive web designs. I'm hoping you'll then have the requisite knowledge to solve most problems that come your way when developing a responsive web design.

Anatomy of a CSS rule

Before exploring some of what CSS3 has to offer, to prevent confusion, let's establish the terminology we use to describe a CSS rule. Consider the following example:

```
.round { /* selector */
  border-radius: 10px; /* declaration */
}
```

This rule is made up of the selector (`.round`) and then the declaration (`border-radius: 10px;`). The declaration is further defined by the property (`border-radius:`) and the value (`10px;`). Happy we're on the same page? Great, let's press on.

Remember to check support for your users

As we delve into CSS3 more and more, don't forget to visit `http://caniuse.com/`, if you ever want to know what the current level of browser support is available for a particular CSS3 or HTML5 feature. Alongside showing browser version support (searchable by feature), it also provides the most recent set of global usage statistics from `http://gs.statcounter.com/`.

Quick and useful CSS tricks

In my day-to-day work, I've found I use some CSS3 features constantly and others hardly ever. I thought it might be useful to share those I've used most often. These are CSS3 goodies that can make life easier, especially in responsive designs. They solve problems that used to be minor headaches with relative ease.

CSS multi-column layouts for responsive designs

Ever needed to make a single piece of text appear in multiple columns? You could solve the problem by splitting the content into different markup elements and then styling accordingly. However, altering markup for purely stylistic purposes is never ideal. The CSS multi-column layout specification describes how we can span one or more pieces of content across multiple columns with ease. Consider the following markup:

```
<main>
    <p>lloremipsimLoremipsum dolor sit amet, consectetur
<!-- LOTS MORE TEXT -->
</p>
    <p>lloremipsimLoremipsum dolor sit amet, consectetur
<!-- LOTS MORE TEXT -->
</p>
</main>
```

With CSS multi-columns you can make all that content flow across multiple columns in a number of ways. You could make the columns a certain column width (for example, 12em) or instead you could specify that the content needs to span a certain number of columns (for example, 3).

Let's look at the code needed to achieve each of those scenarios. For columns of a set width, use the following syntax:

```
main {
  column-width: 12em;
}
```

This will mean, no matter the viewport size, the content will span across columns that are 12em in width. Altering the viewport will adjust the number of columns displayed dynamically. You can view this in the browser by looking at example_05-01 (or at the GitHub repository: https://github.com/benfrain/rwd).

Consider how the page renders on an iPad in portrait orientation (768px wide viewport):

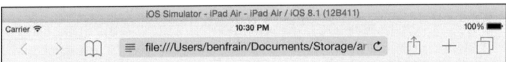

Lorem ipsum dolor sit amet, consectetur adipisicing elit, sed do eiusmod tempor incididunt ut labore et dolore magna aliqua. Ut enim ad minim veniam, quis nostrud exercitation ullamco laboris nisi ut aliquip ex ea commodo consequat. Duis aute irure dolor in reprehenderit in voluptate velit esse cillum dolore eu fugiat nulla pariatur. Excepteur sint occaecat cupidatat non proident, sunt in culpa qui officia deserunt mollit anim id est laborum. Lorem ipsum dolor sit amet, consectetur adipisicing elit, sed do eiusmod tempor incididunt ut labore et dolore magna aliqua. Ut enim ad minim veniam, quis nostrud exercitation ullamco laboris nisi ut aliquip ex ea commodo consequat. Duis aute irure dolor in reprehenderit in voluptate velit esse cillum dolore eu fugiat nulla pariatur. Excepteur sint occaecat cupidatat non proident, sunt in culpa qui officia deserunt mollit anim id est laborum. Lorem ipsum dolor sit amet, consectetur adipisicing elit, sed do eiusmod tempor incididunt ut labore et dolore magna aliqua. Ut enim ad minim veniam, quis nostrud exercitation ullamco laboris nisi ut aliquip ex ea commodo consequat. Duis aute irure dolor in reprehenderit in voluptate velit esse cillum dolore eu fugiat nulla pariatur.Lorem ipsum dolor sit

amet, consectetur adipisicing elit, sed do eiusmod tempor incididunt ut labore et dolore magna aliqua. Ut enim ad minim veniam, quis nostrud exercitation ullamco laboris nisi ut aliquip ex ea commodo consequat. Duis aute irure dolor in reprehenderit in voluptate velit esse cillum dolore eu fugiat nulla pariatur. Excepteur sint occaecat cupidatat non proident, sunt in culpa qui officia deserunt mollit anim id est laborum. Lorem ipsum dolor sit amet, consectetur adipisicing elit, sed do eiusmod tempor incididunt ut labore et dolore magna aliqua. Ut enim ad minim veniam, quis nostrud exercitation ullamco laboris nisi ut aliquip ex ea commodo consequat. Duis aute irure dolor in reprehenderit in voluptate velit esse cillum dolore eu fugiat nulla pariatur. Excepteur sint occaecat cupidatat non proident, sunt in culpa qui officia deserunt mollit anim id est laborum. Lorem ipsum dolor sit amet, consectetur adipisicing elit, sed do eiusmod tempor incididunt ut labore et dolore magna aliqua. Ut enim ad minim veniam, quis nostrud exercitation ullamco laboris nisi ut aliquip ex ea commodo consequat. Duis aute irure dolor in reprehenderit in voluptate velit esse cillum dolore eu fugiat nulla pariatur.Lorem ipsum dolor sit amet, consectetur adipisicing elit, sed

do eiusmod tempor incididunt ut labore et dolore magna aliqua. Ut enim ad minim veniam, quis nostrud exercitation ullamco laboris nisi ut aliquip ex ea commodo consequat. Duis aute irure dolor in reprehenderit in voluptate velit esse cillum dolore eu fugiat nulla pariatur. Excepteur sint occaecat cupidatat non proident, sunt in culpa qui officia deserunt mollit anim id est laborum. Lorem ipsum dolor sit amet, consectetur adipisicing elit, sed do eiusmod tempor incididunt ut labore et dolore magna aliqua. Ut enim ad minim veniam, quis nostrud exercitation ullamco laboris nisi ut aliquip ex ea commodo consequat. Duis aute irure dolor in reprehenderit in voluptate velit esse cillum dolore eu fugiat nulla pariatur. Excepteur sint occaecat cupidatat non proident, sunt in culpa qui officia deserunt mollit anim id est laborum. Lorem ipsum dolor sit amet, consectetur adipisicing elit, sed do eiusmod tempor ncididunt ut labore et dolore magna aliqua. Ut enim ad minim veniam, quis nostrud exercitation ullamco laboris nisi ut aliquip ex ea commodo consequat. Duis aute irure dolor in reprehenderit in voluptate velit esse cillum dolore eu fugiat nulla pariatur.

And then on Chrome in the desktop (approximately 1100px wide viewport):

Simple responsive text columns with minimum work; I like it!

Fixed columns, variable width

If you'd rather keep a fixed number of columns and vary the width, you can write a rule like the following:

```
main {
  column-count: 4;
}
```

Adding a gap and column divider

We can take things even further by adding a specified gap for the columns and a divider:

```
main {
  column-gap: 2em;
  column-rule: thin dotted #999;
  column-width: 12em;
}
```

This gives us a result like the following:

To read the specification on the CSS3 Multi-column Layout Module, visit `http://www.w3.org/TR/css3-multicol/`.

For the time being, despite being at CR status at the W3C, you'll likely still need vendor prefixes on the column declarations for maximum compatibility.

The only caveat I would place on using CSS multi-column is that for longer spans of text it can lead to a flawed user experience. In these instances the user will have to scroll up and down the page to read the columns of text, which can become a little laborious.

Word wrapping

How many times have you had to add a big URL into a tiny space and, well, despaired? Take a look at `http://rwd.education/code/example_05-04`. The problem can also be seen in the following screenshot; notice that the URL is breaking out of its allocated space.

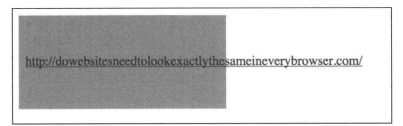

It's easy to fix this issue with a simple CSS3 declaration, which as chance would have it, also works in older versions of Internet Explorer as far back as 5.5! Just add:

```
word-wrap: break-word;
```

to the containing element, which gives an effect as shown in the following screenshot.

Hey presto, the long URL now wraps perfectly!

Text ellipsis

Text truncation used to be the sole domain of server side technology. Nowadays we can do text ellipsis/truncation with CSS alone. Let's consider how.

Consider this markup (you can view this example online at `rwd.education/code/ch5/example_05-03/`):

```
<p class="truncate">OK, listen up, I've figured out the key eternal
happiness. All you need to do is eat lots of scones.</p>
```

But we actually want to truncate the text at 520px wide. So it looks like this:

OK, listen up, I've figured out the key eternal happiness. All you need to do is …

Here is the CSS to make that happen:

```
.truncate {
  width: 520px;
  overflow: hidden;
  text-overflow: ellipsis;
  white-space: no-wrap;
}
```

 You can read the specification for the `text-overflow` property at `http://dev.w3.org/csswg/css-ui-3/`.

Whenever the width of the content exceeds the width defined (the width can just as happily be set as a percentage such as 100% if it's inside a flexible container) it will be truncated. The `white-space: no-wrap` property/value pair is used to ensure that the content doesn't wrap inside the surrounding element.

Creating horizontal scrolling panels

Hopefully you know the kind of thing I mean? Horizontal scrolling panels are common on the iTunes store and Apple TV for showing panels of related content (movies, albums, and so on). Where there is enough horizontal space, all the items are viewable. When space is limited (think mobile devices) the panel is scrollable from side to side.

The scrolling panels work particularly well on modern Android and iOS devices. If you have a modern iOS or Android device to hand, take a look at this next example on that, alongside a desktop browser like Safari or Chrome: `http://rwd.education/code/ch5/example_05-02/`.

I've created a scrolling panel of the top-grossing films of 2014. It looks something like this on an iPhone:

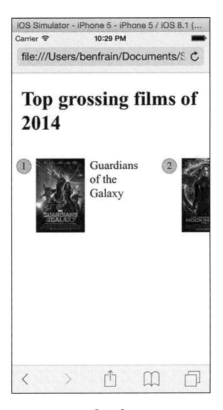

I'm actually cheating a little. The key to this technique is the white-space property, which has actually been around since CSS 2.1 (http://www.w3.org/TR/CSS2/text. html). However, I'm going to use it alongside the new Flexbox layout mechanism, so hopefully you'll indulge me regardless?

To get the basics of this technique working we just need a wrapper narrower than the sum of its contents and to set it's width to auto in the *x* axis. This way, it won't scroll if there is enough space but it will if there isn't.

```
.Scroll_Wrapper {
  width: 100%;
  white-space: nowrap;
  overflow-x: auto;
  overflow-y: hidden;
}

.Item {
  display: inline-flex;
}
```

By using white-space: nowrap we are saying 'do not wrap these elements when you find white space'. Then to keep everything in a single line, we set all the first children of that container to display inline. We're using inline-flex here but it could just as easily be inline, inline-block, or inline-table.

::before and ::after pseudo-elements

If viewing the sample code you will notice that the ::before pseudo element is used to display the number of the item. If using pseudo-elements, remember that for ::before or ::after to display, they must have a content value, even if just whitespace. When these pseudo-elements are displayed, they then behave like the first and last child of that element respectively.

To make things a little more aesthetically pleasing I'm going to hide the scroll bar where I can. Unfortunately these are browser specific so you will need to add these by hand (an Autoprefixer tool won't add them as they are proprietary properties). I'm also going to add touch style inertia scrolling for WebKit browsers (typically iOS devices). Now the updated .Scroll_Wrapper rule looks like this:

```
.Scroll_Wrapper {
  width: 100%;
  white-space: nowrap;
  overflow-x: auto;
  overflow-y: hidden;
```

```
    /*Give us inertia style scrolling on WebKit based touch devices*/
    -webkit-overflow-scrolling: touch;
    /*Remove the scrollbars in supporting versions of IE*/
    -ms-overflow-style: none;
}

/*Stops the scrollbar appearing in WebKit browsers*/
.Scroll_Wrapper::-webkit-scrollbar {
    display: none;
}
```

Where space is limited, we get a nice scrollable horizontal panel. Otherwise, the content just fits.

There are, however, a couple of caveats to this pattern. Firstly, at the time of writing, Firefox has no property that allows you to hide the scroll bars. Secondly, older Android devices can't perform horizontal scrolling (no, really). I therefore tend to qualify this pattern with the help of feature detection. We'll look at how that works next.

Facilitating feature forks in CSS

When you're building out a responsive web design, attempting to provide a single design that works everywhere, on every device, it's a simple fact that you'll frequently encounter situations when features or techniques are not supported on certain devices. In these instances you'll likely want to create a fork in your CSS; if the browser supports a feature, provide one chunk of code, if they don't, they get different code. It's the kind of situation that gets handled by if/else or switch statements in JavaScript.

We currently have two possible approaches. One is entirely CSS based but with fewer browser implementations, and the other is only made possible with the help of a JavaScript library but enjoys far broader support. Let's consider each in turn.

Feature queries

The native solution to forking code in CSS is to use 'Feature Queries', part of the CSS Conditional Rules Module Level 3 (http://www.w3.org/TR/css3-conditional/). However, right now, CSS Conditional Rules lack support in Internet Explorer (as of version 11) and Safari (including iOS devices up to iOS 8.1) so support is hardly ubiquitous.

Feature queries follow a similar syntax to media queries. Consider this:

```
@supports (flashing-sausages: lincolnshire) {
  body {
    sausage-sound: sizzling;
    sausage-color: slighty-burnt;
    background-color: brown;
  }
}
```

Here the styles will only get applied if the browser supports the `flashing-sausages` property. I'm quite confident that no browser is ever going to support a `flashing-sausages` feature (and if they do, I want full credit) so none of the styles inside the `@supports` block will be applied.

Let's consider a more practical example. How about we use Flexbox for when browsers support it, and fallback to another layout technique when they don't. Consider this example:

```
@supports (display: flex) {
  .Item {
    display: inline-flex;
  }
}


@supports not (display: flex) {
  .Item {
    display: inline-block;
  }
}
```

Here we are defining one block of code for when the browser supports a feature, and another lot for when it doesn't. This pattern is fine if the browser supports `@supports` (yes, I realise that is confusing) but if it doesn't, it won't apply any of those styles.

If you want to cover off devices that don't support `@supports`, you're better off writing your default declarations first and then your `@supports` specific one after, so that the prior rule will be overruled if support for `@support` exists, and the `@support` block will be ignored if the browser doesn't support it. Our prior example could therefore be reworked to:

```
.Item {
  display: inline-block;
}
```

```
@supports (display: flex) {
  .Item {
    display: inline-flex;
  }
}
```

Combining conditionals

You can also combine conditionals. Let's suppose we only wanted to apply some rules if both Flexbox and `pointer: coarse` were supported (in case you missed it, we covered the 'pointer' interaction media feature back in *Chapter 2, Media Queries – Supporting Differing Viewports*). Here is what that might look like:

```
@supports ((display: flex) and (pointer: coarse)) {
  .Item {
    display: inline-flex;
  }
}
```

Here we have used the `and` keyword but we could use `or` as well as, or instead of it. For example, if we were happy to apply styles if those two prior property/value combinations were supported, or 3D transforms were supported:

```
@supports ((display: flex) and (pointer: coarse)) or (transform:
translate3d(0, 0, 0)) {
  .Item {
    display: inline-flex;
  }
}
```

Note in that prior example, the extra set of parenthesis that separates the flex and pointer conditional from the transform conditional.

Sadly, as I already mentioned, support for `@support` is far from universal. Boohoo! What's a responsive web designer to do? Fear not, there's a great JavaScript tool that is more than capable of rising to this challenge.

Modernizr

Until `@supports` is more widely implemented in browsers, we can use a JavaScript tool called Modernizr. At present, it's simply the most robust manner in which to facilitate forks in your code.

When forks are needed in CSS, I try and adopt a progressive enhancement approach. Progressive enhancement means starting with simple accessible code; code that will provide, at the very least, a functional design for less capable devices. Then that code is progressively enhanced for more capable devices.

 We'll talk a lot more about progressive enhancement in *Chapter 10, Approaching a Responsive Web Design*.

Let's look how we can facilitate progressive enhancement and forking our CSS code with Modernizr.

Feature detection with Modernizr

If you're a web developer, it's likely you have heard of Modernizr, even if you have perhaps not used it. It's a JavaScript library that you include in your page that feature tests the browser. To start using Modernizr, it's as simple as including a link to the downloaded file in the head section of your pages:

```
<script src="/js/libs/modernizr-2.8.3-custom.min.js"></script>
```

With that in place, when the browser loads the page, any of the included tests are run. If the browser passes the test, Modernizr handily (for our purposes) adds a relevant class to the root HTML tag.

For example, after Mondernizr has done its thing, the classes on the HTML tag for a page might look like this:

```
<html class="js no-touch cssanimations csstransforms csstransforms3d
csstransitions svg inlinesvg" lang="en">
```

In that instance just a few features have been tested: animations, transforms, SVG, inline SVG, and support for touch. With those classes in place, the code can be forked like this:

```
.widget {
  height: 1rem;
}

.touch .widget {
  height: 2rem;
}
```

In the preceding example, the widget item is just 1rem high ordinarily, but if the touch class is present on the HTML (thanks to Modernizr), then the widget would be 2rem high.

We could flip the logic too:

```
.widget {
  height: 2rem;
}

.no-touch .widget {
  height: 1rem;
}
```

This way we would default to the item being 2rem high, and adjust down if the no-touch class was present.

Whichever way you want to structure things, Modernizr provides a widely supported way to fork features. You'll find it especially useful when you want to use features like transform3d but still provide a working substitute for browsers that can't make use of it.

Modernizr can provide accurate tests for most things you'll likely need to fork code on, but not all. For example, overflow-scrolling is notoriously difficult to accurately test for. In situations where a class of devices isn't playing happily, it may make more sense to fork your code on a different feature. For example, as older Android versions have difficulty with horizontal scrolling you might fork with no-svg (as Android 2-2.3 doesn't support SVG either).

Finally, you may wish to combine tests to make your own custom test. That's a little outside the scope here but if that's something that interests you, take a look at http://benfrain.com/combining-modernizr-tests-create-custom-convenience-forks/.

New CSS3 selectors and how to use them

CSS3 gives incredible power for selecting elements within a page. You may not think this sounds very glitzy but trust me, it will make your life easier and you'll love CSS3 for it! I'd better qualify that bold claim.

CSS3 attribute selectors

You've probably used CSS attribute selectors to create rules. For example, consider the following rule:

```
img[alt] {
  border: 3px dashed #e15f5f;
}
```

This would target any image tags in the markup which have an `alt` attribute. Or, let's say we wanted to select all elements with a `data-sausage` attribute:

```
[data-sausage] {
  /* styles */
}
```

All you need is to specify the attribute in squared brackets.

 The `data-*` type attribute was introduced in HTML5 to provide a place for custom data that can't be stored sensibly by any other existing mechanism. The specification description for these can be found at `http://www.w3.org/TR/2010/WD-html5-20101019/elements.html`.

You can also narrow things down by specifying what the attribute value is. For example, consider the following rule:

```
img[alt="sausages"] {
  /* Styles */
}
```

This would only target images which have an `alt` attribute of sausages. For example:

```
<img class="oscarMain" src="img/sausages.png" alt="sausages" />
```

So far, so 'big deal we could do that in CSS2'. What does CSS3 bring to the party?

CSS3 substring matching attribute selectors

CSS3 lets us select elements based upon the substring of their attribute selector. That sounds complicated. It isn't! The three options are whether the attribute is:

- Beginning with the prefix
- Contains an instance of
- Ends with the suffix

Let's see what they look like.

The 'beginning with' substring matching attribute selector

Consider the following markup:

```
<img src="img/ace-film.jpg" alt="film-ace">
<img src="img/rubbish-film.jpg" alt="film-rubbish">
```

We can use the 'beginning with' substring matching attribute selector to select both of those images like this:

```
img[alt^="film"] {
    /* Styles */
}
```

The key character in all this is the ^ symbol (the symbol is called the **caret**, although it is often referred to as the 'hat' symbol too) which means "begins with". Because both `alt` tags begin with `film` our selector selects them.

The 'contains an instance of' substring matching attribute selector

The 'contains an instance of' substring matching attribute selector has the following syntax:

```
[attribute*="value"] {
  /* Styles */
}
```

Like all attribute selectors, you can combine them with a type selector (one that references the actual HTML element used) if needed, although personally I would only do that if I had to (in case you want to change the type of element used).

Let's try an example. Consider this markup:

```
<p data-ingredients="scones cream jam">Will I get selected?</p>
We can select that element like this:
[data-ingredients*="cream"] {
  color: red;
}
```

The key character in all this is the * symbol that in this context means "contains".

The 'begins with' selector would not have worked in with this markup as the string inside the attribute didn't *begin with* 'cream'. It did however *contain* 'cream' so the 'contains an instance of' substring attribute selector finds it.

The 'ends with' substring matching attribute selector

The "ends with" substring matching attribute selector has the following syntax:

```
[attribute$="value"] {
  /* Styles */
}
```

An example should help. Consider this markup:

```
<p data-ingredients="scones cream jam">Will I get selected?</p>
<p data-ingredients="toast jam butter">Will I get selected?</p>
<p data-ingredients="jam toast butter">Will I get selected?</p>
```

Suppose we only want to select the element with scones, cream, and jam in the `data-ingredients` attribute (the first element). We can't use the 'contains an instance of' (it will select all three) or 'begins with' (it will only select the last one) substring attribute selector. However, we can use the 'ends with' substring attribute selector.

```
[data-ingredients$="jam"] {
color: red;
}
```

The key character in all this is the $ (dollar) symbol which means "ends with".

Gotchas with attribute selection

There is a 'gotcha' with attribute selection that's it's important to grasp: attributes are seen as a single string. Consider this CSS rule:

```
[data-film^="film"] {
  color: red;
}
```

It might surprise you to know that it would not select this, even though one of the words inside the attribute begins with `film`:

```
<span data-film="awful moulin-rouge film">Moulin Rouge is dreadful</span>
```

That's because the `data-film` attribute here doesn't begin with `film`, in this case it begins with awful (and if you've seen *Moulin Rouge* you'll know that it begins awfully too—and never improves).

There are a couple of ways around this, in addition to the substring matching selectors we looked at a moment ago. You could use the whitespace separated selector (note the tilde symbol), which has support all the way back to Internet Explorer 7:

```
[data-film~="film"] {
  color: red;
}
```

You could select the entire attribute:

```
[data-film="awful moulin-rouge film"] {
  color: red;
}
```

Or, if you only wanted to select based upon the presence of a couple of strings inside an attribute, you could join a couple (or as many as were needed) of 'contains an instance of' substring attribute selectors:

```
[data-film*="awful"][data-film*="moulin-rouge"] {
  color: red;
}
```

There's no 'right' thing to do, it really just depends on the complexity of the string you are trying to select.

Attribute selectors allow you to select IDs and classes that start with numbers

Before HTML5, it wasn't valid markup to start IDs or class names with a number. HTML5 removes that restriction. When it comes to IDs, there are still some things to remember. There should be no spaces in the ID name and it must be unique on the page. For more information visit `http://www.w3.org/html/wg/drafts/html/master/dom.html`.

Now, although you can start ID and class values with numbers in HTML5, CSS still restricts you from using ID and class selectors that start with a number (`http://www.w3.org/TR/CSS21/syndata.html`).

Lucky for us, we can easily workaround this by using an attribute selector. For example, `[id="10"]`.

CSS3 structural pseudo-classes

CSS3 gives us more power to select elements based upon where they sit in the structure of the DOM.

Let's consider a common design treatment; we're working on the navigation bar for a larger viewport and we want to have all but the last link over on the left.

Historically, we would have needed to solve this problem by adding a class name to the last link so that we could select it, like this:

```
<nav class="nav-Wrapper">
  <a href="/home" class="nav-Link">Home</a>
  <a href="/About" class="nav-Link">About</a>
  <a href="/Films" class="nav-Link">Films</a>
  <a href="/Forum" class="nav-Link">Forum</a>
  <a href="/Contact-Us" class="nav-Link nav-LinkLast">Contact Us</a>
</nav>
```

This in itself can be problematic. For example, sometimes, just getting a content management system to add a class to a final list item can be frustratingly difficult. Thankfully, in those eventualities, it's no longer a concern. We can solve this problem and many more with CSS3 structural pseudo-classes.

The :last-child selector

CSS 2.1 already had a selector applicable for the first item in a list:

```
div:first-child {
  /* Styles */
}
```

However, CSS3 adds a selector that can also match the last:

```
div:last-child {
  /* Styles */
}
```

Let's look how that selector could fix our prior problem:

```
@media (min-width: 60rem) {
  .nav-Wrapper {
    display: flex;
  }
  .nav-Link:last-child {
    margin-left: auto;
  }
}
```

There are also useful selectors for when something is the only item: `:only-child` and the only item of a type: `:only-of-type`.

The nth-child selectors

The `nth-child` selectors let us solve even more difficult problems. With the same markup as before, let's consider how nth-child selectors allow us to select any link(s) within the list.

Firstly, what about selecting every other list item? We could select the odd ones like this:

```
.nav-Link:nth-child(odd) {
  /* Styles */
}
```

Or, if you wanted to select the even ones:

```
.nav-Link:nth-child(even) {
  /* Styles */
}
```

Understanding what nth rules do

For the uninitiated, nth-based selectors can look pretty intimidating. However, once you've mastered the logic and syntax you'll be amazed what you can do with them. Let's take a look.

CSS3 gives us incredible flexibility with a few nth-based rules:

- `nth-child(n)`
- `nth-last-child(n)`
- `nth-of-type(n)`
- `nth-last-of-type(n)`

We've seen that we can use (odd) or (even) values already in an nth-based expression but the (n) parameter can be used in another couple of ways:

As an integer; for example, `:nth-child(2)` would select the second item

As a numeric expression; for example, `:nth-child(3n+1)` would start at 1 and then select every third element

The integer based property is easy enough to understand, just enter the element number you want to select.

The numeric expression version of the selector is the part that can be a little baffling for mere mortals. If math is easy for you, I apologize for this next section. For everyone else, let's break it down.

Breaking down the math

Let's consider 10 spans on a page (you can play about with these by looking at `example_05-05`):

```
<span></span>
<span></span>
<span></span>
<span></span>
<span></span>
<span></span>
<span></span>
<span></span>
<span></span>
<span></span>
```

By default they will be styled like this:

```
span {
    height: 2rem;
    width: 2rem;
    background-color: blue;
    display: inline-block;
}
```

As you might imagine, this gives us 10 squares in a line:

OK, let's look at how we can select different ones with nth-based selections.

For practicality, when considering the expression within the parenthesis, I start from the right. So, for example, if I want to figure out what (2n+3) will select, I start with the right-most number (the three here indicates the third item from the left) and know it will select every second element from that point on. So adding this rule:

```
span:nth-child(2n+3) {
    color: #f90;
    border-radius: 50%;
}
```

Results in this in the browser:

As you can see, our nth selector targets the third list item and then every subsequent second one after that too (if there were 100 list items, it would continue selecting every second one).

How about selecting everything from the second item onwards? Well, although you could write `:nth-child(1n+2)`, you don't actually need the first number 1 as unless otherwise stated, n is equal to 1. We can therefore just write `:nth-child(n+2)`. Likewise, if we wanted to select every third element, rather than write `:nth-child(3n+3)`, we can just write `:nth-child(3n)` as every third item would begin at the third item anyway, without needing to explicitly state it. The expression can also use negative numbers, for example, `:nth-child(3n-2)` starts at -2 and then selects every third item.

You can also change the direction. By default, once the first part of the selection is found, the subsequent ones go down the elements in the DOM (and therefore from left to right in our example). However, you can reverse that with a minus. For example:

```css
span:nth-child(-2n+3) {
  background-color: #f90;
  border-radius: 50%;
}
```

This example finds the third item again, but then goes in the opposite direction to select every two elements (up the DOM tree and therefore from right to left in our example):

Hopefully, the nth-based expressions are making perfect sense now?

The `nth-child` and `nth-last-child` differ in that the `nth-last-child` variant works from the opposite end of the document tree. For example, `:nth-last-child(-n+3)` starts at 3 from the end and then selects all the items after it. Here's what that rule gives us in the browser:

Finally, let's consider :nth-of-type and :nth-last-of-type. While the previous examples count any children regardless of type (always remember the nth-child selector targets all children at the same DOM level, regardless of classes), :nth-of-type and :nth-last-of-type let you be specific about the type of item you want to select. Consider the following markup (example_05-06):

```
<span class="span-class"></span>
<span class="span-class"></span>
<span class="span-class"></span>
<span class="span-class"></span>
<span class="span-class"></span>
<div class="span-class"></div>
<div class="span-class"></div>
<div class="span-class"></div>
<div class="span-class"></div>
<div class="span-class"></div>
```

If we used the selector:

```
.span-class:nth-of-type(-2n+3) {
  background-color: #f90;
  border-radius: 50%;
}
```

Even though all the elements have the same span-class, we will only actually be targeting the span elements (as they are the first type selected). Here is what gets selected:

We will see how CSS4 selectors can solve this issue shortly.

CSS3 doesn't count like JavaScript and jQuery!

If you're used to using JavaScript and jQuery you'll know that it counts from 0 upwards (zero index based). For example, if selecting an element in JavaScript or jQuery, an integer value of 1 would actually be the second element. CSS3 however, starts at 1 so that a value of 1 is the first item it matches.

nth-based selection in responsive web designs

Just to close out this little section I want to illustrate a real life responsive web design problem and how we can use nth-based selection to solve it.

Remember the horizontal scrolling panel from `example_05-02`? Let's consider how that might look in a situation where horizontal scrolling isn't possible. So, using the same markup, let's turn the top 10 grossing films of 2014 into a grid. For some viewports the grid will only be two items wide, as the viewport increases we show three items and at larger sizes still we show four. Here is the problem though. Regardless of the viewport size, we want to prevent any items on the bottom row having a border on the bottom. You can view this code at `example_05-09`.

Here is how it looks with four items wide:

See that pesky border below the bottom two items? That's what we need to remove. However, I want a robust solution so that if there were another item on the bottom row, the border would also be removed on that too. Now, because there are a different number of items on each row at different viewports, we will also need to change the nth-based selection at different viewports. For the sake of brevity, I'll show you the selection that matches four items per row (the larger of the viewports). You can view the code sample to see the amended selection at the different viewports.

```
@media (min-width: 55rem) {
  .Item {
    width: 25%;
```

```
    }
    /*  Get me every fourth item and of those, only ones that are in the
last four items */
    .Item:nth-child(4n+1):nth-last-child(-n+4),
    /* Now get me every one after that same collection too. */
    .Item:nth-child(4n+1):nth-last-child(-n+4) ~ .Item {
      border-bottom: 0;
    }
}
```

You'll notice here that we are chaining the nth-based pseudo-class selectors. It's important to understand that the first doesn't filter the selection for the next, rather the element has to match each of the selections. For our preceding example, the first element has to be the first item of four and also be one of the last four.

Nice! Thanks to nth-based selections we have a defensive set of rules to remove the bottom border regardless of the viewport size or number of items we are showing.

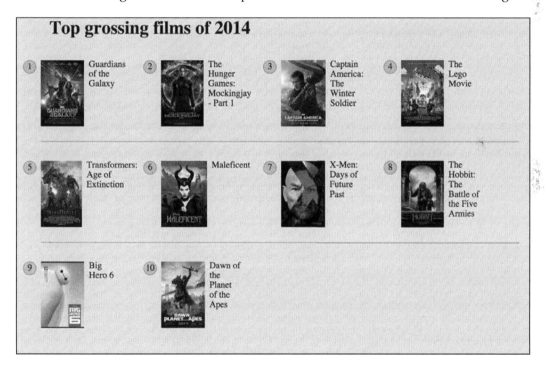

The negation (:not) selector

Another handy selector is the negation pseudo-class selector. This is used to select everything that isn't something else. Consider this:

```
<div class="a-div"></div>
<div class="a-div"></div>
<div class="a-div"></div>
<div class="a-div not-me"></div>
<div class="a-div"></div>
```

And then these styles:

```
div {
   display: inline-block;
   height: 2rem;
   width: 2rem;
   background-color: blue;
}

.a-div:not(.not-me) {
   background-color: orange;
   border-radius: 50%;
}
```

Our final rule will make every element with a class of `.a-div` orange and round, with the exception the `div` that also has the `.not-me` class. You can find that code in the `example_05-07` folder of the code samples (remember, you can grab them all at `http://rwd.education/`).

So far we have looked primarily at what's known as structural pseudo-classes (full information on this is available at `http://www.w3.org/TR/selectors/`). However, CSS3 has many more selectors. If you're working on a web application, it's worth looking at the full list of UI element states pseudo-classes (`http://www.w3.org/TR/selectors/`), as they can, for example, help you target rules based on whether something is selected or not.

The empty (:empty) selector

I've encountered situations where I have an element that includes some padding on the inside and gets content dynamically inserted. Sometimes it gets content, sometimes it doesn't. The trouble is, when it doesn't include content, I still see the padding. Consider the HTML and CSS in `example_05-08`:

```
<div class="thing"></div>
.thing {
  padding: 1rem;
  background-color: violet;
}
```

Without anything content in that `div` I still see the `background-color`. Thankfully, we can easily hide it like this:

```
.thing:empty {
  display: none;
}
```

However, just be careful with the `:empty` selector. For example, you might think this is empty:

```
<div class="thing"> </div>
```

It isn't! Look at the whitespace in there. Whitespace is not no space!

However, just to confuse matters, be aware that a comment doesn't affect whether an element has whitespace or not. For example, this is still considered empty:

```
<div class="thing"><!--I'm empty, honest I am--></div>
```

Amendments to pseudo-elements

Pseudo-elements have been around since CSS2 but the CSS3 specification revises the syntax of their use very slightly. To refresh your memory, until now, `p:first-line` would target the first line in a `<p>` tag. Or `p:first-letter` would target the first letter. Well, CSS3 asks us to separate these pseudo-elements with a double colon to differentiate them from pseudo-classes (such as `nth-child()`). Therefore, we should write `p::first-letter` instead. Note, however, that Internet Explorer 8 and lower versions don't understand the double colon syntax, they only understand the single colon syntax.

Do something with the :first-line regardless of viewport

One thing that you may find particularly handy about the `:first-line` pseudo-element is that it is specific to the viewport. For example, if we write the following rule:

```
p::first-line {
  color: #ff0cff;
}
```

As you might expect, the first line is rendered in an awful shade of pink. However, on a different viewport, it renders a different selection of text.

So, without needing to alter the markup, with a responsive design, there's a handy way of having the first visual line of text (as the browser renders it, not as it appears in the markup) appear differently than the others.

CSS custom properties and variables

Thanks to the popularity of CSS pre-processors, CSS is starting to gain some more 'programmatic' features. The first of which is custom properties. They are more often referred to as variables although that is not necessarily their only use case. You can find the full specification at `http://dev.w3.org/csswg/css-variables/`. Be warned, as of early 2015, browser implementations are few and far between (only Firefox).

CSS custom properties allow us to store information in our style sheets that can then be utilized in that style sheet or perhaps acted upon with JavaScript. An obvious use case would be to store a font-family name and then reference it. Here is how we create a custom property:

```
:root {
  --MainFont: 'Helvetica Neue', Helvetica, Arial, sans-serif;
}
```

Here, we are using the `:root` pseudo-class to store the custom property in the document root (although you can store them inside any rule you like).

> The `:root` pseudo-class always references the top-most parent element in a document structure. In an HTML document this would always be the HTML tag but for an SVG document (we look at SVG in *Chapter 7, Using SVGs for Resolution Independence*), it would reference a different element.

A custom property always begins with two dashes, then the custom name, and then its end, signified like every other property in CSS; with a colon.

We can reference that value with the `var()` notation. Like so:

```
.Title {
  font-family: var(--MainFont);
}
```

You could obviously store as many custom properties as you need in this manner. The main benefit of this approach is that you can change the value inside the variable and every rule that makes use of the variable gets the new value without having to amend them directly.

It's envisaged that in future these properties might be parsed and utilized by JavaScript. For more on that kind of craziness, you might be interested in the new CSS Extensions module:

`http://dev.w3.org/csswg/css-extensions/`

CSS calc

How many times have you been trying to code out a layout and thought something like, "it needs to half the width of the parent element minus exactly 10px"? This is particularly useful with responsive web design, as we never know the size of the screen that will be viewing our web pages. Thankfully CSS now has a way to do this. It's called the `calc()` function. Here's that example in CSS:

```
.thing {
  width: calc(50% - 10px);
}
```

Addition, subtraction, division, and multiplication are supported so it's possible to solve a bunch of problems that have been impossible without JavaScript in the past.

Browser support is quite good, but a notable exception is Android 4.3 and below. Read the specification at `http://www.w3.org/TR/css3-values/`.

CSS Level 4 selectors

There are a number of new selector types being specified for CSS Selectors Level 4 (the latest version available was the Editor's Draft dated December 14, 2014, (`http://dev.w3.org/csswg/selectors-4/`). However, as I write this, there are no implementations of them in browsers. As such we will just look at one example as they are liable/probable to change.

The Relational Pseudo-class selector is from the 'Logical Combinations' (`http://dev.w3.org/csswg/selectors-4/`) section of the latest draft.

The :has pseudo class

This selector takes this format:

```
a:has(figcaption) {
  padding: 1rem;
}
```

This would add padding to any item a tag that contains a `figcaption`. You could invert the selection in combination with the negation pseudo class too:

```
a:not(:has(figcaption)) {
  padding: 1rem;
}
```

This would add the padding if the a tag did not contain a `figcaption` element.

I'll be honest and say that right now, there aren't many new selectors in that draft that get me excited. But who knows what they'll come up with by the time they start being available to use in browsers?

Responsive viewport-percentage lengths (vmax, vmin, vh, vw)

Let's change tack now. We've looked at how we can select items in our responsive world. But how about how we size them? The CSS Values and Units Module Level 3 (`http://www.w3.org/TR/css3-values/`), ushered in viewport relative units. These are great for responsive web design as each unit is a percentage length of the viewport:

- The vw unit (for viewport width)
- vh unit (for viewport height)
- vmin unit (for viewport minimum; equal to the smaller of either vw or vh)
- vmax (viewport maximum; equal to the larger of either vw or vh)

Browser support isn't bad either (`http://caniuse.com/`).

Want a modal window that's 90% of the browser height? It's as easy as:

```
.modal {
  height: 90vh;
}
```

As useful as viewport relative units are, some browsers have curious implementations. Safari in iOS 8, for example, changes the viewable screen area as you scroll from the top of a page (it shrinks the address bar) but doesn't make any changes to the reported viewport height.

However, you can perhaps find more utility for these units when coupled with fonts. For example, it's now trivially easy to create text that scales in size depending upon the viewport.

Now, I could show you that right now. However, I'd like to use a distinct font, so that regardless of whether you are viewing the example on a Windows, Mac, or Linux box we will all see the same thing.

OK, I'll be honest, this is a cheap ploy to allow me to document how we can use web fonts with CSS3.

Web typography

For years the web has had to make do with a boring selection of 'web safe' fonts. When some fancy typography was essential for a design, it was necessary to substitute a graphical element for it and used a text-indent rule to shift the actual text from the viewport. Oh, the joy!

There were also a few inventive methods for adding fancy typography to a page along the way. sIFR (`http://www.mikeindustries.com/blog/sifr/`) and Cufón (`http://cufon.shoqolate.com/generate/`) used Flash and JavaScript respectively to re-make text elements appear as the fonts they were intended to be. Thankfully, CSS3 provides a means of custom web typography that is now ready for the big time.

The @font-face CSS rule

The `@font-face` CSS rule has been around since CSS2 (but subsequently absent in CSS 2.1). It was even supported partially by Internet Explorer 4 (no, really)! So what's it doing here, when we're supposed to be talking about CSS3?

Well, as it turns out, `@font-face` was re-introduced for the CSS3 Fonts module (`http://www.w3.org/TR/css3-fonts`). Due to the historic legal quagmire of using fonts on the web, it's only in recent years that it has started to gain serious traction as the de facto solution for web typography.

Like anything on the web that involves assets, there is no single file format. Just as images can come in JPG, PNG, GIF, and other formats, fonts have their own set of formats to choose from. The Embedded OpenType (files with an .eot extension) font was Internet Explorer's (and not anyone else's) preferred choice. Others favor the more common TrueType (.ttf file extension), whilst there is also SVGs and Web Open Font Format (.woff / .woff2 extension).

Right now, it's necessary to serve multiple file versions of the same font to cover the different browser implementations.

However, the good news is that adding each custom font format for every browser is easy. Let's see how!

Implementing web fonts with @font-face

CSS provides a @font-face 'at-rule' to reference online fonts that can then be used to display text.

There are now a number of great sources for viewing and acquiring web fonts; both free and paid. My personal favorite for free fonts is Font Squirrel (http://www.fontsquirrel.com/) although Google also offers free web fonts, ultimately served with the @font-face rule (http://www.google.com/webfonts). There are also great, paid services from Typekit (http://www.typekit.com/) and Font Deck (http://www.fontdeck.com/).

For this exercise, I'm going to download Roboto. It's the Font used for later Android handsets so if you have one of those it will be familiar. Otherwise, all you need to know is that it's a lovely interface font designed to be highly legible on small screens. You can grab it yourself at http://www.fontsquirrel.com/fonts/roboto.

 If you can download a 'subset' of your font, specific to the language you intend to use, do so. It means, the resultant file size will be much smaller as it won't contain glyphs for languages you have no intention of using.

Having downloaded the @font-face kit, a look inside the ZIP file reveals folders of the different Roboto fonts. I'm choosing the Roboto Regular version and inside that folder the font exists in various file formats (WOFF, TTF, EOT, and SVG), plus a stylesheet.css file containing a font stack. For example, the rule for Roboto Regular looks like this:

```
@font-face {
    font-family: 'robotoregular';
    src: url('Roboto-Regular-webfont.eot');
```

```
        src: url('Roboto-Regular-webfont.eot?#iefix') format('embedded-
opentype'),
           url('Roboto-Regular-webfont.woff') format('woff'),
           url('Roboto-Regular-webfont.ttf') format('truetype'),
           url('Roboto-Regular-webfont.svg#robotoregular')
format('svg');
     font-weight: normal;
     font-style: normal;
}
```

Much like the way vendor prefixes work, the browser will apply styles from that list of properties (with the lower properties, if applicable, taking precedence) and ignore ones it doesn't understand. That way, no matter what the browser, there should be a font that it can use.

Now, although this block of code is great for fans of copy and paste, it's important to pay attention to the paths the fonts are stored in. For example, I tend to copy the fonts from the ZIP file and store them in a folder inventively called `fonts` on the same level as my `css` folder. Therefore, as I'm usually copying this font stack rule into my main style sheet, I need to amend the paths. So, my rule becomes:

```
@font-face {
     font-family: 'robotoregular';
     src: url('../fonts/Roboto-Regular-webfont.eot');
     src: url('../fonts/Roboto-Regular-webfont.eot?#iefix')
format('embedded-opentype'),
           url('../fonts/Roboto-Regular-webfont.woff') format('woff'),
           url('../fonts/Roboto-Regular-webfont.ttf')
format('truetype'),
           url('../fonts/Roboto-Regular-webfont.svg#robotoregular')
format('svg');
     font-weight: normal;
     font-style: normal;
}
```

It's then just a case of setting the correct font and weight (if needed) for the relevant style rule. Look at `example_05-10`, it's the same markup as `example_05-09`, we are merely declaring this `font-family` as the default:

```
body {
  font-family: robotoregular;
}
```

An added bonus with web fonts is that, if the composite uses the same fonts you are using in the code, you can plug the sizes in direct from the composite file. For example, if the font is 24px in Photoshop, we either plug that value straight in or convert it to a more flexible unit such as REM (assuming a root font-size of 16px, 24 / 16 = 1.5rem).

However, as I mentioned before, we now have viewport relative sizes at our disposal. We can use them here to scale the text relative to the amount of viewport space.

```
body {
  font-family: robotoregular;
  font-size: 2.1vw;
}

@media (min-width: 45rem) {
  html,
  body {
    max-width: 50.75rem;
    font-size: 1.8vw;
  }
}

@media (min-width: 55rem) {
  html,
  body {
    max-width: 78.75rem;
    font-size: 1.7vw;
  }
}
```

If you open that example in the browser and resize the viewport you will see that with just a few lines of CSS we have text that scales to the available space. Beautiful!

A note about custom @font-face typography and responsive designs

The @font-face method of web typography is, on the whole, great. The only caveats to be aware of when using the technique with responsive designs are in relation to the font file size. By way of an example, if the device rendering our example required the SVG font format of Roboto Regular, it would need to fetch an extra 34 KB, compared with using the standard web-safe fonts such as Arial. We have used an English subset in our example which reduces the file size but that isn't always an option. Be sure to check the size of custom fonts and be judicious with their use if you want the best possible site performance.

New CSS3 color formats and alpha transparency

So far in this chapter, we have looked at how CSS3 has given us new powers of selection and the ability to add custom typography to our designs. Now, we'll look at ways that CSS3 allows us to work with color that were simply not possible before.

Firstly, CSS3 provides two new ways to declare color: RGB and HSL. In addition, these two formats enable us to use an alpha channel alongside them (RGBA and HSLA respectively).

RGB color

Red, Green, and Blue (RGB) is a coloring system that's been around for decades. It works by defining different values for the red, green, and blue components of a color. For example, a red color might be defined in CSS as a HEX (hexadecimal) value, `#fe0208`:

```
.redness {
  color: #fe0208;
}
```

 For a great post describing how to understand HEX values more intuitively, I can recommend this blog post at Smashing Magazine: `http://www.smashingmagazine.com/2012/10/04/the-code-side-of-color/`

However, with CSS3, that color can equally be described by an RGB value:

```
.redness {
  color: rgb(254, 2, 8);
}
```

Most image editing applications show colors as both HEX and RGB values in their color picker. The Photoshop color picker, has R, G, and B boxes showing the values for each channel. For example, the R value might be 254, the G value 2, and the B value 8. This is easily transferable to the CSS `color` property value. In the CSS, after defining the color mode (for example, RGB) the values for red, green, and blue colors are comma separated in that order within parenthesis (as we have in the previous code).

HSL color

Besides RGB, CSS3 also allows us to declare color values as **Hue, Saturation, and Lightness (HSL)**.

> **HSL isn't the same as HSB!**
>
> Don't make the mistake of thinking that the **Hue, Saturation, and Brightness (HSB)** value shown in the color picker of image editing applications such as Photoshop is the same as HSL—it isn't!

What makes HSL such a joy to use is that it's relatively simple to understand the color that will be represented based on the values given. For example, unless you're some sort of color picking ninja, I'd wager you couldn't instantly tell me what color rgb(255, 51, 204) is? Any takers? No, me neither. However, show me the HSL value of hsl(315, 100%, 60%) and I could take a guess that it is somewhere between Magenta and Red color (it's actually a festive pink color). How do I know this? Simple.

HSL works on a 360° degree color wheel. It looks like this:

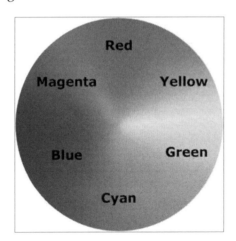

The first figure in a HSL color definition represents Hue. Looking at our wheel we can see that Yellow is at 60°, Green at 120°, Cyan at 180°, Blue at 240°, Magenta at 300°, and finally Red at 360°. So as the aforementioned HSL color had a hue of 315, it's easy to know that it will be between Magenta (at 300°) and Red (at 360°).

The following two values in an HSL definition are for saturation and lightness, specified as percentages. These merely alter the base hue. For a more saturated or 'colorful' appearance, use a higher percentage in the second value. The final value, controlling the Lightness, can vary between 0 percent for black and 100 percent for white.

So, once you've defined a color as an HSL value, it's also easy to create variations on it, merely by altering the saturation and lightness percentages. For example, our red color can be defined in HSL values as follows:

```
.redness {
  color: hsl(359, 99%, 50%);
}
```

If we wanted to make a slightly darker color, we could use the same HSL value and merely alter the lightness (the final value) percentage value only:

```
.darker-red {
  color: hsl(359, 99%, 40%);
}
```

In conclusion, if you can remember the mnemonic 'Young Guys Can Be Messy Rascals' (or any other mnemonic you care to memorize) for the HSL color wheel, you'll be able to approximately write HSL color values without resorting to a color picker, and also create variations upon it. Show that trick to the savant Ruby, Node, and .NET guys and gals at the office party and earn some quick kudos!

Alpha channels

So far you'd be forgiven for wondering why on earth we'd bother using HSL or RGB instead of our trusty HEX values we've been using for years. Where HSL and RGB differ from HEX is that they allow the use of an alpha transparency channel so something beneath an element can 'show through'.

An HSLA color declaration is similar in syntax to a standard HSL rule. However, in addition, you must declare the value as hsla (rather than merely hsl) and add an additional opacity value, given as a decimal value between 0 (completely transparent) and 1 (completely opaque). For example:

```
.redness-alpha {
  color: hsla(359, 99%, 50%, .5);
}
```

The RGBA syntax follows the same convention as the HSLA equivalent:

```
.redness-alpha-rgba {
  color: rgba(255, 255, 255, 0.8);
}
```

Why not just use opacity?

CSS3 also allows elements to have opacity set with the opacity declaration. A value is set between 0 and 1 in decimal increments (for example, opacity set to .1 is 10 percent). However, this differs from RGBA and HSLA in that setting an opacity value on an element effects the entire element. Whereas, setting a value with HSLA or RGBA meanwhile allows particular parts of an element to have an alpha layer. For example, an element could have an HSLA value for the background but a solid color for the text within it.

Color manipulation with CSS Color Module Level 4

Although in the very early specification stages, it should be possible in the not too distant future to enjoy color manipulations in CSS using the `color()` function.

Until there is wide browser support, this kind of thing is best handled by CSS pre/post processors (do yourself a favor and buy yourself a book on the subject right now; I recommend *Sass and Compass for Designers* by that wonderful chap, Ben Frain).

You can follow the progress of the CSS Color Module Level 4 at `http://dev.w3.org/csswg/css-color-4/`.

Summary

In this chapter, we've learned how to easily select almost anything we need on the page with CSS3's new selectors. We've also looked at how we can make responsive columns and scrolling panels for content in record time and solve common and annoying problems such as long URL wrapping. We now also have an understanding of CSS3's new color module and how we can apply colors with RGB and HSL complete with transparent alpha layers for great aesthetic effects.

In this chapter, we've also learned how to add web typography to a design with the `@font-face` rule, finally freeing us from the shackles of the humdrum selection of web-safe fonts. Despite all these great new features and techniques, we've only picked at the surface of what we can do with CSS3. Let's move on now and look at even more ways CSS3 can make a responsive design as fast, efficient, and maintainable as possible with CSS3 text shadows, box shadows, gradients, and multiple backgrounds.

6
Stunning Aesthetics
with CSS3

The aesthetically focused features of CSS3 are so useful in responsive design because using CSS3 lets us replace images in many situations. This saves you time, makes your code more maintainable and flexible and results in less page 'weight' for the end user. Those benefits would be useful even on a typical fixed-width desktop design but it's even more important with a responsive design as using CSS in these situations makes it trivial to create different aesthetic effects at different viewports.

In this chapter we will cover:

- How to create text shadows with CSS3
- How to create box shadows with CSS3
- How to make gradient backgrounds with CSS3
- How to use multiple backgrounds with CSS3
- Using CSS3 background gradients to make patterns
- How to implement high-resolution background images with media queries
- How to use CSS filters (and their performance implications)

Let's dig in.

Vendor prefixes

When implementing experimental CSS, just remember to add relevant vendor prefixes via a tool, rather than by hand. This ensures the broadest cross-browser compatibility and also negates you adding in prefixes that are no longer required. I'm mentioning Autoprefixer (`https://github.com/postcss/autoprefixer`) in most chapters as, at the time of writing, I think it's the best tool for the job.

Text shadows with CSS3

One of the most widely implemented CSS3 features is `text-shadow`. Like `@font-face`, it had a previous life but was dropped in CSS 2.1. Thankfully it's back and widely supported (for all modern browsers and Internet Explorer 9 onwards). Let's look at the basic syntax:

```
.element {
    text-shadow: 1px 1px 1px #ccc;
}
```

Remember, the values in shorthand rules always go right and then down (or think of it as clockwise if you prefer). Therefore, the first value is the amount of shadow to the right, the second is the amount down, the third value is the amount of blur (the distance the shadow travels before fading to nothing), and the final value is the color.

Shadows to the left and above can be achieved using negative values. For example:

```
.text {
    text-shadow: -4px -4px 0px #dad7d7;
}
```

The color value doesn't need to be defined as a HEX value. It can just as easily be HSL(A) or RGB(A):

```
text-shadow: 4px 4px 0px hsla(140, 3%, 26%, 0.4);
```

However, keep in mind that the browser must then also support HSL/RGB color modes along with `text-shadow` in order to render the effect.

You can also set the shadow values in any other valid CSS length units such as em, rem, ch, rem, and so on. Personally, I rarely use em or rem units for `text-shadow` values. As the values are always really low, using 1px or 2px generally looks good across all viewports.

Thanks to media queries, we can easily remove text shadows at different viewport sizes too. The key here is the none value:

```
.text {
    text-shadow: .0625rem .0625rem 0 #bfbfbf;
}
@media (min-width: 30rem) {
    .text {
        text-shadow: none;
    }
}
```

 As an aside, it's worth knowing that in CSS, where a value starts with a zero, such as 0.14s, there is no need to write the leading zero: .14s is exactly the same.

Omitting the blur value when not needed

If there is no blur to be added to a text-shadow the value can be omitted from the declaration, for example:

```
.text {
    text-shadow: -4px -4px #dad7d7;
}
```

That is perfectly valid. The browser assumes that the first two values are for the offsets if no third value is declared.

Multiple text shadows

It's possible to add multiple text shadows by comma separating two or more shadows. For example:

```
.multiple {
    text-shadow: 0px 1px #fff,4px 4px 0px #dad7d7;
}
```

Also, as CSS is forgiving of whitespace, you can lay out the values like this if it helps with readability:

```
.text {
    font-size: calc(100vmax / 40); /* 100 of vh or vw, whichever is
larger divided by 40 */
    text-shadow:
```

```
    3px 3px #bbb, /* right and down */
    -3px -3px #999; /* left and up */
}
```

 You can read the W3C specification for the text-shadow property at http://www.w3.org/TR/css3-text/.

Box shadows

Box shadows allow you to create a box-shaped shadow around the outside or inside of the element it is applied to. Once text shadows are understood, box shadows are a piece of cake; principally, they follow the same syntax: horizontal offset, vertical offset, blur, spread (we will get to spread in a moment), and color.

Only two of the possible four length values are required (in the absence of the last two, the value of color defines the shadow color and a value of zero is used for the blur radius). Let's look at a simple example:

```
.shadow {
    box-shadow: 0px 3px 5px #444;
}
```

The default box-shadow is set on the outside of the element. Another optional keyword, inset allows the box-shadow to be applied inside the element.

An inset shadow

The box-shadow property can also be used to create an inset shadow. The syntax is identical to a normal box shadow except that the value starts with the keyword inset:

```
.inset {
    box-shadow: inset 0 0 40px #000;
}
```

Everything functions as before but the `inset` part of the declaration instructs the browser to set the effect on the inside. If you look at `example_06-01` you'll see an example of each type:

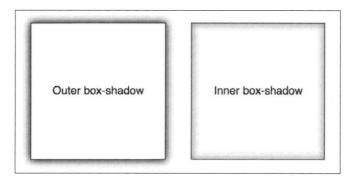

Multiple shadows

Like `text-shadow`, you can apply multiple `box-shadow`. Separate the `box-shadow` with a comma and they are applied bottom to top (last to first) as they are listed. Remind yourself of the order by thinking that the declaration nearest to the top in the rule (in the code) appears nearest to the 'top' of the order when displayed in the browser. As with `text-shadow`, you may find it useful to use whitespace to visually stack the different `box-shadow`:

```
box-shadow: inset 0 0 30px hsl(0, 0%, 0%),
            inset 0 0 70px hsla(0, 97%, 53%, 1);
```

> Stacking longer, multiple values, one under the other in the code, has an added benefit when using version control systems; it makes it easy to spot differences when you 'diff' two versions of a file. That's the primary reason I stack groups of selectors one under the other too.

Understanding spread

I'll be honest, for literally years I didn't truly understand what the spread value of a `box-shadow` actually did. I don't think the name 'spread' is useful. Think of it more as an offset. Let me explain.

Look at the box on the left in `example_06-02`. This has a standard `box-shadow` applied. The one on the right has a negative spread value applied. It's set with the fourth value. Here is the relevant code:

```
.no-spread {
  box-shadow: 0 10px 10px;
}

.spread {
  box-shadow: 0 10px 10px -10px;
}
```

Here is the effect of each (element with spread value on the right):

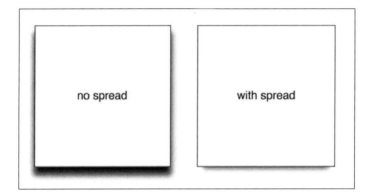

The spread value lets you extend or contract the shadow in all directions by the amount specified. In this example, a negative value is pulling the shadow back in all directions. The result being that we see the shadow at the bottom, only instead of seeing the blur 'leak' out on all sides (as the blur is being counter-balanced by the negative spread value).

You can read the W3C specification for the `box-shadow` property at `http://www.w3.org/TR/css3-background/`.

Background gradients

In days gone by, to achieve a background gradient on an element, it was necessary to tile a thin graphical slice of the gradient. As graphics resources go, it's quite an economical trade-off. An image, only a pixel or two wide, isn't going to break the bandwidth bank and on a single site it can be used on multiple elements.

However, if we need to tweak the gradient it still requires round-trips to the graphics editor. Plus, occasionally, content might 'break out' of the gradient background, extending beyond the images' fixed size limitations. This problem is compounded with a responsive design, as sections of a page may increase at different viewports.

With a CSS background-image gradient however, things are far more flexible. As part of the CSS Image Values and Replaced Content Module Level 3, CSS enables us to create linear and radial background gradients. Let's look how we can define them.

 The specification for CSS Image Values and Replaced Content Module Level 3 can be found at http://www. w3.org/TR/css3-images/.

The linear-gradient notation

The linear-gradient notation, in its simplest form, looks like this:

```
.linear-gradient {
    background: linear-gradient(red, blue);
}
```

This will create a linear gradient that starts at red (the gradient starts from the top by default) and fades to blue.

Specifying gradient direction

Now, if you want to specify a direction for the gradient, there are a couple of ways. The gradient will always begin in the opposite direction to where you are sending it. However, when no direction is set, a gradient will always default to a top to bottom direction. For example:

```
.linear-gradient {
    background: linear-gradient(to top right, red, blue);
}
```

In this instance, the gradient heads to the top right. It starts red in the bottom-left corner and fades to blue at the top right.

If you're more mathematically minded, you may believe it would be comparable to write the gradient like this:

```
.linear-gradient {
    background: linear-gradient(45deg, red, blue);
}
```

However, keep in mind that on a rectangular box, a gradient that heads 'to top right' (always the top right of the element it's applied to) will end in a slightly different position than `45deg` (always 45 degrees from its starting point).

It's worth knowing you can also start gradients before they are visible within a box. For example:

```
.linear-gradient {
    background: linear-gradient(red -50%, blue);
}
```

This would render a gradient as if it had started before it is even visible inside the box.

We've actually used a color stop in that last example to define a place where a color should begin and end so let's look at those more fully.

Color stops

Perhaps the handiest thing about background gradients is color stops. They provide the means to set which color is used at which point in a gradient. With color stops you can specify something as complex as you are likely to need. Consider this example:

```
.linear-gradient {
  margin: 1rem;
  width: 400px;
  height: 200px;
  background: linear-gradient(#f90 0, #f90 2%, #555 2%, #eee 50%, #555
98%, #f90 98%, #f90 100%);
}
```

Here's how that `linear-gradient` renders:

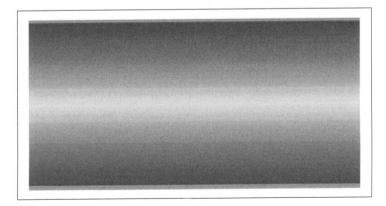

In this example (`example_06-03`), a direction has not been specified so the default top to bottom direction applies.

Color stops inside a gradient are written comma separated and defined by giving first the color, and then the position of the stop. It's generally advisable not to mix units in one notation but you can. You can have as many color stops as you like and colors can be written as a keyword, HEX, RGBA, or HSLA value.

 Note that there have been a number of different background gradient syntaxes over the years so this is one area that is particularly difficult to write fallbacks for by hand. At the risk of sounding like a broken record (kids, if you don't know what a 'record' is, ask mom or dad), make your life easier with a tool such as Autoprefixer. This lets you write the current W3C standard syntax (as detailed earlier) and it will automatically create the prior versions for you.

Read the W3C specification for linear background gradients at `http://www.w3.org/TR/css3-images/`.

Adding fallback for older browsers

As a simple fallback for older browsers that don't support background gradients, just define a solid background color first. That way older browsers will at least render a solid background if they don't understand the gradient that's defined afterwards. For example:

```
.thing {
  background: red;
  background: linear-gradient(45deg, red, blue);
}
```

Radial background gradients

It's equally simple to create a radial gradient in CSS. These typically begin from a central point and spread out smoothly in an elliptical or circular shape.

Here's the syntax for a radial background gradient (you can play with it in `example_06-04`):

```
.radial-gradient {
    margin: 1rem;
    width: 400px;
    height: 200px;
```

```
      background: radial-gradient(12rem circle at bottom,  yellow,
orange, red);
}
```

Breakdown of the radial-gradient syntax

After specifying the property (`background:`) we begin the `radial-gradient` notation. To start with, before the first comma, we define the shape or size of the gradient and the position. We have used 12rem circle for the shape and size above but consider some other examples:

- `5em` would be a circle 5em in size. It's possible to omit the 'circle' part if giving just a size.
- `circle` would be a circle the full size of the container (the size of a radial gradient defaults to 'farthest corner' if omitted—more on sizing keywords shortly)
- `40px 30px` would be a ellipse as if drawn inside a box 40px wide by 30px tall
- `ellipse` would create an ellipse shape that would fit within the element

Next, after the size and/or shape, we define the position. The default position is center but let's look at some other possibilities and how they can be defined:

- **at top right** starts the radial gradient from the top right
- **at right 100px top 20px** starts the gradient 100px from the right edge and 20px from the top edge
- **at center left** starts it halfway down the left side of the element

We end our size, shape, and position 'parameters' with a comma and then define any color stops; which work in exactly the same manner as they do with `linear-gradient`.

To simplify the notation: size, shape, and position before the first comma, then as many color stops as needed after it (with each stop separated with commas).

Handy 'extent' keywords for responsive sizing

For responsive work, you may find it advantageous to size gradients proportionally rather than using fixed pixel dimensions. That way you know you are covered (both literally and figuratively) when the size of elements change. There are some handy sizing keywords that can be applied to gradients. You would write them like this, in place of any size value:

```
background: radial-gradient(closest-side circle at center, #333,
blue);
```

Here is what each of them does:

- `closest-side`: The shape meets the side of the box nearest to the center (in the case of circles), or meets both the horizontal and vertical sides that are closest to the center (in the case of ellipses)
- `closest-corner`: The shape meets exactly the closest corner of the box from its center
- `farthest-side`: The opposite of `closest-side`, in that rather than the shape meeting the nearest size, it's sized to meet the one farthest from its center (or both the furthest vertical and horizontal side in the case of an ellipse)
- `farthest-corner`: The shape expands to the farthest corner of the box from the center
- `cover`: Identical to `farthest-corner`
- `contain`: Identical to `closest-side`

Read the W3C specification for radial background gradients at `http://www.w3.org/TR/css3-images/`.

The cheat's way to perfect CSS3 linear and radial gradients

If defining gradients by hand seems like hard work, there are some great online gradient generators. My personal favorite is `http://www.colorzilla.com/gradient-editor/`. It uses a graphics editor style GUI, allowing you to pick your colors, stops, gradient style (linear and radial gradients are supported), and even the color space (HEX, RGB(A), HSL(A)) you'd like the final gradient in. There are also loads of preset gradients to use as starting points. If that wasn't enough, it even gives you optional code for fixing up Internet Explorer 9 to show the gradient and a fallback flat color for older browsers. Still not convinced? How about the ability to generate a CSS gradient based on upon the gradient values in an existing image? Thought that might swing it for you.

Repeating gradients

CSS3 also gives us the ability to create repeating background gradients. Let's take a look at how it's done:

```
.repeating-radial-gradient {
    background: repeating-radial-gradient(black 0px, orange 5px, red 10px);
}
```

Here's how that looks (don't look for long, may cause nausea):

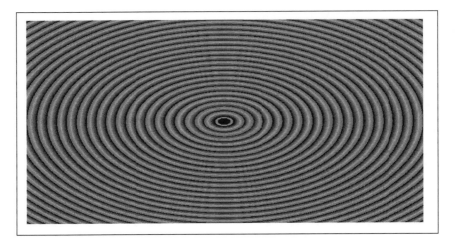

Firstly, prefix the `linear-gradient` or `radial-gradient` with repeating, then it follows the same syntax as a normal gradient. Here I've used pixel distances between the black, orange, and red colors (0px, 5px, and 10px respectively) but you could also choose to use percentages. For best results, it's recommended to stick to the same measurement units (such as pixels or percentages) within a gradient.

> Read the W3C information on repeating gradients at http://www.w3.org/TR/css3-images/.

There's one more way of using background gradients I'd like to share with you.

Background gradient patterns

Although I've often used subtle linear gradients in designs, I've found less practical use for radial gradients and repeating gradients. However, clever folks out there have harnessed the power of gradients to create background gradient patterns. Let's look at an example from CSS Ninja, Lea Verou's collection of CSS3 background patterns, available at http://lea.verou.me/css3patterns/:

```
.carbon-fibre {
    margin: 1rem;
    width: 400px;
    height: 200px;
    background:
    radial-gradient(black 15%, transparent 16%) 0 0,
    radial-gradient(black 15%, transparent 16%) 8px 8px,
```

```
    radial-gradient(rgba(255,255,255,.1) 15%, transparent 20%) 0 1px,
    radial-gradient(rgba(255,255,255,.1) 15%, transparent 20%) 8px
9px;
    background-color:#282828;
    background-size:16px 16px;
}
```

Here's what that gives us in the browser, a `carbon-fibre` background effect:

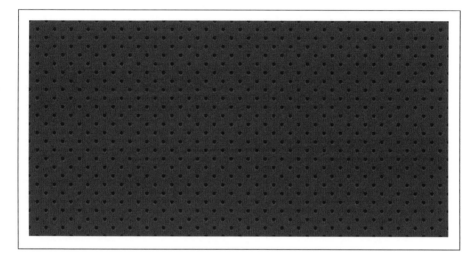

How about that? Just a few lines of CSS3 and we have an easily editable, responsive, and scalable background pattern.

 You might find it useful to add `background-repeat: no-repeat` at the end of the rule to better understand how it works.

As ever, thanks to media queries, different declarations can be used for different responsive scenarios. For example, although a gradient pattern might work well at smaller viewports, it might be better to go with a plain background at larger ones:

```
@media (min-width: 45rem) {
    .carbon-fibre {
        background: #333;
    }
}
```

You can view this example at `example_06-05`.

Multiple background images

Although a little out of fashion at the moment, it used to be a fairly common design requirement to build a page with a different background image at the top of the page than at the bottom. Or perhaps to use different background images for the top and bottom of a content section within a page. Back in the day, with CSS2.1, achieving the effect typically required additional markup (one element for the header background and another for the footer background).

With CSS3 you can stack as many background images as you need on an element.

Here's the syntax:

```css
.bg {
    background:
        url('../img/1.png'),
        url('../img/2.png'),
        url('../img/3.png');
}
```

As with the stacking order of multiple shadows, the image listed first appears nearest to the top in the browser. You can also add a general color for the background in the same declaration if you wish, like this:

```css
.bg {
    background:
    url('../img/1.png'),
    url('../img/2.png'),
    url('../img/3.png') left bottom, black;
}
```

Specify the color last and this will show below every image specified above.

 When specifying multiple background elements, you don't have to stack the different images on different lines; I just find it easier to read code when written this way.

Browsers that don't understand the multiple backgrounds rule (such as Internet Explorer 8 and below) will ignore the rule altogether, so you may wish to declare a 'normal' background property immediately before a CSS3 multiple background rule as a fallback for really old browsers.

With the multiple background images, as long as you're using PNG files with transparency, any partially transparent background images that sit on top of another will show through below. However, background images don't have to sit on top of one another, nor do they all have to be the same size.

Background size

To set different sizes for each image, use the `background-size` property. When multiple images have been used, the syntax works like this:

```
.bg {
    background-size: 100% 50%, 300px 400px, auto;
}
```

The size values (first width, then height) for each image are declared, separated by commas, in the order they are listed in the background property. As in the example above, you can use percentage or pixel values for each image alongside the following:

- `auto`: Which sets the element at its native size
- `cover`: Which expands the image, preserving its aspect ratio, to cover the area of the element
- `contain`: Which expands the image to fit its longest side within the element while preserving the aspect ratio

Background position

If you have different background images, at different sizes, the next thing you'll want is the ability to position them differently. Thankfully, the `background-position` property facilitates that too.

Let's put all this background image capability together, alongside some of the responsive units we have looked at in previous chapters.

Let's create a simple space scene, made with a single element and three background images, set at three different sizes, and positioned in three different ways:

```
.bg-multi {
    height: 100vh;
    width: 100vw;
    background:
        url('rosetta.png'),
        url('moon.png'),
        url('stars.jpg');
    background-size: 75vmax, 50vw, cover;
    background-position: top 50px right 80px, 40px 40px, top center;
    background-repeat: no-repeat;
}
```

You'll see something like this in the browser:

We have the stars image at the bottom, then the moon on top, and finally an image of the Rosetta space probe on top. View this for yourself in `example_06-06`. Notice that if you adjust the browser window, the responsive length units work well (vmax, vh, and vw) and retain proportion, while pixel based ones do not.

 Where no `background-position` is declared, the default position of top left is applied.

Background shorthand

There is a shorthand method of combining the different background properties together. You can read the specification for it at `http://www.w3.org/TR/css3-background/`. However, my experience so far has been that it produces erratic results. Therefore, I recommend the longhand method and declare the multiple images first, then the size, and then the position.

 Read the W3C documentation on multiple background elements at `http://www.w3.org/TR/css3-background/`.

High-resolution background images

Thanks to media queries, we have the ability to load in different background images, not just at different viewport sizes but also different viewport resolutions.

For example, here is the official way of specifying a background image for a 'normal' and a high DPI screen. You can find this in `example_06-07`:

```
.bg {
    background-image: url('bg.jpg');
}
@media (min-resolution: 1.5dppx) {
    .bg {
        background-image: url('bg@1_5x.jpg');
    }
}
```

The media query is written exactly as it is with width, height, or any of the other capability tests. In this example, we are defining the minimum resolution that `bg@1_5x.jpg` should use as 1.5dppx (device pixels per CSS pixel). We could also use **dpi (dots per inch)** or **dpcm (dots per centimeter)** units if preferable. However, despite the poorer support, I find dppx the easiest unit to think about; as 2dppx is twice the resolution, 3dppx would be three times the resolution. Thinking about that in dpi is trickier. 'Standard' resolution would be 96dpi, twice that resolution would be 192dpi and so on.

Support for the 'dppx' unit isn't great right now (check your target browsers at `http://caniuse.com/`) so to get this working everywhere smoothly, you'll need to write a few versions of the media query resolution or, as ever, rely on a tool to do the prefixing for you.

A brief note on performance

Just remember that large images can potentially slow down the feel of your site and lead to a poor experience for users. While a background image won't block the rendering of the page (you'll still see the rest of the site drawn to the page while you wait for the background image), it will add to the total weight of the page, which is important if users are paying for data.

CSS filters

There is a glaring problem with box-shadow. As the name implies, it is limited to the rectangular CSS box shape of the element it is applied to. Here's a screen grab of a triangle shape made with CSS (you can view the code in example_06-08) with a box shadow applied:

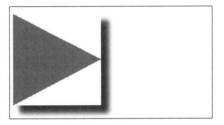

Not exactly what I was hoping for. Thankfully, we can overcome this issue with CSS filters, part of the Filter Effects Module Level 1 (http://www.w3.org/TR/filter-effects/). They are not as widely supported as box-shadow, but work great with a progressive enhancement approach. If a browser doesn't understand what to do with the filter it simply ignores it. For supporting browsers, the fancy effects are rendered.

Here is that same element with a CSS drop-shadow filter applied instead of a box-shadow:

Here is the format for CSS filters:

```
.filter-drop-shadow {
    filter: drop-shadow(8px 8px 6px #333);
}
```

After the filter property we specify the filter we want to use, drop-shadow in this example, and then pass in the arguments for the filter. The drop-shadow follows a similar syntax to box-shadow so this one is easy; x and y offset, blur, then spread radius (both optional), and finally color (also optional, although I recommend specifying a color for consistency).

CSS filters are actually based upon SVG filters which have a wider support. We'll look at the SVG based equivalent in *Chapter 7, Using SVGs for Resolution Independence.*

Available CSS filters

There are a few filters to choose from. We will look at each. While images of most of the filters follow, readers reading a hard copy of this book (with monochrome images) may struggle to notice the differences. If you're in that situation, remember you can still view the various filters in the browser by opening example_06-08. I'm going to list each out now with a suitable value specified. As you might imagine, more of a value means more of the filter applied. Where images are used, the image is shown after the relevant code.

- `filter: url ('./img/filters.svg#filterRed')`: Lets you specify an SVG filter to use.

- `filter: blur(3px)`: Use a single length value (but not as a percentage).

- `filter: brightness(2)`: Use a value from 0 to 1 or 0% to 100%. 0/0% is black, 1/100% is 'normal,' and anything beyond brightens the element further.

- `filter: contrast(2)`: Use a value from 0 to 1 or 0% to 100%. 0/0% is black, 1/100% is 'normal,' and anything beyond raises the color contrast.

- `filter: drop-shadow(4px 4px 6px #333)`: We looked at `drop-shadow` in detail earlier.

- `filter: grayscale(.8)`: Use a value from 0 to 1, or 0% to 100% to apply varying amounts of grayscale to the element. A value of 0 would be no grayscale while a value of 1 would be fully grayscale.

- `filter: hue-rotate(25deg)`: Use a value between 0 and 360 degrees to adjust the colors around the color wheel.

- `filter: invert(75%)`: Use a value from 0 to 1, or 0% to 100% to define the amount the element has its colors inverted.

- `filter: opacity(50%)`: Use a value from 0 to 1, or 0% to 100% to alter the opacity of the element. This is similar to the `opacity` property you will already be familiar with. However, filters, as we shall see, can be combined and this allows opacity to be combined with other filters in one go.

- `filter: saturate(15%)`: Use a value from 0 to 1, or 0% to 100% to de-saturate an image and anything above 1/100% to add extra saturation.

- `filter: sepia(.75)`: Use a value from 0 to 1, or 0% to 100% to make the element appear with a more sepia color. 0/0% leaves the element 'as is' while anything above that applies greater amounts of sepia up to a maximum of 1/100%.

Combining CSS filters

You can also combine filters easily; simply space separate them. For example, here is how you would apply `opacity`, `blur`, and `sepia` filters at once:

```
.MultipleFilters {
    filter: opacity(10%) blur(2px) sepia(35%);
}
```

 Note: Apart from `hue-rotate`, when using filters, negative values are not allowed.

I think you'll agree, CSS filters offer some pretty powerful effects. They are also effects we can transition and transform from situation to situation. We'll look at how to do that in *Chapter 8, Transitions, Transformations, and Animations*.

However, before you go crazy with these new toys, we need to have a grown up conversation about performance.

A warning on CSS performance

When it comes to CSS performance, I would like you to remember this one thing:

"Architecture is outside the braces, performance is inside."

– Ben Frain

Let me expand on my little maxim:

As far as I am able to prove, worrying about whether a CSS selector (the part outside the curly braces), is fast or slow is pointless. I set out to prove this at `http://benfrain.com/css-performance-revisited-selectors-bloat-expensive-styles/`.

However, one thing that really can grind a page to a halt, CSS wise, is 'expensive' properties (the parts inside the curly braces). When we use the term 'expensive', in relation to certain styles, it simply means it costs the browser a lot of overhead. It's something that the browser finds overly taxing to do.

It's possible to take a common sense guess about what will likely cause the browser extra work. It's basically anything it would have to compute before it can paint things to the screen. For example, compare a standard div with a flat solid background, against a semi-opaque image, on top of a background made up of multiple gradients, with rounded corners and a `drop-shadow`. The latter is more expensive; it will result in far more computational work for the browser and subsequently cause more overhead.

Therefore, when you apply effects like filters, do so judiciously and, if possible, test whether the page speed suffers on the lowest powered devices you are hoping to support. At the least, switch on development tool features such as continuous page repainting in Chrome and toggle any affects you think may cause problems. This will provide you with data (in the form of a millisecond reading of how long the current viewport is taking to paint) to make a more educated decision on which effects to apply. The lower the figure, the faster the page will perform (although be aware that browsers/platforms vary so, as ever, test on real devices where possible).

For more on this subject I recommend the following resource:

`https://developers.google.com/web/fundamentals/performance/rendering/`

A note on CSS masks and clipping

In the near future, CSS will be able to offer masks and clipping as part of the CSS Masking Module Level 1. These features will enable us to clip an image with a shape or arbitrary path (specified via SVG or a number of polygon points). Sadly, despite the specification being at the more advanced CR stage, as I write this, the browser implementations are just too buggy to recommend. However, it's a fluid situation so by the time you are reading this, there's every chance the implementations will be solid. For the curious, I'll therefore refer you to the specification at `http://www.w3.org/TR/css-masking/`.

I also think Chris Coyier does a great job of explaining where things are at support wise in this post:

`http://css-tricks.com/clipping-masking-css/`

Finally, a good overview and explanation of what will be possible is offered by Sara Soueidan in this post:

`http://alistapart.com/article/css-shapes-101`

Summary

In this chapter we've looked at a selection of the most useful CSS features for creating lightweight aesthetics in responsive web designs. CSS3's background gradients curb our reliance on images for background effects. We have even considered how they can be used to create infinitely repeating background patterns. We've also learned how to use text-shadows to create simple text enhancements and box-shadows to add shadows to the outside and inside of elements. We've also looked at CSS filters. They allow us to achieve even more impressive visual effects with CSS alone and can be combined for truly impressive results.

In the next chapter we're going to turn our attention to creating and using SVGs as they are more simply called. While it's a very mature technology, it is only in the current climate of responsive, and high-performing websites that it has really come of age.

7
Using SVGs for Resolution Independence

Entire books have, are being, and will be written about SVG (an abbreviation for scalable vector graphics). SVG is an important technology for responsive web design as it provides pin-sharp and future-proof graphical assets for all screen resolutions.

Images on the web, with formats such as JPEG, GIF, or PNG have their visual data saved as set pixels. If you save a graphic in any of those formats with a set width and height, and zoom the image to twice its original size or more, their limitations can be easily exposed.

Here's a screen grab of just that. A PNG image I've zoomed into in the browser:

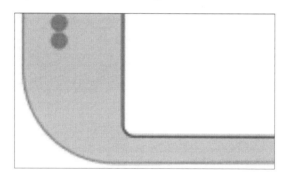

Can you see how the image looks obviously pixelated? Here is the exact same image saved as a vector image, in SVG format, and zoomed to a similar level:

Hopefully the difference is obvious.

Beyond the smallest graphical assets, where at all possible, using SVG rather than JPEG, GIF, or PNG will produce resolution independent graphics that require far smaller file sizes compared to bitmap images.

While we will touch upon many aspects of SVG in this chapter, the focus will be on how to integrate them into your workflow, while also providing an overview of what is possible with SVG.

In this chapter we will cover:

- SVG, a brief history, and an anatomy of a basic SVG document
- Creating SVGs with popular image editing packages and services
- Inserting SVGs into a page with `img` and `object` tags
- Inserting SVGs as background images
- Inserting SVGs directly (inline) into HTML
- Re-using SVG symbols
- Referencing external SVG symbols
- What capabilities are possible with each insertion method
- Animating SVGs with SMIL
- Styling SVGs with an external style sheet
- Styling SVGs with internal styles
- Amending and animating SVGs with CSS
- Media queries and SVGs
- Optimizing SVGs
- Using SVGs to define filters for CSS

- Manipulating SVGs with JavaScript and JavaScript libraries
- Implementation tips
- Further resources

SVG is a dense subject. Which portions of this chapter are most relevant to your needs will depend on what you actually need from SVG. Hopefully, I can offer a few shortcuts right up front.

If you simply want to replace static graphical assets on a website with SVG versions, for sharper images and/or smaller file sizes, then look at the shorter sections on using SVG as background images and within `img` tags.

If you're curious about what applications and services can help you generate and manage SVG assets, skip down to the section, *Creating SVGs with popular image editing packages and services*, for some useful links and pointers.

If you want to understand SVG more fully, or animate and manipulate SVG, you had better get yourself comfy and get a double size of your favorite beverage as this is quite a long one.

To begin our journey of understanding, step with me back into 2001.

A brief history of SVG

The first release of SVG was in 2001. That was not a typo. SVG has been 'a thing' since 2001. While it gained traction along the way, it's only since the advent of high-resolution devices that they have received widespread interest and adoption. Here is the introduction to SVGs from the 1.1 specification (`http://www.w3.org/TR/SVG11/intro.html`):

SVG is a language for describing two-dimensional graphics in XML [XML10]. SVG allows for three types of graphic objects: vector graphic shapes (for example, paths consisting of straight lines and curves), images, and text.

As the name implies, SVGs allow two-dimensional images to be described in code as vector points. This makes them a great candidate for icons, line drawings, and charts.

As vectors describe relative points, they can scale to any size, without loss of fidelity. Furthermore, in terms of data, as SVG are described as vector points, it tends to make them tiny, compared to a comparably sized JPEG, GIF, or PNG file.

Browser support for SVG is now also very good. Android 2.3 and above, and Internet Explorer 9 and above, support them (`http://caniuse.com/#search=svg`).

The graphic that is a document

Ordinarily, if you try and view the code of a graphics file in a text editor the resultant text is completely unintelligible.

Where SVG graphics differ is that they are actually described in a markup style language. SVG is written in **Extensible Markup Language (XML)**, a close relative of HTML. Although you may not realize it, XML is actually everywhere on the Internet. Do you use an RSS reader? That's XML right there. XML is the language that wraps up the content of an RSS feed and makes it easily consumable to a variety of tools and services.

So not only can machines read and understand SVG graphics, but we can too.

Let me give you an example. Take a look at this star graphic:

This is an SVG graphic, called `Star.svg` inside `example_07-01`. You can either open this example in the browser where it will appear as the star or you can open it in a text editor and you can see the code that generates it. Consider this:

```
<?xml version="1.0" encoding="UTF-8" standalone="no"?>
<svg width="198px" height="188px" viewBox="0 0 198 188" version="1.1"
xmlns="http://www.w3.org/2000/svg" xmlns:xlink="http://www.
w3.org/1999/xlink" xmlns:sketch="http://www.bohemiancoding.com/sketch/
ns">
    <!-- Generator: Sketch 3.2.2 (9983) - http://www.bohemiancoding.
com/sketch -->
    <title>Star 1</title>
    <desc>Created with Sketch.</desc>
    <defs></defs>
    <g id="Page-1" stroke="none" stroke-width="1" fill="none" fill-
rule="evenodd" sketch:type="MSPage">
        <polygon id="Star-1" stroke="#979797" stroke-width="3"
fill="#F8E81C" sketch:type="MSShapeGroup" points="99 154 40.2214748
184.901699 51.4471742 119.45085 3.89434837 73.0983006 69.6107374
63.5491503 99 4 128.389263 63.5491503 194.105652 73.0983006 146.552826
119.45085 157.778525 184.901699 "></polygon>
    </g>
</svg>
```

That is the entirety of the code needed to generate that star as an SVG graphic.

Now, ordinarily, if you've never looked at the code of an SVG graphic before, you may be wondering why you would ever want to. If all you want is vector graphics displayed on the web, you certainly don't need to. Just find a graphics application that will save your vector artwork as an SVG and you're done. We will list a few of those packages in the coming pages.

However, although it's certainly common and possible to only work with SVG graphics from within a graphics editing application, understanding exactly how an SVG fits together and how you can tweak it to your exact will can become very useful if you need to start manipulating and animating an SVG.

So, let's take a closer look at that SVG markup and get an appreciation of what exactly is going on in there. I'd like to draw your attention to a few key things.

The root SVG element

The root SVG element here has attributes for `width`, `height`, and `viewbox`.

```
<svg width="198px" height="188px" viewBox="0 0 198 188"
```

Each of these plays an important role in how an SVG is displayed.

Hopefully at this point you understand the term 'viewport'. It's been used in most chapters of this book to describe the area of a device through which content is viewed. For example, a mobile device might have a 320px by 480px viewport. A desktop computer might have a 1920px by 1080px viewport.

The `width` and `height` attributes of the SVG effectively create a viewport. Through this defined viewport we can peek in to see the shapes defined inside the SVG. Just like a web page, the contents of the SVG may be bigger than the viewport but that doesn't mean the rest isn't there, it's merely hidden from our current view.

The viewbox on the other hand defines the coordinate system in which all the shapes of the SVG are governed:

You can think of the viewbox values 0 0 198 188 as describing the top left and bottom right area of a rectangle. The first two values, known technically as **min-x** and **min-y**, describe the top left corner, while the second two, known technically as width and height, describe the bottom right corner.

Having the `viewbox` attribute allows you to do things like zoom an image in or out. For example, if you halve the width and height in the `viewbox` attribute like this:

```
<svg width="198px" height="188px" viewBox="0 0 99 94"
```

The shape will 'zoom' to fill the size of the SVG width and height.

 To really understand the viewbox and SVG coordinate system and the opportunities it presents, I recommend this post by Sara Soueidan: `http://sarasoueidan.com/blog/svg-coordinate-systems/` and this post by Jakob Jenkov: `http://tutorials.jenkov.com/svg/svg-viewport-view-box.html`

Namespace

This SVG has an additional namespace defined for the Sketch graphics program that generated it (`xmlns` is short for XML namespace).

```
xmlns:sketch="http://www.bohemiancoding.com/sketch/ns"
```

These namespace references tend to only be used by the program that generated the SVG, so they are often unneeded when the SVGs are bound for the web. Optimization processes for reducing the size of SVGs will often strip them out.

The title and desc tags

There are `title` and `desc` tags which make an SVG document highly accessible:

```
<title>Star 1</title>
    <desc>Created with Sketch.</desc>
```

These tags can be used to describe the contents of the graphics when they cannot be seen. However, when SVG graphics are used for background graphics, these tags can be stripped to further reduce file size.

The defs tag

There is an empty `defs` tag in our example code:

```
<defs></defs>
```

Despite being empty in our example, this is an important element. It is used to store definitions of all manner of reusable content such as gradients, symbols, paths, and more.

The g element

The g element is used to group other elements together. For example, if you were drawing an SVG of a car, you might group the shapes that make up an entire wheel inside a g tag.

```
<g id="Page-1" stroke="none" stroke-width="1" fill="none" fill-
rule="evenodd" sketch:type="MSPage">
```

In our g tag we can see the earlier namespace of sketch reused here. This will help that graphics application open this graphic again but it serves no further purpose should this image be bound elsewhere.

SVG shapes

The innermost node in this example is a polygon.

```
<polygon id="Star-1" stroke="#979797" stroke-width="3" fill="#F8E81C"
sketch:type="MSShapeGroup" points="99 154 40.2214748 184.901699
51.4471742 119.45085 3.89434837 73.0983006 69.6107374 63.5491503 99
4 128.389263 63.5491503 194.105652 73.0983006 146.552826 119.45085
157.778525 184.901699 "></polygon>
```

SVGs have a number of readymade shapes available (path, rect, circle, ellipse, line, polyline, and polygon).

SVG paths

SVG paths differ from the other shapes of SVG as they are composed of any number of connected points (giving you the freedom to create any shape you like).

So that's the guts of an SVG file, and hopefully now you have a high-level understanding of what's going on. While some will relish the opportunity to hand write or edit SVG files in code, a great many more would rather generate SVGs with a graphics package. Let's consider some of the more popular choices.

Creating SVGs with popular image editing packages and services

While SVGs can be opened, edited, and written in a text editor, there are plenty of applications offering a **graphical user interface** (**GUI**) that make authoring complex SVG graphics easier if you come from a graphics editing background. Perhaps the most obvious choice is Adobe's Illustrator (PC/Mac). However, it is expensive for casual users so my own preference is Bohemian Coding's Sketch (Mac only: `http://bohemiancoding.com/sketch/`). That itself isn't cheap (currently at $99), but it's still the option I would recommend if you use a Mac.

If you use Windows/Linux or are looking for a cheaper option, consider the free and open-source, Inkscape (`https://inkscape.org/en/`). It's by no means the prettiest tool to work with but it is very capable (if you want any proof, view the Inkscape gallery at `https://inkscape.org/en/community/gallery/`).

Finally, there are a few online editors. Google has SVG-edit (`http://svg-edit.googlecode.com/svn/branches/stable/editor/svg-editor.html`). There is also Draw SVG (`http://www.drawsvg.org`), and Method Draw, an arguably better looking fork of SVG-edit (`http://editor.method.ac/`).

Save time with SVG icon services

The aforementioned applications all give you the capability to create SVG graphics from scratch. However, if it's icons you're after, you can probably save a lot of time (and for me, get better results) by downloading SVG versions of icons from an online icon service. My personal favorite is `http://icomoon.io/` is also great.

To quickly illustrate the benefits of an online icon service, loading the icomoon.io application gives you a searchable library of icons (some free, some paid):

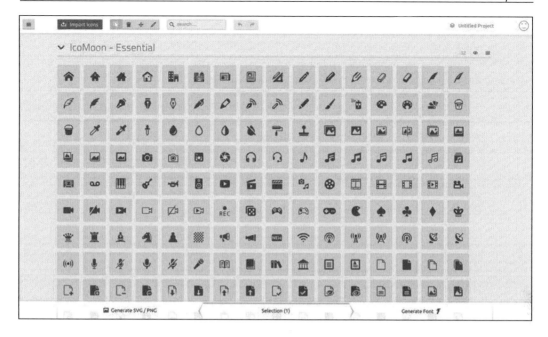

You select the ones you want and then click download. The resultant file contains the icons as SVGs, PNGs, and also SVG symbols for placement in the defs element (remember the defs element is a container element for referenced elements).

To see for yourself, open example_07-02 and you can see the resultant download files after I'd chosen five icons from http://icomoon.io/.

Inserting SVGs into your web pages

There are a number of things that you can do (browser dependent) with SVG images that you can't do with normal image formats (JPEG, GIF, PNG). The range of what's possible is largely dependent upon the way that the SVG is inserted into the page. So, before we get to what we can actually do with SVGs, we'll consider the various ways we can actually get them on the page in the first place.

Using an img tag

The most straightforward way to use an SVG graphic is exactly how you would insert any image into an HTML document. We just use a good ol' `img` tag:

```
<img src="mySconeVector.svg" alt="Amazing line art of a scone" />
```

This makes the SVG behave more or less like any other image. Not much more to say about that.

Using an object tag

The `object` tag is the container recommended by the W3C for holding non-HTML content in a web page (the specification for object is at `http://www.w3.org/TR/html5/embedded-content-0.html`). We can make use of it to insert an SVG into our page like this:

```
<object data="img/svgfile.svg" type="image/svg+xml">
    <span class="fallback-info">Your browser doesn't support SVG</span>
</object>
```

Either a `data` or `type` attribute is required, although I would always recommend adding both. The `data` attribute is where you link out to the SVG asset in the same manner you would link to any other asset. The `type` attribute describes the MIME type relevant for the content. In this instance, `image/svg+xml` is the MIME (Internet media type) type to indicate the data is SVG. You can also add a `width` and `height` attribute too if you want to constrain the size of the SVG with this container.

An SVG inserted into the page via an `object` tag is also accessible with JavaScript so that's one reason to insert them this way. However, an additional bonus of using the `object` tag is that it provides a simple mechanism for when a browser doesn't understand the data type. For example, if that prior `object` element was viewed in Internet Explorer 8 (which has no support for SVG), it would simply see the message 'Your browser doesn't support SVG'. You can use this space to provide a fallback image in an `img` tag. However, be warned that from my cursory testing, the browser will always download the fallback image, regardless of whether it actually needs it. Therefore, if you want your site to load in the shortest possible time (you do, trust me) this might not actually be the best choice.

 If you want to manipulate an SVG inserted via an `object` tag with jQuery, you'll need to use the native `.contentDocument` JavaScript property. You can then use the jQuery `.attr` to change things like `fill`.

An alternative approach to providing a fallback would be to add a `background-image` via the CSS. For example, in our example above, our fallback span has a class of `.fallback-info`. We could make use of this in CSS to link to a suitable `background-image`. That way the `background-image` will only be downloaded if required.

Insert an SVG as a background image

SVGs can be used as a background image in CSS, much the same way as any other image format (PNG, JPG, GIF). There's nothing special about the way you reference them:

```
.item {
    background-image: url('image.svg');
}
```

For older browsers that don't support SVG, you might want to include a 'fallback' image in a more widely supported format (typically PNG). Here's one way to do that for Internet Explorer 8 and Android 2, as IE8 doesn't support SVG or `background-size`, and Android 2.3 doesn't support SVG and requires a vendor prefix for `background-size`:

```
.item {
    background: url('image.png') no-repeat;
    background: url('image.svg') left top / auto auto no-repeat;
}
```

In CSS, where two equivalent properties are applied, the one further down the style sheet will always overrule those above. In CSS, a browser will always disregard a property/value pair in a rule it cannot make sense of. Therefore, in this case the older browsers get the PNG, as they cannot make use of the SVG or understand an un-prefixed `background-size` property, while newer browsers that could actually use either, take the bottom one as it supersedes the first.

You can also provide fallbacks with the aid of Modernizr; the JavaScript tool for feature testing the browser (Modernizr is discussed more fully in *Chapter 5*, *CSS3 – Selectors, Typography, Color Modes, and New Features*). Modernizr has individual tests for some of the different SVG insertion methods, and the next version of Modernizr (unreleased at the time of writing) may have something more specific for SVG in CSS. For now however, you can do this:

```
.item {
    background-image: url('image.png');
}
.svg .item {
    background-image: url('image.svg');
}
```

Or invert the logic if preferred:

```
.item {
    background-image: url('image.svg');
}
.no-svg .item {
    background-image: url('image.png');
}
```

When Feature Queries are more fully supported, you could also do this:

```
.item {
    background-image: url('image.png');
}

@supports (fill: black) {
    .item {
        background-image: url('image.svg');
    }
}
```

The @supports rule works here because fill is a SVG property so if the browser understands that, it would take the lower rule over the first.

If your needs for SVG are primarily static background images, perhaps for icons and the like, I highly recommend implementing SVGs as background images. That's because there are a number of tools that will automatically create image sprites or style sheet assets (which means including the SVGs as data URIs), fallback PNG assets, and requisite style sheets from any individual SVGs you create. Using SVGs this way is very well supported, the images themselves cache well (so performance wise they work very well), and it's simple to implement.

A brief aside on data URIs

If you're reading that prior section and wondering what on earth a data **Uniform Resource Identifier (URI)** is, in relation to CSS, it's a means of including what would ordinarily be an external asset, such as an image, within the CSS file itself. Therefore, where we might do this to link at an external image file:

```
.external {
  background-image: url('Star.svg');
}
```

We could simply include the image inside our style sheet with a data URI like this:

```
.data-uri {
  background-image: url(data:image/svg+xml,%3C%3Fxml%20
version%3D%221.0%22%20encoding%3D%22UTF-8%22%20standalone%3D%22
no%22%3F%3E%0A%3Csvg%20width%3D%22198px%22%20height%3D%22188px-
%22%20viewBox%3D%220%200%20198%20188%22%20version%3D%221.1%22%20
xmlns%3D%22http%3A%2F%2Fwww.w3.org%2F2000%2Fsvg%22%20xmlns%3Axlink
%3D%22http%3A%2F%2Fwww.w3.org%2F1999%2Fxlink%22%20xmlns%3Asketch%3
D%22http%3A%2F%2Fwww.bohemiancoding.com%2Fsketch%2Fns%22%3E%0A%20
%20%20%20%3C%21--%20Generator%3A%20Sketch%203.2.2%20%289983%29%20
-%20http%3A%2F%2Fwww.bohemiancoding.com%2Fsketch%20--%3E%0A%20
%20%20%20%3Ctitle%3EStar%201%3C%2Ftitle%3E%0A%20%20%20%20
%3Cdesc%3ECreated%20with%20Sketch.%3C%2Fdesc%3E%0A%20%20%20%20-
%3Cdefs%3E%3C%2Fdefs%3E%0A%20%20%20%20%3Cg%20id%3D%22Page-1%22%20
stroke%3D%22none%22%20stroke-width%3D%221%22%20fill%3D%22none%22%20
fill-rule%3D%22evenodd%22%20sketch%3Atype%3D%22MSPage%22%3E%
0A%20%20%20%20%20%20%20%20%3Cpolygon%20id%3D%22Star-1%22%20
stroke%3D%22%23979797%22%20stroke-width%3D%223%22%20
fill%3D%22%23F8E81C%22%20sketch%3Atype%3D%22MSShapeGroup%22%20
points%3D%2299%20154%2040.2214748%20184.901699%2051.4471742%20
119.45085%203.89434837%2073.0983006%2069.6107374%2063.5491503%2099%20
4%20128.389263%2063.5491503%20194.105652%2073.0983006%20146.552826%20
119.45085%20157.778525%20184.901699%20%22%3E%3C%2Fpolygon%3E%0A%20%20
%20%20%3C%2Fg%3E%0A%3C%2Fsvg%3E);
}
```

It's not pretty but it provides a way to negate a separate request over the network. There are different encoding methods for data URIs and plenty of tools available to create data URIs from your assets.

If encoding SVGs in this manner, I would suggest avoiding the base64 method as it doesn't compress as well as text for SVG content.

Generating image sprites

My personal recommendation, tool wise, for generating image sprites or data URI assets, is Iconizr (`http://iconizr.com/`). It gives you complete control over how you would like your resultant SVG and fallback PNG assets. You can have the SVGs and fallback PNG files output as data URIs or image sprites and it even includes the requisite JavaScript snippet for loading the correct asset if you opt for data URIs; highly recommended.

Also, if you are wondering whether to choose data URIs or image sprites for your projects, I did further research on the pros and cons of data URIs or image sprites that you may be interested in should you be facing the same choice: `http://benfrain.com/image-sprites-data-uris-icon-fonts-v-svgs/`

While I'm a big fan of SVGs as background images, if you want to animate them dynamically, or inject values into them via JavaScript, then it will be best to opt for inserting SVG data 'inline' into the HTML.

Inserting an SVG inline

As SVG is merely an XML document, you can insert it directly into the HTML. For example:

```
<div>
    <h3>Inserted 'inline':</h3>
    <span class="inlineSVG">
        <svg id="svgInline" width="198" height="188" viewBox="0 0
198 188" xmlns="http://www.w3.org/2000/svg" xmlns:xlink="http://www.
w3.org/1999/xlink">
        <title>Star 1</title>
            <g class="star_Wrapper" fill="none" fill-rule="evenodd">
                <path id="star_Path" stroke="#979797" stroke-
width="3" fill="#F8E81C" d="M99 1541-58.78 30.902 11.227-65.45L3.894
73.097165.717-9.55L99 4129.39 59.55 65.716 9.548-47.553 46.353 11.226
65.452z" />
            </g>
        </svg>
    </span>
</div>
```

There is no special wrapping element needed, you literally just insert the SVG markup inside the HTML markup. It's also worth knowing that if you remove any `width` and `height` attributes on the `svg` element, the SVG will scale fluidly to fit the containing element.

Inserting SVGs into your documents is probably the most versatile in terms of SVG features.

Re-using graphical objects from symbols

Earlier in the chapter I mentioned that I had picked and downloaded some icons from IcoMoon (`http://icomoon.io`). They were icons depicting touch gesture: swipe, pinch, drag, and so on. Suppose in a website you are building you need to make use of them multiple times. Remember I mentioned that there was a version of those icons as SVG symbol definitions? That's what we will make use of now.

In `example_07-09` we will insert the various symbol definitions inside the `defs` element of an SVG in the page. You'll notice that on the SVG element, an inline style is used: `display:none` and the `height` and `width` attributes have both been set to zero (those styles could be set in CSS if you would rather). This is so that this SVG takes up no space. We are only using this SVG to house symbols of the graphical objects we want to use elsewhere.

So, our markup starts like this:

```
<body>
    <svg display="none" width="0" height="0" version="1.1"
xmlns="http://www.w3.org/2000/svg" xmlns:xlink="http://www.
w3.org/1999/xlink">
    <defs>
    <symbol id="icon-drag-left-right" viewBox="0 0 1344 1024">
        <title>drag-left-right</title>
        <path class="path1" d="M256 192v-160l-224 224 224
224v-160h256v-128z"></path>
```

Notice the `symbol` element inside the `defs` element? This is the element to use when we want to define a shape for later reuse.

After the SVG defining all necessary symbols for our work, we have all our 'normal' HTML markup. Then, when we want to make use of one of those symbols, we can do this:

```
<svg class="icon-drag-left-right">
  <use xlink:href="#icon-drag-left-right"></use>
</svg>
```

That will display the drag left and right icon:

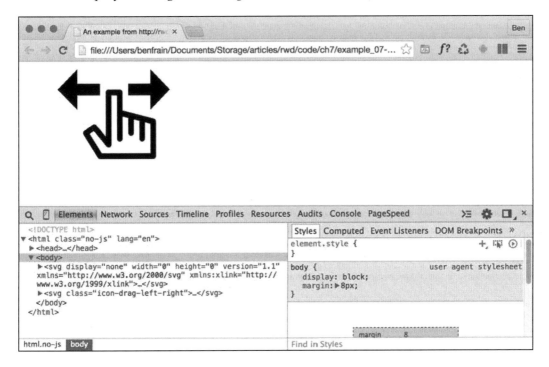

The magic here is the `use` element. As you might have guessed from the name, it's used to make use of existing graphical objects that have already been defined elsewhere. The mechanism for choosing what to reference is the `xlink` attribute that in this case is referencing the symbol ID of the 'drag left and right' icon (`#icon-drag-left-right`) we have inline at the beginning of the markup.

When you re-use a symbol, unless you explicitly set a size (either with attributes on the element itself or with CSS) the `use` will be set to width and height 100%. So, to re-size our icon we could do this:

```
.icon-drag-left-right {
    width: 2.5rem;
    height: 2.5rem;
}
```

The `use` element can be used to re-use all sorts of SVG content: gradients, shapes, symbols, and more.

Inline SVGs allow different colors in different contexts

With inline SVGs you can also do useful things like change colors based on context, and that's great when you need multiple versions of the same icon in different colors:

```css
.icon-drag-left-right {
    fill: #f90;
}

.different-context .icon-drag-left-right {
    fill: #ddd;
}
```

Make dual-tone icons that inherit the color of their parent

With inline SVGs you can also have some fun and create a two-tone effects from a single color icon (as long as the SVG is made up of more than one path) with the use of currentColor, the oldest CSS variable. To do this, inside the SVG symbol, set the fill of the path you want to be one color as currentColor. Then use the color value in your CSS to color the element. For the paths in the SVG symbol without the fill, set as currentColor, they will receive the fill value. To exemplify:

```css
.icon-drag-left-right {
    width: 2.5rem;
    height: 2.5rem;
    fill: #f90;
    color: #ccc; /* this gets applied to the path that has it's fill
attribute set to currentColor in the symbol */
}
```

Here's that same symbol re-used three times, each with different colors and sizes:

Remember you can dig around the code in `example_07-09`. It's also worth knowing that the color doesn't have to be set on that element itself, it can be on any parent element; the `currentColor` will inherit a value from up the DOM tree to the nearest parent with a color value set.

There are a lot of positives to using SVG in this way. The only downside being that it's necessary to include the same SVG data on every page you want to use the icons. Sadly, this is bad for performance, as the assets (the SVG data) isn't going to be cached easily. However, there is another option (if you are happy to add a script to support Internet Explorer).

Re-using graphical objects from external sources

Rather than paste in an enormous set of SVG symbols in each page, while still using the `use` element, it's possible to link out to external SVG files and grab the portion of the document you want to use. Take a look at `example-07-10` and the same three icons as we had in `example_07-09` are put on the page in this manner:

```
<svg class="icon-drag-left-right">
    <use xlink:href="defs.svg#icon-drag-left-right"></use>
</svg>
```

The important part to understand is the `href`. We are linking to an external SVG file (the `defs.svg` part) and then specifying the ID of the symbol within that file we want to use (the `#icon-drag-left-right` part).

The benefits of this approach are that the asset is cached by the browser (just like any other external image would/could be) and it saves littering our markup with an SVG full of symbol definitions. The downside is that, unlike when the `defs` are placed inline, any dynamic changes made to the `defs.svg` (for example, if a path was being manipulated by JavaScript) won't be updated in the `use` tags.

Sadly, Internet Explorer does not allow referencing symbols from external assets. However, there's a polyfill script for IE9-11, called **SVG For Everybody** that allows us to use this technique regardless. Head over to `https://github.com/jonathantneal/svg4everybody` for more information.

When using that piece of JavaScript, you can happily reference external assets and the polyfill will insert the SVG data directly into the body of the document for Internet Explorer.

What you can do with each SVG insertion method (inline, object, background-image, and img)

As mentioned previously, SVGs differ from other graphical assets. They can behave differently, depending upon the way they are inserted into a page. As we have seen, there are four main ways in which to place SVG onto the page:

- Inside an `img` tag
- Inside an `object` tag
- As a background image
- Inline

And depending upon the insertion method, certain capabilities will or will not be available to you.

To understand what should be possible with each insertion method, it might be simpler to consider this table.

Feature	img	object	inline	bg image
SMIL	Y	Y	Y	Y
External CSS	N	*1	Y	N
Internal CSS	Y	Y	Y	Y
Access via JS	N	Y	Y	N
Cacheable	Y	Y	*2	Y
MQ in SVG	Y	Y	*3	Y
Use possible	N	Y	Y	N

Now there are caveats to consider, marked within numbers:

- ***1**: When using an SVG inside an object you can use an external style sheet to style the SVG but you have to link to that style sheet from within the SVG
- ***2**: You can use SVGs in an external asset (which is cacheable) but it doesn't work by default in Internet Explorer
- ***3**: A media query inside the styles section of an 'inlined' SVG works on the size of the document it lives in (not the size of the SVG itself)

Browser schisms

Be aware that browser implementations of SVG also vary. Therefore, just because those things should be possible (as indicated above), doesn't mean they actually will be in every browser, or that they will behave consistently!

For example, the results in the preceding table are based upon the test page in `example_07-03`.

The behavior of the test page is comparable in the latest version of Firefox, Chrome, and Safari. However, Internet Explorer sometimes does things a little differently.

For example, in all the SVG capable versions of Internet Explorer (at this point, that's 9, 10, and 11), as we have already seen, it is not possible to reference external SVG sources. Furthermore, Internet Explorer applies the styles from the external style sheet onto the SVGs regardless of how they have been inserted (all the other browsers only apply styles from external style sheets if the SVGs have been inserted via an `object` or inline). Internet Explorer also doesn't allow any animation of SVG via CSS; animation of SVG in Internet Explorer has to be done via JavaScript. I'll say that one again for the folks at the back in the cheap seats: you cannot animate SVGs in Internet Explorer by any means other than JavaScript.

Extra SVG capabilities and oddities

Let's put aside the foibles of browsers for a moment and consider what some of these features in the table actually allow and why you may or may not want to make use of them.

SVGs will always render as sharp as the viewing device will allow and regardless of the manner of insertion. For most practical situations, resolution independence is usually reason enough to use SVG. It's then just a question of choosing whichever insertion method suits your workflow and the task at hand.

However, there are other capabilities and oddities that are worth knowing about such as SMIL animation, different ways to link to external style sheets, marking internal styles with character data delimiters, amending an SVG with JavaScript, and making use of media queries within an SVG. Let's cover those next.

SMIL animation

SMIL animations (`http://www.w3.org/TR/smil-animation/`) are a way to define animations for an SVG within the SVG document itself.

SMIL (pronounced 'smile' in case you were wondering) stands for synchronized multimedia integration language and was developed as a method of defining animations inside an XML document (remember, SVG is XML based).

Here's an example of how to define a SMIL based animation:

```
<g class="star_Wrapper" fill="none" fill-rule="evenodd">
    <animate xlink:href="#star_Path" attributeName="fill"
attributeType="XML" begin="0s" dur="2s" fill="freeze" from="#F8E81C"
to="#14805e" />

    <path id="star_Path" stroke="#979797" stroke-width="3"
fill="#F8E81C" d="M99 154l-58.78 30.902 11.227-65.45L3.894
73.097l65.717-9.55L99 4l29.39 59.55 65.716 9.548-47.553 46.353 11.226
65.452z" />
</g>
```

I've grabbed a section of the earlier SVG we looked at. The `g` is a grouping element in SVG, and this one includes both a star shape (the `path` element with the `id="star_Path"`) and the SMIL animation within the `animate` element. That simple animation tweens the fill color of the star from yellow to green over two seconds. What's more, it does that whether the SVG is put on the page in an `img`, `object`, `background-image`, or inline (no, honestly, open up `example_07-03` in any recent browser other than Internet Explorer to see).

Tweening

In case you didn't already know (I didn't), 'tweening' as a term is simply a shortening of 'inbetweening' as it merely indicates all the inbetween stages from one animation point to another.

Wow! Great, right? Well, it could have been. Despite being a standard for some time, it looks like SMILs days are numbered.

The end of SMIL

SMIL has no support in Internet Explorer. None. Nada. Zip. Zilch. I could go on with other words that amount to very little but I trust you understand there's not much support for SMIL in Internet Explorer at this point.

Worse still (I know, I'm giving you both barrels here) Microsoft have no plans to introduce it either. Take a look at the platform status: `https://status.modern.ie/svgsmilanimation?term=SMIL`

Plus Chrome have now indicated an intent to deprecate SMIL in the Chrome browser: `https://groups.google.com/a/chromium.org/forum/#!topic/blink-dev/5o0yiO440LM`

Mic. Dropped.

 If you still have a need to use SMIL, Sara Soueidan wrote an excellent, in-depth article about SMIL animations at `http://css-tricks.com/guide-svg-animations-smil/`.

Thankfully, there are plenty of other ways we can animate SVGs, which we will come to shortly. So if you have to support Internet Explorer hang on in there.

Styling an SVG with an external style sheet

It's possible to style an SVG with CSS. This can be CSS enclosed in the SVG itself, or in the CSS style sheets you would write all your 'normal' CSS in.

Now, if you refer back to our features table from earlier in the chapter, you can see that styling SVG with external CSS isn't possible when the SVG is included via an `img` tag or as a background-image (apart from Internet Explorer). It's only possible when SVGs are inserted via an `object` tag or `inline`.

There are two syntaxes for linking to an external style sheet from an SVG. The most straightforward way is like this (you would typically add this in the `defs` section):

```
<link href="styles.css" type="text/css" rel="stylesheet"/>
```

It's akin to the way we used to link to style sheets prior to HTML5 (for example, note the `type` attribute is no longer necessary in HTML5). However, despite this working in many browsers, it isn't the way the specifications define how external style sheets should be linked in SVG (`http://www.w3.org/TR/SVG/styling.html`). Here is the correct/official way, actually defined for XML back in 1999 (`http://www.w3.org/1999/06/REC-xml-stylesheet-19990629/`):

```
<?xml-stylesheet href="styles.css" type="text/css"?>
```

You need to add that above the opening SVG element in your file. For example:

```
<?xml-stylesheet href="styles.css" type="text/css"?>
<svg width="198" height="188" viewBox="0 0 198 188" xmlns="http://www.
w3.org/2000/svg" xmlns:xlink="http://www.w3.org/1999/xlink">
```

Interestingly, the latter syntax is the only one that works in Internet Explorer. So, when you need to link out to a style sheet from your SVG, I'd recommend using this second syntax for wider support.

You don't have to use an external style sheet; you can use inline styles directly in the SVG itself if you would rather.

Styling an SVG with internal styles

You can place styles for an SVG within the SVG itself. They should be placed within the `defs` element. As SVG is XML based, it's safest to include the **Character Data (CDATA)** marker. The CDATA marker simply tells the browser that the information within the character data delimited section could possibly be interpreted as XML markup but should not be. The syntax is like this:

```
<defs>
    <style type="text/css">
        <![CDATA[
            #star_Path {
                stroke: red;
            }
        ]]>
    </style>
</defs>
```

SVG properties and values within CSS

Notice that `stroke` property in that prior code block. That isn't a CSS property, it's an SVG property. There are quite a few specific SVG properties you can use in styles (regardless of whether they are declared inline or via an external style sheet). For example, with an SVG, you don't specify a `background-color`, instead you specify a `fill`. You don't specify a `border`, you specify a `stroke-width`. For the full list of SVG specific properties, take a look at the specification here: http://www.w3.org/TR/SVG/styling.html

With either inline or external CSS, it's possible to do all the 'normal' CSS things you would expect; change an elements appearance, animate, transform elements, and so on.

Animate an SVG with CSS

Let's consider a quick example of adding a CSS animation inside an SVG (remember, these styles could just as easily be in an external style sheet too).

Let's take the star example we have looked at throughout this chapter and make it spin. You can look at the finished example in example_07-07:

```
<div class="wrapper">
    <svg width="198" height="188" viewBox="0 0 220 200" xmlns="http://
www.w3.org/2000/svg" xmlns:xlink="http://www.w3.org/1999/xlink">
        <title>Star 1</title>
        <defs>
            <style type="text/css">
                <![CDATA[
                @keyframes spin {
                    0% {
                        transform: rotate(0deg);
                    }
                    100% {
                        transform: rotate(360deg);
                    }
                }
                .star_Wrapper {
                    animation: spin 2s 1s;
                    transform-origin: 50% 50%;
                }
                .wrapper {
                    padding: 2rem;
                    margin: 2rem;
                }
                ]]>
            </style>
            <g id="shape">
                <path fill="#14805e" d="M50 50h50v50H50z"/>
                <circle fill="#ebebeb" cx="50" cy="50" r="50"/>
            </g>
        </defs>
        <g class="star_Wrapper" fill="none" fill-rule="evenodd">
            <path id="star_Path" stroke="#333" stroke-width="3"
fill="#F8E81C" d="M99 1541-58.78 30.902 11.227-65.45L3.894
73.097l65.717-9.55L99 4129.39 59.55 65.716 9.548-47.553 46.353 11.226
65.453z"/>
        </g>
    </svg>
</div>
```

If you load that example in the browser, after a 1 second delay, the star will spin a full circle over the course of 2 seconds.

 Notice how a transform origin of `50% 50%` has been set on the SVG? That's because, unlike CSS, the default `transform-origin` of an SVG is not 50% 50% (center in both axis), it's actually 0 0 (top left). Without that property set, the star would rotate around the top left point.

You can get quite far animating SVGs with CSS animations alone (well, assuming you don't need to worry about Internet Explorer). However, when you want to add interactivity, support Internet Explorer, or synchronize a number of events, it's generally best to lean on JavaScript. And the good news is that there are great libraries that make animating SVGs really easy. Let's look at an example of that now.

Animating SVG with JavaScript

With an SVG inserted into the page via an `object` tag or inline, it's possible to manipulate the SVG directly or indirectly with JavaScript.

By indirectly, I mean it's possible with JavaScript to change a class on or above the SVG that would cause an CSS animation to start. For example:

```
svg {
    /* no animation */
}

.added-with-js svg {
    /* animation */
}
```

However, it's also possible to animate an SVG via JavaScript directly.

If animating just one or two things independently, it's probable things would be lighter, code wise, by writing the JavaScript by hand. However, if you need to animate lots of elements or synchronize the animation of elements as if on a timeline, JavaScript libraries can really help. Ultimately, you will need to judge whether the weight of including the library in your page can be justified for the goal you are trying to achieve.

My recommendation for animating SVGs via JavaScript is the GreenSock animation platform (`http://greensock.com`), Velocity.js (`http://julian.com/research/velocity/`), or Snap.svg (`http://snapsvg.io/`). For the next example, we'll cover a very simple example using GreenSock.

A simple example of animating an SVG with GreenSock

Suppose we want to make an interface dial, that animates around when we click a button from zero to whatever value we input. We want not only the stroke of the dial to animate in both length and color, but also the number from zero to the value we input. You can view the completed implementation in `example_07-08`.

So, if we entered a value of 75, and clicked animate, it would fill around to look like this:

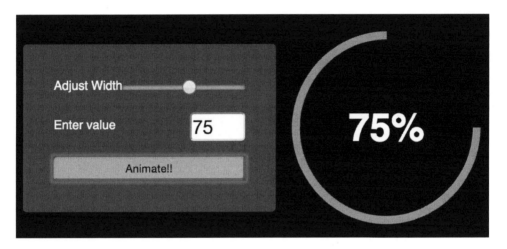

Instead of listing out the entire JavaScript file (which is heavily commented so should make some sense to read in isolation), for brevity's sake, we'll just consider the key points.

The basic idea is that we have made a circle as an SVG `<path>` (rather than a `<circle>` element). As it's a path it means we can animate the path as if it were being drawn using the `stroke-dashoffset` technique. There's more info on this technique in the boxed out section below but briefly, we use JavaScript to measure the length of the path and then use the `stroke-dasharray` attribute to specify the length of the rendered part of the line and the length of the gap. Then we use `stroke-dashoffset` to change where that `dasharray` starts. This means you can effectively start the stroke 'off' the path and animate it in. This gives the illusion that the path is being drawn.

If the value to animate the `dasharray` to was a static, known value, this effect would be relatively simple to achieve with a CSS animation and a little trial and error (more on CSS animations in the next chapter).

However, besides a dynamic value, at the same time as we are 'drawing' the line we want to fade in the stroke color from one value to another and visually count up to the input value in the text node. This is an animation equivalent of patting our heads, rubbing our tummy, and counting backwards from 10,000. GreenSock makes those things trivially easy (the animation part; it won't rub your tummy or pat your head, although it can count back from 10,000 should you need to). Here are the lines of JavaScript needed to make GreenSock do all three:

```
// Animate the drawing of the line and color change
TweenLite.to(circlePath, 1.5, {'stroke-dashoffset': "-"+amount,
stroke: strokeEndColour});
// Set a counter to zero and animate to the input value
var counter = { var: 0 };
TweenLite.to(counter, 1.5, {
    var: inputValue,
    onUpdate: function () {
        text.textContent = Math.ceil(counter.var) + "%";
    },
    ease:Circ.easeOut
});
```

In essence, with the `TweenLite.to()` function you pass in the thing you want to animate, the time over which the animation should occur, and then the values you want to change (and what you want them to change to).

The GreenSock site has excellent documentation and support forums so if you find yourself needing to synchronize a number of animations at once, be sure to clear a day from your diary and familiarize yourself with GreenSock.

In case you haven't come across the SVG 'line drawing' technique before it was popularized by Polygon magazine when Vox Media animated a couple of line drawings of the Xbox One and Playstation 4 games consoles. You can read the original post at `http://product.voxmedia.com/2013/11/25/5426880/polygon-feature-design-svg-animations-for-fun-and-profit`

There's also an excellent and more thorough explanation of the technique by Jake Archibald at `http://jakearchibald.com/2013/animated-line-drawing-svg/`.

Optimising SVGs

As conscientious developers, we want to ensure that assets are as small as possible. The easiest way to do this with SVGs is to make use of automation tools that can optimize various particulars of SVG documents. Besides obvious economies such as removing elements (for example, stripping the title and description elements) it's also possible to perform a raft of micro-optimizations that, when added up, make for far leaner SVG assets.

Presently, for this task I would recommend SVGO (`https://github.com/svg/svgo`). If you have never used SVGO before I would recommend starting with SVGOMG (`https://jakearchibald.github.io/svgomg/`). It's a browser-based version of SVGO that enables you to toggle the various optimization plugins and get instant feedback on the file savings.

Remember our example star SVG markup from the beginning of the chapter? By default, that simple SVG is 489 bytes in size. By passing that through SVGO, it's possible to get the size down to just 218 bytes, and that's leaving the `viewBox` in. That's a saving of 55.42%. If you're using a raft of SVG images, these savings can really add up. Here's what the optimized SVG markup looks like:

```
<svg width="198" height="188" viewBox="0 0 198 188" xmlns="http://
www.w3.org/2000/svg"><path stroke="#979797" stroke-width="3"
fill="#F8E81C" d="M99 154l-58.78 30.902 11.227-65.45L3.894
73.097l65.717-9.55L99 4l29.39 59.55 65.716 9.548-47.553 46.353 11.226
65.454z"/></svg>
```

Before you spend too long with SVGO, be aware that such is the popularity of SVGO, plenty of other SVG tools also make use of it. For example, the aforementioned Iconizr (`http://iconizr.com/`) tool runs your SVG files through SVGO by default anyway, before creating your assets so ensure you aren't unnecessarily double-optimizing.

Using SVGs as filters

In *Chapter 6, Stunning Aesthetics with CSS3*, we looked at the CSS filter effects. However, they are not currently supported in Internet Explorer 10 or 11. That can be frustrating if you want to enjoy filter effects in those browsers. Luckily, with help from SVG, we can create filters that work in Internet Explorer 10 and 11 too but as ever, it's perhaps not as straight forward as you might imagine. For example, in `example_07-05`, we have a page with the following markup inside the `body`:

```
<img class="HRH" src="queen@2x-1024x747.png"/>
```

It's an image of the Queen of England. Ordinarily, it looks like this:

Now, also in that example folder, is an SVG with a filter defined in the `defs` elements. The SVG markup looks like this:

```
<svg xmlns="http://www.w3.org/2000/svg" version="1.1">
    <defs>
        <filter id="myfilter" x="0" y="0">
            <feColorMatrix in="SourceGraphic" type="hueRotate"
values="90" result="A"/>
            <feGaussianBlur in="A" stdDeviation="6"/>
        </filter>
    </defs>
</svg>
```

Within the filter, we are first defining a hue rotation of 90 (using the `feColorMatrix`, and then passing that effect, via the `result` attribute, to the next filter (the `feGaussianBlur`) with a blur value of 6. Be aware that I've been deliberately heavy handed here. This doesn't produce a nice aesthetic, but it should leave you in no doubt that the effect has worked!

Now, rather than add that SVG markup to the HTML, we can leave it where it is and reference it using the same CSS filter syntax we saw in the last chapter.

```
.HRH {
    filter: url('filter.svg#myfilter');
}
```

In most evergreen browsers (Chrome, Safari, Firefox) this is the effect:

Sadly, this method doesn't work in IE 10 or 11. However, there is another way to achieve our goal, and that's using SVGs own image tag to include the image within the SVG. Inside `example_07-06`, we have the following markup:

```
<svg height="747px" width="1024px" viewbox="0 0 1024 747"
xmlns="http://www.w3.org/2000/svg" version="1.1">
    <defs>
        <filter id="myfilter" x="0" y="0">
            <feColorMatrix in="SourceGraphic" type="hueRotate"
values="90" result="A"/>
            <feGaussianBlur in="A" stdDeviation="6"/>
```

```
        </filter>
    </defs>
    <image x="0" y="0" height="747px" width="1024px"
xmlns:xlink="http://www.w3.org/1999/xlink" xlink:href="queen@2x-
1024x747.png" filter="url(#myfilter)"></image>
    </svg>
```

The SVG markup here is very similar to the external `filter.svg` filter we used in the previous example but `height`, `width`, and `viewbox` attributes have been added. In addition, the image we want to apply the filter to is the only content in the SVG outside of the `defs` element. To link to the filter, we are using the `filter` attribute and passing the ID of the filter we want to use (in this case from within the `defs` element above).

Although this approach is a little more involved, it means you can get the many and varied filter effects that SVG affords, even in versions 10 and 11 of Internet Explorer.

A note on media queries inside SVGs

All browsers that understand SVG should respect the CSS media queries defined inside. However, when it comes to media queries inside SVGs there are a few things to remember.

For example, suppose you insert a media query inside an SVG like this:

```
<style type="text/css"><![CDATA[
    #star_Path {
        stroke: red;
    }
    @media (min-width: 800px) {
        #star_Path {
            stroke: violet;
        }
    }
]]></style>
```

And that SVG is displayed on the page at a width of 200px while the viewport is 1200px wide.

We might expect the stroke of the star to be violet when the screen is 800px and above. After all, that's what we have our media query set to. However, when the SVG is placed in the page via an `img` tag, as a background image or inside an `object` tag, it is has no knowledge of the outer HTML document. Hence, in this situation, `min-width` means the min-width of the SVG itself. So, unless the SVG itself was displaying on the page at a width of 800px or more, the stroke wouldn't be violet.

Conversely, when you insert an SVG inline, it merges, (in a manner of speaking), with the outer HTML document. The `min-width` media query here is looking to the viewport (as is the HTML) to decide when the media query matches.

To solve this particular problem and make the same media query behave consistently, we could amend our media query to this:

```
@media (min-device-width: 800px) {
    #star_Path {
        stroke: violet;
    }
}
```

That way, regardless of the SVG size or how it is embedded it is looking to the device width (effectively the viewport).

Implementation tips

We're almost at the end of the chapter now and there is still so much we could talk about regarding SVG. Therefore, at this point I'll just list a few unrelated considerations. They aren't necessarily worthy of protracted explanations but I'll list them here in note form in case they save you from an hour of Googling:

- If you have no need to animate your SVGs, opt for an image sprite of your assets or a data URI style sheet. It's far easier to provide fallback assets and they almost always perform better from a performance perspective.

- Automate as many steps in the asset creation process as possible; it reduces human error and produces predictable results faster.

- To insert static SVGs in a project, try and pick a single delivery mechanism and stick to it (image sprite, data URI, or inline). It can become a burden to produce some assets one way and some another and maintain the various implementations.

- There is no easy 'one size fits all' choice with SVG animation. For occasional and simple animations, use CSS. For complex interactive or timeline style animations, that will also work in Internet Explorer, lean on a proven library such as Greensock, Velocity.js, or Snap.svg.

Further resources

As I mentioned at the start of this chapter, I have neither the space, nor the knowledge, to impart all there is to know about SVG. Therefore, I'd like to make you aware of the following excellent resources which provide additional depth and range on the subject:

- *SVG Essentials, 2nd Edition* by J. David Eisenberg, Amelia Bellamy-Royds (`http://shop.oreilly.com/product/0636920032335.do`)

- *A Guide to SVG Animations (SMIL)* by Sara Soueidan (`http://css-tricks.com/guide-svg-animations-smil/`)

- *Media Queries inside SVGs Test* by Jeremie Patonnier (`http://jeremie.patonnier.net/experiences/svg/media-queries/test.html`)

- *An SVG Primer for Today's Browsers* (`http://www.w3.org/Graphics/SVG/IG/resources/svgprimer.html`)

- *Understanding SVG Coordinate Systems and Transformations (Part 1)* by Sara Soueidan (`http://sarasoueidan.com/blog/svg-coordinate-systems/`)

- *Hands On: SVG Filter Effects* (`http://ie.microsoft.com/testdrive/graphics/hands-on-css3/hands-on_svg-filter-effects.htm`)

- Full set of SVG tutorials by Jakob Jenkov (`http://tutorials.jenkov.com/svg/index.html`)

Summary

In this chapter we have covered a lot of the essential information needed to start making sense of, and implementing, SVGs in a responsive project. We have considered the different graphics applications and online solutions available to create SVG assets, then the various insertion methods possible and the capabilities each allows, along with the various browser peculiarities to be aware of.

We've also considered how to link to external style sheets and re-use SVG symbols from within the same page and when referenced externally. We even looked at how we can make filters with SVG that can be referenced and used in CSS for wider support than CSS filters.

Finally, we considered how to make use of JavaScript libraries to aid animating SVGs and also how to optimize SVGs with the aid of the SVGO tool.

In the next chapter, we'll be looking at CSS transitions, transforms and animations. It's also worth reading that chapter in relation to SVG, as many of the syntaxes and techniques can be used and applied in SVG documents too. So grab yourself a hot beverage (you're worth it) and I'll see you again in a moment.

8

Transitions, Transformations, and Animations

Historically, whenever elements needed to be moved or animated around the screen, it was the sole domain of JavaScript. Nowadays, CSS can handle the majority of motion jobs via three principal agents: CSS transitions, CSS transforms, and CSS animations. In fact, only transitions and animations are directly related to motion, transforms simply allow us to change elements, but as we shall see, they are often integral to successful motion effects.

To clearly understand what each of these things is responsible for, I will offer this, perhaps overly simplistic summary:

- Use a CSS transition when you already have the beginning and end state of the things you want to apply motion to, and need a simple way to 'tween' from one state to another.

- Use a CSS transform if you need to visually transform an item, without affecting the layout of the page.

- Use a CSS animation if you want to perform a series of changes to an element at various key points over time.

Right, so we had better crack on and get our heads around how we can wield all these capabilities. In this chapter, we'll cover:

- What CSS3 transitions are and how we can use them
- How to write a CSS3 transition and its shorthand syntax
- CSS3 transition timing functions (ease, cubic-bezier, and so on)
- Fun transitions for responsive websites
- What CSS3 transforms are and how we can use them

- Understanding different 2D transforms (`scale`, `rotate`, `skew`, `translate`, and so on)
- Understanding 3D transforms
- How to animate with CSS3 using `keyframes`

What CSS3 transitions are and how we can use them

Transitions are the simplest way to create some visual 'effect' between one state and another with CSS. Let's consider a simple example, an element that transitions from one state to another when hovered over.

When styling hyperlinks in CSS, it's common practice to create a hover state; an obvious way to make users aware that the item they are hovering over is a link. Hover states are of little relevance to the growing number of touch screen devices but for mouse users, they're a great and simple interaction between website and user. They're also handy for illustrating transitions, so that's what we will start with.

Traditionally, using only CSS, hover states are an on/off affair. There is one set of properties and values on an element as the default, and when a pointer is hovered over that element, the properties and values are instantly changed. However, CSS3 transitions, as the name implies, allow us to transition between one or more properties and values to other properties and values.

 A couple of important things to know up front. Firstly, you can't transition from `display: none;`. When something is set to `display: none;` it isn't actually 'painted' on the screen so has no existing state you can transition from. In order to create the effect of something fading in, you would have to transition opacity or position values. Secondly, not all properties can be transitioned. To ensure you're not attempting the impossible, here is the list of transitionable (I know, it's not even a word) properties: `http://www.w3.org/TR/css3-transitions/`

If you open up `example_08-01` you'll see a few links in a `nav`. Here's the relevant markup:

```
<nav>
    <a href="#">link1</a>
    <a href="#">link2</a>
    <a href="#">link3</a>
```

```
    <a href="#">link4</a>
    <a href="#">link5</a>
</nav>
```

And here's the relevant CSS:

```
a {
    font-family: sans-serif;
    color: #fff;
    text-indent: 1rem;
    background-color: #ccc;
    display: inline-flex;
    flex: 1 1 20%;
    align-self: stretch;
    align-items: center;
    text-decoration: none;
    transition: box-shadow 1s;
}

a + a {
    border-left: 1px solid #aaa;
}

a:hover {
    box-shadow: inset 0 -3px 0 #CC3232;
}
```

And here are the two states, first the default:

And then here's the hover state:

In this example, when the link is hovered over, we add a red box-shadow at the bottom (I chose a box-shadow as it won't affect the layout of the link like a border might). Ordinarily, hovering over the link snaps from the first state (no red line) to the second (red line); it's an on/off affair. However, this line:

```
transition: box-shadow 1s;
```

Adds a transition to the `box-shadow` from the existing state to the hover state over 1 second.

 You'll notice in the CSS of the preceding example we're using the adjacent sibling selector +. This means if a selector (an anchor tag in our example) directly follows another selector (another anchor tag) then apply the enclosed styles. It's useful here as we don't want a left border on the first element.

Note that the transition property is applied in the CSS to the original state of the element, not the state the element ends up as. More succinctly, apply the transition declaration on the 'from' state, not the 'to' state. This is so that different states such as `:active` can also have different styles set and enjoy the same transition.

The properties of a transition

A transition can be declared using up to four properties:

- `transition-property`: The name of the CSS property to be transitioned (such as `background-color`, `text-shadow`, or `all` to transition every possible property).

- `transition-duration`: The length of time over which the transition should occur (defined in seconds, for example `.3s`, `2s`, or `1.5s`).

- `transition-timing-function`: How the transition changes speed during the duration (for example `ease`, `linear`, `ease-in`, `ease-out`, `ease-in-out`, or `cubic-bezier`).

- `transition-delay`: An optional value to determine a delay before the transition commences. Alternatively, a negative value can be used to commence a transition immediately but part way through its transition 'journey'. It's defined in seconds, for example, `.3s`, `1s`, or `2.5s`.

Used separately, the various transition properties can be used to create a transition like this:

```
.style {
    /*...(more styles)...*/
    transition-property: all;
    transition-duration: 1s;
    transition-timing-function: ease;
    transition-delay: 0s;
}
```

The transition shorthand property

We can roll these individual declarations into a single, shorthand version:

```
transition: all 1s ease 0s;
```

One important point to note when writing the shorthand version is that the first time related value is given is always taken to be the `transition-duration`. The second time related value is taken to be the `transition-delay`. The shorthand version is the one I tend to favor as I generally only need to define the duration of the transition and the properties that should be transitioned.

It's a minor point, but only define the property or properties you actually need to transition. It's really handy to just set `all` but if you only need to transition the opacity, then only define the opacity as the transition property. Otherwise you're making the browser work harder than necessary. In most cases this isn't a big deal but if you're hoping to have the best performing site possible, especially on older devices, then every little helps.

Transitions are very well supported but, as ever, ensure you have a tool like Autoprefixer set up to add any vendor prefixes relevant to the browsers you need to support. You can also check which browsers support the various capabilities at `caniuse.com`.

The short version:

Transitions and 2D transforms work everywhere apart from IE9 and below, 3D transforms work everywhere except IE9 and below, Android 2.3 and below, and Safari 3.2 and below.

Transition different properties over different periods of time

Where a rule has multiple properties declared you don't have to transition all of them in the same way. Consider this rule:

```
.style {
    /* ...(more styles)... */
    transition-property: border, color, text-shadow;
    transition-duration: 2s, 3s, 8s;
}
```

Here we have specified with the `transition-property` that we'd like to transition the `border`, `color`, and `text-shadow`. Then with the `transition-duration` declaration, we are stating that the border should transition over 2 seconds, the color over 3 seconds, and the text-shadow over 8 seconds. The comma-separated durations match the comma-separated order of the transition properties.

Understanding timing functions

When you declare a transition, the properties, durations, and delays are relatively simple to understand. However, understanding what each timing function does can be a little trickier. Just what do `ease`, `linear`, `ease-in`, `ease-out`, `ease-in-out`, and `cubic-bezier` actually do? Each of them is actually a pre-defined cubic-bezier curve, essentially the same as an easing function. Or, more simplistically, a mathematical description of how the transition should look. It's generally easier to visualize these curves so I recommend you head over to `http://cubic-bezier.com/` and `http://easings.net/`.

Both these sites let you compare timing functions and see the difference each one makes. Here is a screenshot of `http://easings.net` — you can hover over each line for a demonstration of the easing function.

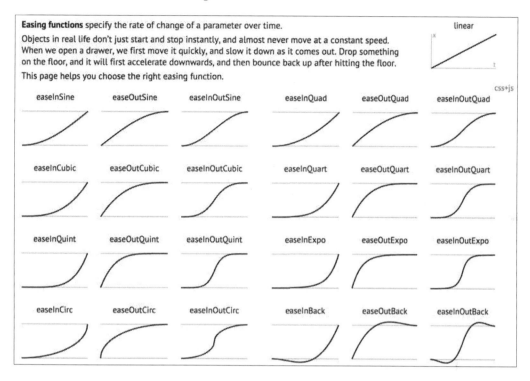

However, even if you can write your own cubic-bezier curves blindfolded, the likelihood is, for most practical situations, it makes little difference. The reason being that, like any enhancement, it's necessary to employ transition effects subtly. For 'real world' implementations, transitions that occur over too great a period of time tend to make a site feel slow. For example, navigation links that take 5 seconds to transition are going to frustrate, rather than wow your users. The perception of speed is incredibly important for our users and you and I must concentrate on making websites and applications feel as fast as possible.

Therefore, unless there is a compelling reason to do so, using the default transition (ease) over a short interval is often best; a maximum of 1 second is my own preference.

Fun transitions for responsive websites

Did you ever have one of those occasions growing up when one parent was out for the day and the other parent said something to the effect of, "OK, while your mom/dad are out we're going to put sugar all over your breakfast cereal but you have to promise not to tell them when they come back"? I'm certainly guilty of that with my little ankle biters. So here's the thing. While no one is looking, let's have a bit of fun. I don't recommend this for production, but try adding this to your responsive project.

```
* {
    transition: all 1s;
}
```

Here, we are using the CSS universal selector * to select everything and then setting a transition on all properties for 1 second (1s). As we have omitted to specify the timing function, ease will be used by default and there will be no delay as again, a default of 0 is assumed if an alternative value is not added. The effect? Well, try resizing your browser window and most things (links, hover states, and the like) behave as you would expect. However, because everything transitions, it also includes any rules within media queries, so as the browser window is resized, elements sort of flow from one state to the next. Is it essential? Absolutely not! Is it fun to watch and play around with? Certainly! Now, remove that rule before your mom sees it!

CSS3 2D transforms

Despite sounding similar, CSS transforms are entirely different to CSS transitions. Think of it like this: transitions smooth the change from one state to another, while transforms are defining what the element will actually become. My own (admittedly childish) way of remembering the difference is like this: imagine a transformer robot such as Optimus Prime. When he has changed into a truck he has transformed. However, the period between robot and truck is a transition (he's transitioning from one state to another).

Obviously, if you have no idea who or what Optimus Prime even is, feel free to mentally discard the last few sentences. Hopefully all will become clear momentarily.

There are two groups of CSS3 transforms available: 2D and 3D. 2D variants are far more widely implemented, browser wise, and certainly easier to write so let's look at those first. The CSS3 2D Transforms Module allows us to use the following transforms:

- `scale`: Used to scale an element (larger or smaller)
- `translate`: Move an element on the screen (up, down, left, and right)
- `rotate`: Rotate the element by a specified amount (defined in degrees)
- `skew`: Used to skew an element with its x and y co-ordinates
- `matrix`: Allows you to move and shape transformations with pixel precision

> It's important to remember that transforms occur outside of the document flow. Any element that is transformed will not affect the position of an element nearby that is not being transformed.

Let's try out the various 2D transitions. You can test each of these out by opening `example_08-02` in the browser. There's a transition applied to all of the transforms so you get a better idea of what's happening.

Scale

Here's the syntax for `scale`:

```
.scale:hover {
    transform: scale(1.4);
}
```

Hovering over the 'scale' link in our example produces this effect:

We've told the browser that when this element is hovered over, we want the element to scale to 1.4 times its original value.

Besides the values we've already used to enlarge elements, by using values below 1, we can shrink elements; the following will shrink the element to half its size:

```
transform: scale(0.5);
```

Translate

Here's the syntax for `translate`:

```
.translate:hover {
    transform: translate(-20px, -20px);
}
```

Here's the effect that rule has in our example:

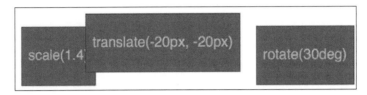

The `translate` property tells the browser to move an element by an amount, defined in either pixels or percentages. The first value is the *x* axis and the second value is the *y* axis. Positive values given within parentheses move the element right or down; negative values move it left or up.

If you only pass one value then it is applied to the *x* axis. If you want to specify just one axis to translate an element you can also use `translateX` or `translateY`.

Using translate to center absolutely positioned elements

The `translate` provides a really useful way to center absolutely positioned elements within a relatively positioned container. You can view this example at `example_08-03`.

Consider this markup:

```
<div class="outer">
    <div class="inner"></div>
</div>
```

And then this CSS:

```
.outer {
    position: relative;
    height: 400px;
    background-color: #f90;
}

.inner {
    position: absolute;
```

```
    height: 200px;
    width: 200px;
    margin-top: -100px;
    margin-left: -100px;
    top: 50%;
    left: 50%;
}
```

You've perhaps done something similar to this yourself. When the dimensions of the absolutely positioned element are known (200px x 200px in this case) we can use negative margins to 'pull' the item back to the center. However, what happens when you want to include content and have no way of knowing how tall it will be? Transform to the rescue.

Let's add some random content into the inner box:

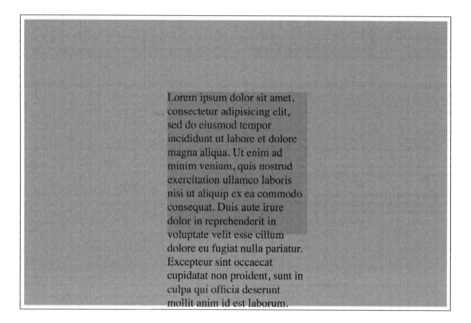

Yes, that problem! Right, let's use `transform` to sort this mess out.

```
.inner {
    position: absolute;
    width: 200px;
    background-color: #999;
    top: 50%;
    left: 50%;
    transform: translate(-50%, -50%);
}
```

And here is the result:

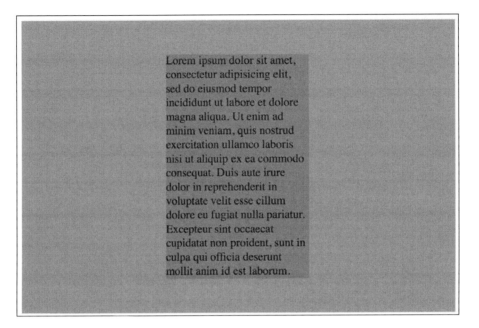

Here, `top` and `left` are positioning the inner box inside its container so that the top left corner of the inner box starts at a point 50% along and 50% down the outer. Then the `transform` is working on the inner element and positioning it negatively in those axis by half (-50%) of its own width and height. Nice!

Rotate

The `rotate` transform allows you to rotate an element. Here's the syntax:

```
.rotate:hover {
    transform: rotate(30deg);
}
```

In the browser, here's what happens:

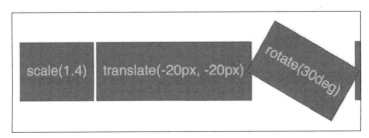

The value in parentheses should always be in degrees (for example, 90deg). While positive values always apply clockwise, using negative values will rotate the element counter-clockwise. You can also go crazy and make elements spin by specifying a value like the following:

```
transform: rotate(3600deg);
```

This will rotate the element 10 times in a complete circle. Practical uses for this particular value are few and far between but you know, if you ever find yourself designing websites for a windmill company, it may come in handy.

Skew

If you've spent any time working in Photoshop, you'll have a good idea what `skew` will do. It allows an element to be skewed on either or both of its axes. Here's the code for our example:

```
.skew:hover {
    transform: skew(40deg, 12deg);
}
```

Setting this on the hover link produces the following effect on hover:

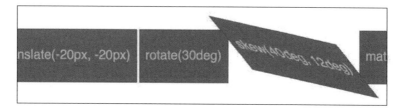

The first value is the `skew` applied to the *x* axis (in our example, 40deg), while the second (12deg) is for the *y* axis. Omitting the second value means any value will merely be applied to the *x* axis (horizontal). For example:

```
transform: skew(10deg);
```

Matrix

Did somebody mention a completely over-rated film? No? What's that? You want to know about the CSS3 matrix, not the film? Oh, okay.

I'm not going to lie. I think the matrix transform syntax looks scary. Here's our example code:

```css
.matrix:hover {
    transform: matrix(1.678, -0.256, 1.522, 2.333, -51.533, -1.989);
}
```

It essentially allows you to combine a number of other transforms (`scale`, `rotate`, `skew`, and so on) into a single declaration. The preceding declaration results in the following effect in the browser:

Now, I like a challenge like the best of them (unless, you know, it's sitting through the *Twilight* films) but I'm sure we can agree that syntax is a bit testing. For me, things got worse when I looked at the specification and realized that it involved mathematics knowledge beyond my rudimentary level to fully understand: `http://www.w3.org/TR/css3-2d-transforms/`

> If you find yourself doing work with animations in JavaScript without the help of an animation library, you'll probably need to become a little more acquainted with the matrix. It's the syntax all the other transforms get computed into so if you're grabbing the current state of an animation with JavaScript, it will be the matrix value you will need to inspect and understand.

Matrix transformations for cheats and dunces

I'm not a mathematician by any stretch of the imagination, so when faced with the need to create a matrix-based transformation, I cheat. If your mathematical skills are also found wanting, I'd suggest heading over to `http://www.useragentman.com/matrix/`.

The Matrix Construction Set website allows you to drag and drop the element exactly where you want it and then includes good ol' copy and paste code (including vendor-prefixes) for your CSS file.

The transform-origin property

Notice how with CSS, the default transform origin (the point at which the browser uses as the center for the transform) is in the middle: 50% along the x axis and 50% along the y axis of the element. This differs from SVG which defaults to top left (or 0 0).

Using the `transform-origin` property we can amend the point from which transforms originate.

Consider our earlier matrix transform. The default `transform-origin` is '50% 50%' (the center of the element). The Firefox developer tools show how the `transform` is applied:

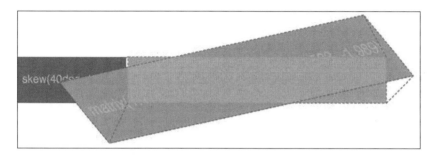

Now, if we adjust the `transform-origin` like this:

```css
.matrix:hover {
    transform: matrix(1.678, -0.256, 1.522, 2.333, -51.533, -1.989);
    transform-origin: 270px 20px;
}
```

Then you can see the effect this has:

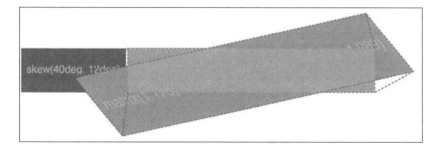

The first value is the horizontal offset and the second value is the vertical offset. You can use keywords. For example, left is equal to 0% horizontal, right is equal to 100% horizontal, top is equal to 0% vertical, and bottom is equal to 100% vertical. Alternatively, you can use a length, using any of the CSS length units.

If you use a percentage for the `transform-origin` values, then the horizontal/ vertical offset is relative to the height/width of the elements bounding box.

If you use a length, then the values are measured from the top-left corner of the elements bounding box.

Full information on the `transform-origin` property can be found at `http://www.w3.org/TR/css3-2d-transforms/`.

That covers the essentials of 2D transforms. They are far more widely implemented than their 3D brethren and provide a far better means to move elements around the screen than older methods such as absolute positioning.

Read the full specification on CSS3 2D Transforms Module Level 3 at `http://www.w3.org/TR/css3-2d-transforms/`.

For more on the benefits of moving element with `transform`, here's a great post by Paul Irish (`http://www.paulirish. com/2012/why-moving-elements-with-translate- is-better-than-posabs-topleft/`) that provides some good data.

And, for a fantastic overview of how browsers actually deal with transitions and animations, and why transforms can be so effective, I highly recommend the following blog post: `http://blogs.adobe.com/webplatform/2014/03/18/ css-animations-and-transitions-performance/`

CSS3 3D transformations

Let's look at our first example. An element that flips when we hover over it. I've used hover here to invoke the change as it's simple for the sake of illustration, however the flipping action could just as easily be initiated with a class change (via JavaScript) or when an element received focus.

We will have two of these elements; a horizontal flipping element and a vertical flipping element. You can view the final example at `example_08-04`. Images fail to fully convey this technique but the idea is that the element flips from the green 'face' to the red 'face' and gives the illusion of doing so through 3D space with the aid of perspective. Here's a grab partway through the transition from green to red which hopefully conveys some of the effect.

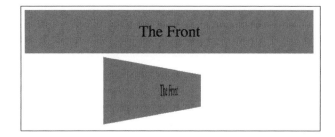

 It's also worth knowing that while positioning an element absolutely with top/left/bottom/right values operates pixel by pixel, a transform can interpolate at sub-pixel positions.

Here's the markup for the flipping element:

```
<div class="flipper">
    <span class="flipper-object flipper-vertical">
        <span class="panel front">The Front</span>
        <span class="panel back">The Back</span>
    </span>
</div>
```

The only difference with the horizontal one, markup wise is the `flipper-horizontal` class instead of `flipper-vertical`.

As the majority of the styles relate to aesthetics, we'll merely look at the essential ingredients in our styles to make the flipping effect possible. Refer to the full style sheet in the example for the aesthetic styles.

First of all, we need to set some perspective for the `.flipper-object` to flip within. For that we use the `perspective` property. This takes a length attempting to simulate the distance from the viewer's screen to the edge of the elements 3D space.

If you set a low number like 20px for the perspective value, the 3D space of the element will extend right out to only 20px from your screen; the result being a very pronounced 3D effect. Setting a high number on the other hand, will mean the edge of that imaginary 3D space will be further away, and therefore produce a less pronounced 3D effect.

```
.flipper {
    perspective: 400px;
    position: relative;
}
```

We are positioning the outer element relatively to create a context for the `flipper-object` to be positioned within:

```
.flipper-object {
    position: absolute;
    transition: transform 1s;
    transform-style: preserve-3d;
}
```

Besides positioning the `.flipper-object` absolutely at the top left of its closest relatively positioned parent (the default position for absolutely positioned elements), we have set a transition for the transform. The key thing here, 3D wise, though is the `transform-styles: preserve-3d`. This tells the browser that when we transform this element, we want any children elements to preserve the 3D effect.

If we didn't set `preserve-3d` on the `.flipper-object`, we would never get to see the back (the red part) of the flipping element. You can read the specification for this property at `http://www.w3.org/TR/2009/WD-css3-3d-transforms-20090320/`.

Each 'panel' in our flipping element needs positioning at the top of its container but we also want to make sure that if rotated, we don't see the 'rear' of it (otherwise we would never see the green panel as it sits 'behind' the red one). To do that we use the `backface-visibility` property. We set this to hidden so that the back face of the element is, you guessed it, hidden:

```
.panel {
    top: 0;
    position: absolute;
    backface-visibility: hidden;
}
```

 I've found that `backface-visibility` actually has a few surprising side effects in some browsers. It's particularly useful for improving the performance of fixed position elements on older Android devices. For more on this and why it does what it does, take a look at this post: `http://benfrain.com/easy-css-fix-fixed-positioning-android-2-2-2-3/` and this one: `http://benfrain.com/improving-css-performance-fixed-position-elements/`

Next we want to make our back panel flipped by default (so that when we flip the whole thing it will actually be in the correct position). To do that we apply a `rotate` transform:

```
.flipper-vertical .back {
    transform: rotateX(180deg);
```

```
}

.flipper-horizontal .back {
    transform: rotateY(180deg);
}
```

Now everything is in place, now all we want to do is flip the entire inner element when the outer one is hovered over:

```
.flipper:hover .flipper-vertical {
    transform: rotateX(180deg);
}

.flipper:hover .flipper-horizontal {
    transform: rotateY(180deg);
}
```

As you can imagine there are a bazillion (by the way, that's definitely not a real amount, I just checked) ways you can use these principals. If you're wondering what a fancy navigation effect, or off-canvas menu, might look like with a spot of perspective, I highly recommend paying Codrops a visit: `http://tympanus.net/Development/PerspectivePageViewNavigation/index.html`.

 Read about the latest W3C developments on CSS Transforms Module Level 1 at `http://dev.w3.org/csswg/css-transforms/`.

The transform3d property

In addition to using perspective, I've also found great utility in the `transform3d` value. With a single property and value, this allows you to move an element in the X (left/right), Y (up/down), and Z (forwards/backwards) axis. Let's amend our last example and make use of the `translate3d` transform. You can view this example at `example_08-06`.

Besides setting the elements in with a little padding, the only changes from our previous example can be seen here:

```
.flipper:hover .flipper-vertical {
    transform: rotateX(180deg) translate3d(0, 0, -120px);
    animation: pulse 1s 1s infinite alternate both;
}

.flipper:hover .flipper-horizontal {
    transform: rotateY(180deg) translate3d(0, 0, 120px);
    animation: pulse 1s 1s infinite alternate both;
}
```

We're still applying a transform but this time, in addition to our rotate we have also added a translate3d. The syntax for the comma-separated 'arguments' you can pass into translate3d are *x* axis movement, *y* axis movement, and *z* axis movement.

In our two examples I'm not moving the element in the *x* or *y* axis (left to right, and up and down) instead I'm moving towards or further away from you as you look at it.

If you look at the top example you will see it flip behind the bottom button and end 120px closer to the screen (minus values effectively pull it backwards towards you).

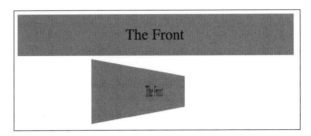

On the other hand, the bottom button flips around horizontally and ends with the button 120px further away from you.

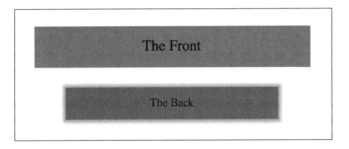

 You can read the specification for translate3d at http://www.w3.org/TR/css3-3d-transforms/.

Use transforms with progressive enhancement

The area I have found the greatest utility for transform3d is in sliding panels on and off the screen, particularly 'off-canvas' navigation patterns. If you open example_08-07 you'll see I have created a basic, progressively enhanced off-canvas pattern.

Whenever you create interaction with JavaScript and modern CSS features like transforms it makes sense to try and consider things from the lowest possible device you want to support. What about the two people that don't have JavaScript (yes, those guys) or if there is a problem with the JavaScript loading or executing? What if somebody's device doesn't support transform (Opera Mini for example)? Don't worry, it's possible, with a little effort, to ensure a working interface for every eventuality.

When building these kind of interface patterns I find it most useful to start with the lowest set of features and enhance from there. So, first establish what someone sees if they don't have JavaScript available. After all, it's no use parking a menu off-screen if the method for displaying the menu relies upon JavaScript. In this case, we are relying upon markup to place the navigation area in the normal document flow. Worst case, whatever the viewport width, they can merely scroll down the page and click a link:

If JavaScript is available, for smaller screens we 'pull' the menu off to the left. When the menu button is clicked, we add a class onto the `body` tag (with JavaScript) and use this class as a hook to move the navigation back into view with CSS.

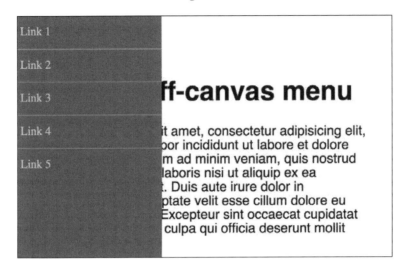

For larger viewports we hide the menu button and merely position the navigation to the left and move the main content over to accommodate.

A basic off-canvas menu

Lorem ipsum dolor sit amet, consectetur adipisicing elit, sed do eiusmod tempor incididunt ut labore et dolore magna aliqua. Ut enim ad minim veniam, quis nostrud exercitation ullamco laboris nisi ut aliquip ex ea commodo consequat. Duis aute irure dolor in reprehenderit in voluptate velit esse cillum dolore eu fugiat nulla pariatur. Excepteur sint occaecat cupidatat non proident, sunt in culpa qui officia deserunt mollit anim id est laborum.

Lorem ipsum dolor sit amet, consectetur adipisicing elit, sed do eiusmod tempor incididunt ut labore et dolore magna aliqua. Ut enim ad minim veniam, quis nostrud exercitation ullamco laboris nisi ut aliquip ex ea commodo consequat. Duis aute irure dolor in reprehenderit in voluptate velit esse cillum dolore eu fugiat nulla pariatur. Excepteur sint occaecat cupidatat non proident, sunt in culpa qui officia deserunt mollit anim id est laborum.

Lorem ipsum dolor sit amet, consectetur adipisicing elit, sed do eiusmod tempor incididunt ut labore et dolore magna aliqua. Ut enim ad minim veniam, quis nostrud exercitation ullamco laboris nisi ut aliquip ex ea commodo consequat. Duis aute irure dolor in reprehenderit in voluptate velit esse cillum dolore eu fugiat nulla pariatur. Excepteur sint occaecat cupidatat non proident, sunt in culpa qui officia deserunt mollit anim id est laborum.

We then progressively enhance the navigation show/hide effect. This is where a tool like Modernizr really earns its place; adding classes to the HTML tag we can use as styling hooks (Modernizr is discussed in greater detail in *Chapter 5, CSS3 – Selectors, Typography, Color Modes, and New Features*).

First, for browsers that only support translate transforms (old Android for example), a simple translateX:

```
.js .csstransforms .navigation-menu {
    left: auto;
    transform: translateX(-200px);
}
```

For browsers that support translate3d we use translate3d instead. This will perform far better, where supported, thanks to being offloaded to the graphics processors on most devices:

```
.js .csstransforms3d .navigation-menu {
    left: auto;
    transform: translate3d(-200px, 0, 0);
}
```

Embracing a progressive enhancement approach ensures the widest possible audience will get a workable experience from your design. Remember, your users don't need visual parity but they might appreciate capability parity.

Animating with CSS3

If you've worked with applications like Flash, Final Cut Pro or After Effects, you'll have an instant advantage when working with CSS3 animations. CSS3 employs animation keyframing conventions found in timeline-based applications.

Animations are widely implemented; supported in Firefox 5+, Chrome, Safari 4+, Android (all versions), iOS (all versions), and Internet Explorer 10+. There are two components to a CSS3 animation; firstly a keyframes declaration and then employing that keyframes declaration in an animation property. Let's take a look.

In a previous example, we made a simple flip effect on elements that combined transforms and transitions. Let's bring together all the techniques we have learned in this chapter and add an animation to that previous example. In this next example, example_08-05, let's add a pulsing animation effect once the element has flipped.

Firstly we will create a `keyframes` at-rule:

```
@keyframes pulse {
  100% {
    text-shadow: 0 0 5px #bbb;
    box-shadow: 0 0 3px 4px #bbb;
  }
}
```

As you can see, after writing at `@keyframes` to define a new `keyframes` at-rule we name this particular animation (pulse in this instance).

It's generally best to use a name that represents what the animation does, not where you intend to use the animation, as a single `@keyframes` rule can be used as many times as you need throughout a project.

We have used a single keyframe selector here: 100%. However, you can set as many keyframe selectors (defined as percentage points) as you like within a `keyframes` rule. Think of these as points along a timeline. For example, at 10%, make the background blue, at 30% make the background purple, at 60%, make the element semi-opaque. On and on as you need. There is also the keyword which is equivalent to 0% and to which is equivalent to100%. You can use them like this:

```
@keyframes pulse {
  to {
    text-shadow: 0 0 5px #bbb;
    box-shadow: 0 0 3px 4px #bbb;
  }
}
```

Be warned, however, that WebKit browsers (iOS, Safari) don't always play happily with from and to values (preferring 0% and 100%) so I'd recommend sticking with percentage keyframe selectors.

You'll notice here that we haven't bothered to define a starting point. That's because the starting point is the state each of those properties is already at. Here's the part of the specification that explains that: `http://www.w3.org/TR/css3-animations/`

> If a `0%` or `from` keyframe is not specified, then the user agent constructs a `0%` keyframe using the computed values of the properties being animated. If a `100%` or `to` keyframe is not specified, then the user agent constructs a `100%` keyframe using the computed values of the properties being animated. If a keyframe selector specifies negative percentage values or values higher than `100%`, then the keyframe will be ignored.

In this `keyframes` at-rule we've added a text-shadow and box-shadow at 100%. We can then expect the `keyframes`, when applied to an element to animate the text-shadow and box-shadow to the defined amount. But how long does the animation last? How do we make it repeat, reverse, and other eventualities I hope to have the answer for? This is how we actually apply a `keyframes` animation:

```
.flipper:hover .flipper-horizontal {
    transform: rotateY(180deg);
    animation: pulse 1s 1s infinite alternate both;
}
```

The `animation` property here is being used as a shorthand for a number of animation related properties. In this example, we are actually declaring (in order), the name of the `keyframes` declaration to use (pulse), the `animation-duration` (1 second), the delay before the animation begins (1 second, to allow time for our button to first flip), the amount of times the animation will run (infinitely), the direction of the animation (alternate, so it animates first one way and then back the other) and that we want the `animation-fill-mode` to retain the values that are defined in the `keyframes` whether going forwards or backwards (both).

The shorthand property can actually accept all seven animation properties. In addition to those used in the preceding example, it's also possible to specify `animation-play-state`. This can be set to running or paused to effectively play and pause an animation. Of course, you don't need to use the shorthand property; sometimes it can make more sense (and help when you revisit the code in the future) to set each property separately. Below are the individual properties and where appropriate, alternate values separated with the pipe symbol:

```
.animation-properties {
    animation-name: warning;
    animation-duration: 1.5s;
    animation-timing-function: ease-in-out;
    animation-iteration-count: infinite;
    animation-play-state: running | paused;
    animation-delay: 0s;
    animation-fill-mode: none | forwards | backwards | both;
    animation-direction: normal | reverse | alternate | alternate-
reverse;
}
```

 You can read the full definition for each of these animation properties at http://www.w3.org/TR/css3-animations/.

As mentioned previously, it's simple to reuse a declared `keyframes` on other elements and with completely different settings:

```
.flipper:hover .flipper-vertical {
    transform: rotateX(180deg);
    animation: pulse 2s 1s cubic-bezier(0.68, -0.55, 0.265, 1.55) 5
alternate both;
}
```

Here the `pulse` animation would run over 2 seconds and uses an ease-in-out-back timing function (defined as a cubic-bezier curve). It runs five times in both directions. This declaration has been applied to the vertically flipping element in the example file.

This is just one very simple example of using CSS animations. As virtually anything can be key-framed, the possibilities are pretty endless. Read about the latest developments on CSS3 animations at `http://dev.w3.org/csswg/css3-animations/`.

The animation-fill-mode property

The `animation-fill-mode` property is worthy of a special mention. Consider an animation that starts with a yellow background and animates to a red background over 3 seconds. You can view this in `example_08-08`.

We apply the animation like this:

```
.background-change {
  animation: fillBg 3s;
  height: 200px;
  width: 400px;
  border: 1px solid #ccc;
}

@keyframes fillBg {
  0% {
    background-color: yellow;
  }
  100% {
    background-color: red;
  }
}
```

However, once the animation completes, the background of the `div` will return to nothing. That's because by default 'what happens outside of animations, stays outside of animations'! In order to override this behavior, we have the `animation-fill-mode` property. In this instance we could apply this:

```
animation-fill-mode: forwards;
```

This makes the item retain any values that have been applied at the animation end. In our case, the `div` would retain the red background color that the animation ended on. More on the `animation-fill-mode` property here: `http://www.w3.org/TR/css3-animations/#animation-fill-mode-property`

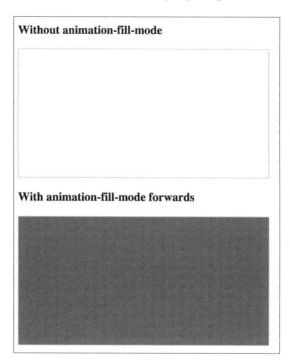

Summary

It would be entirely possible to fill multiple books covering the possibilities of CSS transforms, transitions, and animations. However, hopefully, by dipping your toe in the water with this chapter you'll be able to pick up the basics and run with them. Ultimately, by embracing these newer features and techniques of CSS, the aim is to make a responsive design even leaner and richer than ever by using CSS, rather than JavaScript, for some of the fancier aesthetic enhancements.

In this chapter we've learned what CSS3 transitions are and how to write them. We've got a handle on timing functions like ease and linear, and then used them to create simple but fun effects. We then learned all about 2D transforms such as `scale` and `skew` and then how to use them in tandem with transitions. We also looked briefly at 3D transformations before learning all about the power and relative simplicity of CSS animations. You'd better believe our CSS3 muscles are growing!

However, if there's one area of site design that I always avoid where possible, it's making forms. I don't know why, I've just always found making them a tedious and largely frustrating task. Imagine my joy when I learned that HTML5 and CSS3 can make the whole form building, styling, and even validating (yes, validating!), process easier than ever before. I was quite joyous. As joyous as you can be about building web forms that is. In the next chapter I'd like to share this knowledge with you.

9
Conquer Forms with HTML5 and CSS3

Before HTML5, adding things such as date pickers, placeholder text, and range sliders into forms has always needed JavaScript. Similarly, there has been no easy way to tell users what we expect them to input into certain input fields, for example, whether we want users to input telephone numbers, e-mail addresses, or URLs. The good news is that HTML5 largely solves these common problems.

We have two main aims in this chapter. Firstly, to understand HTML5 form features and secondly, to understand how we can lay out forms more simply for multiple devices with the latest CSS features.

In this chapter, we will learn how to:

- Easily add placeholder text into relevant form input fields
- Disable auto-completion of form fields where necessary
- Set certain fields to be required before submission
- Specify different input types such as e-mail, telephone number, and URL
- Create number range sliders for easy value selection
- Place date and color pickers into a form
- Learn how we can use a regular expression to define an allowed form value
- How to style forms using Flexbox

HTML5 forms

I think the easiest way to get to grips with HTML5 forms is to work our way through an example form. From the finest of daytime TV examples, I have one I made earlier. A minor introduction is needed.

Two facts: firstly, I love films. Secondly, I'm very opinionated on what is a good film and what is not.

Every year, when the Oscar nominations are announced, I can't help feeling the wrong films have got 'the nod' from the Academy. Therefore, we will start with an HTML5 form that enables fellow cinephiles to vent their frustrations at the continual travesties of the Oscar nominations.

It's made up of a few `fieldset` elements, within which we are including a raft of the HTML5 form input types and attributes. Besides standard form input fields and text areas, we have a number spinner, a range slider, and placeholder text for many of the fields.

Here's how it looks with no styles applied in Chrome:

If we 'focus' on the first field and start inputting text, the placeholder text is removed. If we blur focus without entering anything (by clicking outside of the input box again) the placeholder text re-appears. If we submit the form (without entering anything), the following happens:

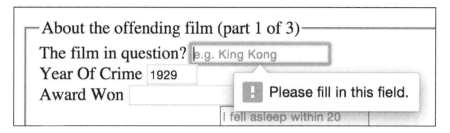

The great news is that all these user interface elements, including the aforementioned slider, placeholder text, and spinner, and the input validation, are all being handled natively by the browser via HTML5, and no JavaScript. Now, the form validation isn't entirely cross browser compatible, but we will get to that shortly. First of all, let's get a handle on all the new capabilities of HTML5 that relate to forms and make all this possible. Once we understand all the mechanics, we can get to work styling it up.

Understanding the component parts of HTML5 forms

There's a lot going on in our HTML5 powered form, so let's break it down. The three sections of the form are each wrapped in a `fieldset` with a legend:

```
<fieldset>
<legend>About the offending film (part 1 of 3)</legend>
<div>
   <label for="film">The film in question?</label>
   <input id="film" name="film" type="text" placeholder="e.g. King
Kong" required>
</div>
```

You can see from the previous code snippet that each input element of the form is also wrapped in a `div` with a label associated with each input (we could have wrapped the input with the label element if we wanted to too). So far, so normal. However, within this first input we've just stumbled upon our first HTML5 form feature. After common attributes of ID, name, and type, we have `placeholder`.

placeholder

The `placeholder` attribute looks like this:

```
placeholder="e.g. King Kong"
```

Placeholder text within form fields is such a common requirement that the folks creating HTML5 decided it should be a standard feature of HTML. Simply include the `placeholder` attribute within your input and the value will be displayed by default until the field gains focus. When it loses focus, if a value has not been entered it will re-display the placeholder text.

Styling the placeholder text

You can style the `placeholder` attribute with the `:placeholder-shown` pseudo selector. Be aware that this selector has been through a number of iterations so ensure you have the prefixer tool set up to provide the fallback selectors for already implemented versions.

```
input:placeholder-shown {
    color: #333;
}
```

After the `placeholder` attribute, in the previous code snippet, the next HTML5 form feature is the `required` attribute.

required

The `required` attribute looks like this:

```
required
```

In supporting HTML5 capable browsers, by adding the Boolean (meaning you simply include the attribute or not) attribute `required` within the `input` element, it indicates that a value is required. If the form is submitted without the field containing the requisite information, a warning message should be displayed. The message displayed is specific (both in content and styling) to both the browser and the input type used.

We've already seen what the `required` field browser message looks like in Chrome. The following screenshot shows the same message in Firefox:

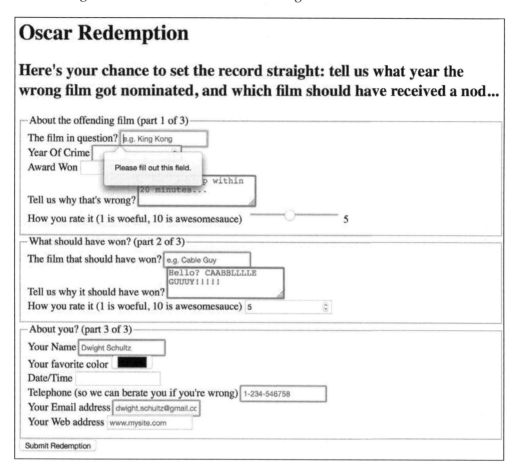

The `required` value can be used alongside many input types to ensure a value is entered. Notable exceptions are the `range`, `color`, `button`, and `hidden` input types as they almost always have a default value.

autofocus

The HTML5 `autofocus` attribute allows a form to have a field already focused, ready for user input. The following code is an example of an `input` field wrapped in a `div` with the `autofocus` attribute added at the end:

```
<div>
  <label for="search">Search the site...</label>
  <input id="search" name="search" type="search" placeholder="Wyatt
Earp" autofocus>
</div>
```

Be careful when using this attribute. Cross browser confusion can reign if multiple fields have the `autofocus` attribute added. For example, if multiple fields have `autofocus` added, in Safari, the last field with the `autofocus` attributed is focused on page load. However, Firefox and Chrome do the opposite with the first `autofocus` field selected.

It's also worth considering that some users use the spacebar to quickly skip down the content of a web page once it's loaded. On a page where a form has an autofocused input field, it prevents this capability; instead it adds a space into the focused input field. It's easy to see how that could be a source of frustration for users.

If using the `autofocus` attribute, be certain it's only used once in a form and be sure you understand the implications for those who scroll with the spacebar.

autocomplete

By default, most browsers aid user input by auto-completing the value of form fields where possible. While the user can turn this preference on and off within the browser, we can now also indicate to the browser when we don't want a form or field to allow auto-completion. This is useful not just for sensitive data (bank account numbers for example) but also if you want to ensure users pay attention and enter something by hand. For example, for many forms I complete, if a telephone number is required, I enter a 'spoof' telephone number. I know I'm not the only one that does that (doesn't everyone?) but I can ensure that users don't enter an autocompleted spoof number by setting the `autocomplete` attribute to off on the relevant input field. The following is a code example of a field with the `autocomplete` attribute set to `off`:

```
<div>
  <label for="tel">Telephone (so we can berate you if you're wrong)</
  label>
```

```
    <input id="tel" name="tel" type="tel" placeholder="1-234-546758"
autocomplete="off" required>
</div>
```

We can also set entire forms (but not fieldsets) to not autocomplete by using the attribute on the form itself. The following is a code example:

```
<form id="redemption" method="post" autocomplete="off">
```

List and the associated datalist element

This `list` attribute and the associated `datalist` element allow a number of selections to be presented to a user once they start entering a value in the field. The following is a code example of the `list` attribute in use with an associated `datalist`, all wrapped in a `div`:

```
<div>
  <label for="awardWon">Award Won</label>
  <input id="awardWon" name="awardWon" type="text" list="awards">
  <datalist id="awards">
    <select>
      <option value="Best Picture"></option>
      <option value="Best Director"></option>
      <option value="Best Adapted Screenplay"></option>
      <option value="Best Original Screenplay"></option>
    </select>
  </datalist>
</div>
```

The value given in the `list` attribute (`awards`) refers to the ID of the `datalist`. Doing this associates the `datalist` with the input field. Although wrapping the options with a `<select>` element isn't strictly necessary, it helps when applying polyfills for browsers that haven't implemented the feature.

Amazingly, in mid-2015, the `datalist` element still isn't supported natively in iOS, Safari, or Android 4.4 and below (`http://caniuse.com/`)

You can read the specification for `datalist` at `http://www.w3.org/TR/html5/forms.html`.

While the input field seems to be just a normal text input field, when typing in the field, a selection box appears below it (in supporting browsers) with matching results from the datalist. In the following screenshot, we can see the list in action (Firefox). In this instance, as B is present in all options within the datalist, all the values are shown for the user to select from:

However, when typing D instead, only the matching suggestions appear as shown in the following screenshot:

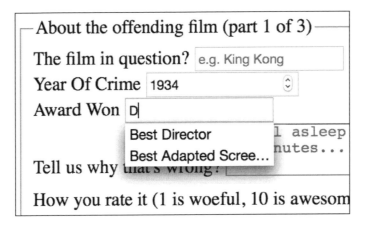

The list and datalist don't prevent a user entering different text in the input box but they do provide another great way of adding common functionality and user enhancement through HTML5 markup alone.

HTML5 input types

HTML5 adds a number of extra input types, which amongst other things, enable us to limit the data that users input without the need for extraneous JavaScript code. The most comforting thing about these new input types is that by default, where browsers don't support the feature, they degrade to a standard text input box. Furthermore, there are great polyfills available to bring older browsers up to speed, which we will look at shortly. In the meantime, let's look at these new HTML5 input types and the benefits they provide.

email

You can set an input to the `email` type like this:

```
type="email"
```

Supporting browsers will expect a user input that matches the syntax of an e-mail address. In the following code example `type="email"` is used alongside `required` and `placeholder`:

```
<div>
  <label for="email">Your Email address</label>
  <input id="email" name="email" type="email" placeholder="dwight.
schultz@gmail.com" required>
</div>
```

When used in conjunction with required, submitting a non-conforming input will generate a warning message:

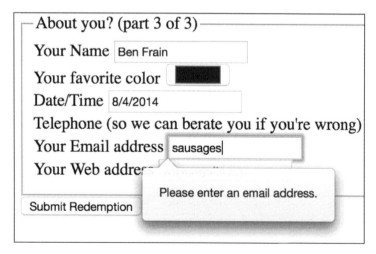

Furthermore, many touch screen devices (for example, Android, iPhone, and so on) change the input display based upon this input type. The following screenshot shows how an input `type="email"` screen looks on the iPad. Notice the @ symbol for been added to the software keyboard for easy email address completion:

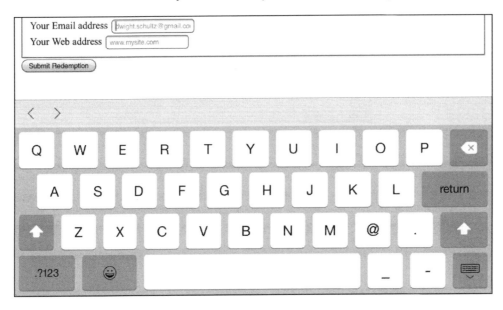

number

You can set an input field to a type of number like this:

```
type="number"
```

A supporting browser expects a number to be entered here. Supporting browsers also provide what's called **spinner controls**. These are tiny pieces of user interface that allow users to easily click up or down to alter the value input. The following is a code example:

```
<div>
  <label for="yearOfCrime">Year Of Crime</label>
  <input id="yearOfCrime" name="yearOfCrime" type="number"
min="1929"  max="2015" required>
</div>
```

And the following screenshot shows how it looks in a supporting browser (Chrome):

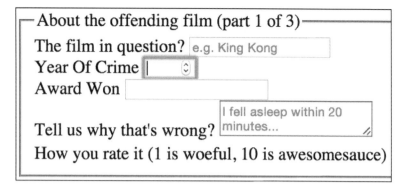

Implementation of what happens if you don't enter a number varies. For example, Chrome and Firefox do nothing until the form is submitted, at which point they pop up a warning above the field. Safari on the other hand, simply does nothing, and merely lets the form be submitted. Internet Explorer 11 simply empties the field as soon as focus leaves it.

min and max ranges

You'll notice in the previous code example, we have also set a minimum and maximum allowed range, similar to the following code:

```
type="number" min="1929" max="2015"
```

Numbers outside of this range (should) get special treatment.

You probably won't be surprised to learn that browser implementation of min and max ranges is varied. For example, Internet Explorer 11, Chrome, and Firefox, display a warning while Safari does nothing.

Changing the step increments

You can alter the step increments (granularity) for the spinner controls of various input types with the use of the step attribute. For example, to step 10 units at a time:

```
<input type="number" step="10">
```

url

You can set an input field to expect a URL like this:

```
type="url"
```

As you might expect, the `url` input type is for URL values. Similar to the `tel` and `email` input types; it behaves almost identically to a standard text input. However, some browsers add specific information to the warning message provided when submitted with incorrect values. The following is a code example including the `placeholder` attribute:

```
<div>
    <label for="web">Your Web address</label>
    <input id="web" name="web" type="url" placeholder="www.mysite.com">
</div>
```

The following screenshot shows what happens when an incorrectly entered URL field is submitted in Chrome:

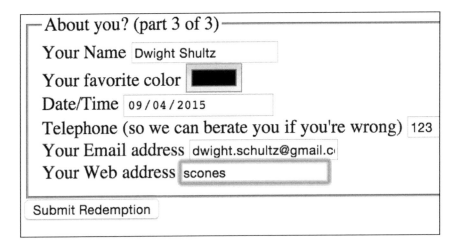

Like `type="email"`, touch screen devices often amend the input display based upon this input type. The following screenshot shows how an input `type="url"` screen looks on the iPad:

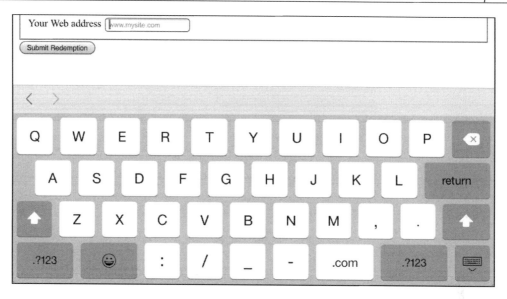

Notice the *.com* key? Because we've used a URL input type they are presented by the device for easy URL completion (on iOS, if you're not going to a .com site you can press and hold for a few other popular top level domains).

tel

Set an input field to expect a telephone number like this:

```
type="tel"
```

Here's a more complete example:

```
<div>
  <label for="tel">Telephone (so we can berate you if you're wrong)</label>
  <input id="tel" name="tel" type="tel" placeholder="1-234-546758"
autocomplete="off" required>
</div>
```

Although, a number format is expected on many browsers, even modern evergreen ones such as Internet Explorer 11, Chrome, and Firefox, it merely behaves like a text input field. When an incorrect value is input, they fail to provide a suitable warning message when the field loses focus or on form submission.

However, better news is that, like the `email` and `url` input types, touch screen devices often thoughtfully accommodate this kind of input with an amended input display for easy completion; here's the `tel` input when accessed with an iPad (running iOS 8.2):

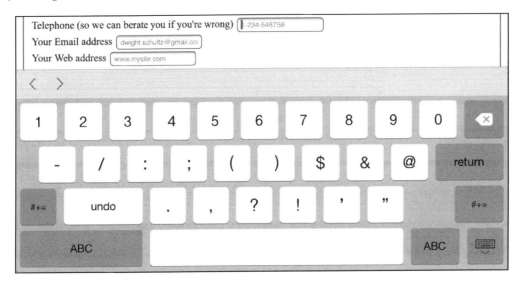

Notice the lack of alphabet characters in the keyboard area? This makes it much faster for users to enter a value in the correct format.

Quick tip

If the default blue color of telephone numbers in iOS Safari annoys you when you use a `tel` input, you can amend it with the following selector:

```
a[href^=tel] { color: inherit; }
```

search

You can set an input as a search type like this:

```
type="search"
```

The `search` input type works like a standard text input. Here's an example:

```
<div>
  <label for="search">Search the site...</label>
  <input id="search" name="search" type="search" placeholder= "Wyatt
Earp">
</div>
```

However, software keyboards (such as those found on mobile devices) often provided a more tailored keyboard. Here's the iOS 8.2 keyboard that appears when a `search` input type gets focus:

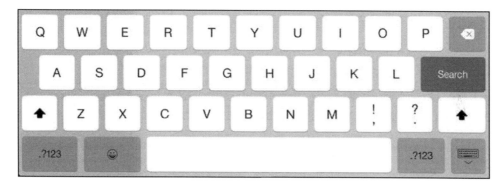

pattern

You can set an input to expect a certain pattern input like this:

```
pattern=""
```

The `pattern` attribute allows you to specify, via a regular expression, the syntax of data that should be allowed in a given input field.

Learn about regular expressions

If you've never encountered regular expressions before, I'd suggest starting here: `http://en.wikipedia.org/wiki/Regular_expressions`

Regular expressions are used across many programming languages as a means of matching possible strings. While the format is intimidating at first, they are incredibly powerful and flexible. For example, you could build a regular expression to match a password format, or select a certain style CSS class naming pattern. To help build up your own regex pattern and get a visual understanding of how they work, I'd recommend starting with a browser based tool like `http://www.regexr.com/`.

The following code is an example:

```
<div>
  <label for="name">Your Name (first and last)</label>
  <input id="name" name="name" pattern="([a-zA-Z]{3,30}\s*)+[a-zA- Z]
{3,30}" placeholder="Dwight Schultz" required>
</div>
```

Such is my commitment to this book, I searched the Internet for approximately 458 seconds to find a regular expression that would match a first and last name syntax. By entering the regular expression value within the `pattern` attribute, it makes supporting browsers expect a matching input syntax. Then, when used in conjunction with the `required` attribute, incorrect entries get the following treatment in supporting browsers. In this instance, I tried submitting the form without providing a last name.

Again, browsers do things differently. Internet Explorer 11 requests that the field is entered correctly, Safari, Firefox, and Chrome do nothing (they just behave like a standard text input).

color

Want to set an input field to receive a hexadecimal color value? You can do this:

```
type="color"
```

The `color` input type invokes a color picker in supporting browsers (currently just Chrome and Firefox), allowing users to select a color value in a hexadecimal value. The following code is an example:

```
<div>
  <label for="color">Your favorite color</label>
  <input id="color" name="color" type="color">
</div>
```

Date and time inputs

The thinking behind the new `date` and `time` input types is to provide a consistent user experience for choosing dates and times. If you've ever bought tickets to an event online, chances are that you have used a date picker of one sort or another. This functionality is almost always provided via JavaScript (typically jQuery UI library) but the hope is to make this common necessity possible merely with HTML5 markup.

date

The following code is an example:

```
<input id="date" type="date" name="date">
```

Similar to the `color` input type, native browser support is thin on the ground, defaulting on most browsers to a standard text input box. Chrome and Opera are the only two of the modern browsers to have implemented this functionality. That's not surprising as they both use the same engine (known as **Blink** in case you were interested).

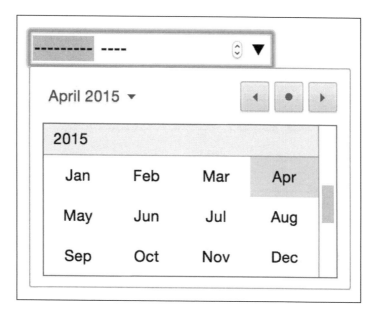

There are a variety of different `date` and `time` related input types available. What follows is a brief overview of the others.

month

The following code is an example:

```
<input id="month" type="month" name="month">
```

The interface allows the user to select a single month and provides the input as a year and month for example 2012-06. The following screenshot shows how it looks in the browser:

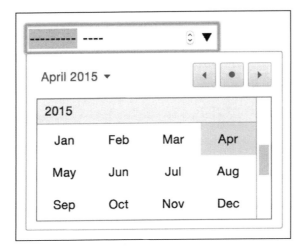

week

The following code is an example:

```
<input id="week" type="week" name="week">
```

When the week input type is used, the picker allows the user to select a single week within a year and provides the input in the 2012-W47 format.

The following screenshot shows how it looks in the browser:

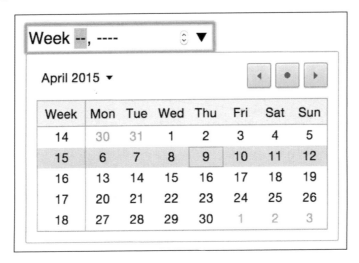

time

The following code is an example:

```
<input id="time" type="time" name="time">
```

The `time` input type allows a value in the 24-hour format, for example 23:50.

It displays in supporting browsers with spinner controls but only allows relevant time values.

range

The `range` input type creates a slider interface element. Here's an example:

```
<input type="range" min="1" max="10" value="5">
```

And the following screenshot shows how it looks in Firefox:

The default range is from 0 to 100. However, by specifying a `min` and `max` value in our example we have limited it to between 1 and 10.

One big problem I've encountered with the `range` input type is that the current value is never displayed to the user. Although the range slider is only intended for vague number selections, I've often wanted to display the value as it changes. Currently, there is no way to do this using HTML5. However, if you absolutely must display the current value of the slider, it can be achieved easily with some simple JavaScript. Amend the previous example to the following code:

```
<input id="howYouRateIt" name="howYouRateIt" type="range" min="1"
max="10" value="5" onchange="showValue(this.value)"><span
id="range">5</span>
```

We've added two things, an `onchange` attribute and also a `span` element with the ID of range. Now, we'll add the following tiny piece of JavaScript:

```
<script>
  function showValue(newValue)
  {
    document.getElementById("range").innerHTML=newValue;
  }
</script>
```

All this does is get the current value of the range slider and display it in the element with an ID of range (our span tag). You can then use whatever CSS you deem appropriate to change the appearance of the value.

There are a few other form related features that are new in HTML5. You can read the full specification at http://www.w3.org/TR/html5/forms.html.

How to polyfill non-supporting browsers

All this HTML5 form malarkey is all well and good. There seems however, to be two things that put a serious dent in our ability to use them: disparity between how supporting browsers implement the features, and how to deal with browsers that don't support the features at all.

If you need to support some of these features in older or non-supporting browsers then consider Webshims Lib, which you can download at http://afarkas.github. com/webshim/demos/. It is a polyfill library written by Alexander Farkas that can load form polyfills to make non-supporting browsers handle HTML5 based form features.

Exercise caution with polyfills

Whenever you reach for a polyfill script remember to consider carefully. While they can be very handy, they add weight to your project. For example, Webshims also requires jQuery so there's yet another dependency needed if you weren't using jQuery before. Unless polyfilling older browsers is essential, I steer clear.

The handy thing about Webshims is that it only adds polyfills as needed. If being viewed by a browser that supports these HTML5 features natively it adds very little. Older browsers, although they need to load more code (as they are less capable by default), get a similar user experience, albeit with the relevant functionality created with the help of JavaScript.

But it isn't just older browsers that benefit. As we've seen, many modern browsers haven't implemented the HTML5 form features fully. Employing Webshims lib to the page also fills any gaps in their capability. For example, Safari doesn't offer any warning when a HTML5 form is submitted with required fields empty. No feedback is given to the user as to what the problem is: hardly ideal. With Webshims lib added to the page, the following happens in the aforementioned scenario.

So when Firefox isn't able to provide a spinner for a `type="number"` attribute, Webshims lib provides a suitable, jQuery powered, fallback. In short, it's a great tool, so let's get this beautiful little package installed and hooked up and then we can carry on writing forms with HTML5, safe in the knowledge that all users will see what they need to use our form (except those two people using IE6 with JavaScript turned off—you know who you are—now pack it in!).

First download Webshims lib (`http://github.com/aFarkas/webshim/downloads`) and extract the package. Now copy the `js-webshim` folder to a relevant section of your web page. For simplicity, for this example I've copied it into the website root.

Now add the following code into the section of your page:

```
<script src="js/jquery-2.1.3.min.js"></script>
<script src="js-webshim/minified/polyfiller.js"></script>
<script>
   //request the features you need:
   webshim.polyfill('forms');
</script>
```

Let's go through this a section at a time. Firstly, we link to a local copy of the jQuery library (get the latest version at `www.jquery.com`) and the Webshim script:

```
<script src="js/jquery-2.1.3.min.js"></script>
<script src="js-webshim/minified/polyfiller.js"></script>
```

Finally, I'm telling the script to load all needed polyfills:

```
<script>
   //request the features you need:
   webshim.polyfill('forms');
</script>
```

And that's all there is to it. Now, missing functionality is automatically added by the relevant polyfill. Excellent!

Styling HTML5 forms with CSS3

Our form is now fully functional across browsers so now we need to make it a little more appealing across different viewport sizes. Now, I don't consider myself a designer, but by applying some of the techniques we've learned throughout the previous chapters, I still think we can improve the aesthetics of our form.

You can view the styled form at `example_09-02`, and remember, if you don't already have the example code, you can grab it at `http://rwd.education`.

In this example, I've also included two versions of the style sheet: `styles.css` is the version that includes vendor prefixes (added via Autoprefixer) and `styles-unprefixed.css` is the CSS as written. The latter is probably easier to look at if you want to see how anything is being applied.

Here's how the form looks in a small viewport with some basic styling applied:

And here it is at a larger viewport:

If you look at the CSS you'll see many of the techniques we've looked at throughout previous chapters applied. For example, Flexbox (*Chapter 3, Fluid Layouts and Responsive Images*) has been used to create uniform spacing and flexibility for elements; transforms and transitions (*Chapter 8, Transitions, Transformations, and Animations*) so that the focused input fields grow and the ready/submit button flips vertically when it gains focus. Box-shadows and gradients (*Chapter 6, Stunning Aesthetics with CSS3*) are used to emphasize different areas of the form. Media queries (*Chapter 2, Media Queries – Supporting Differing Viewports*) are being used to switch the Flexbox direction for different viewport sizes and CSS Level 3 selectors (*Chapter 5, CSS3 – Selectors, Typography, Color Modes, and New Features*) are being used for selector negation.

We won't go over those techniques in detail here again. Instead, we will focus on a couple of peculiarities. Firstly, how to visually indicate required fields (and for bonus points indicate a value has been entered) and secondly, how to create a 'fill' effect when a field gets user focus.

Indicating required fields

We can indicate required input fields to a user using CSS alone. For example:

```
input:required {
  /* styles */
}
```

With that selector we could add a border or outline to the required fields or add a `background-image` inside the field. Basically the sky's the limit! We could also use a specific selector to target an input field that is required, only when it gains focus. For example:

```
input:focus:required {
  /* styles */
}
```

However, that would apply styles to the input box itself. What if we want to amend styles on the associated `label` element? I've decided I'd like to indicate required fields with a little asterisk symbol to the side of the label. But this presents a problem. Generally, CSS only lets us affect a change on elements if they are children of an element, the element itself, or a general or adjacent sibling of an element that receives 'state' (when I say state I'm talking about `hover`, `focus`, `active`, `checked`, and so on). In the following examples I'm using `:hover` but that would obviously be problematic for touch based devices.

```
.item:hover .item-child {}
```

With the preceding selector, styles are applied to `item-child` when item is hovered over.

```
.item:hover ~ .item-general-sibling {}
```

With this selector, when the item is hovered over, styles are applied to `item-general-sibling` if it is at the same DOM level as item and follows it.

```
.item:hover + .item-adjacent-sibling {}
```

Here, when the item is hovered over, styles are applied to `item-adjacent-sibling` if it is the adjacent sibling element of item (straight after it in the DOM).

So, back to our issue. If we have a form with labels and fields like this, with the label above the input (to give us the requisite basic layout), it leaves us a little stuck:

```
<div class="form-Input_Wrapper">
  <label for="film">The film in question?</label>
  <input id="film" name="film" type="text" placeholder="e.g. King
Kong" required/>
</div>
```

In this situation, using just CSS, there is no way to change the style of the label based upon whether the input is required or not (as it comes after the label in the markup). We could switch the order of those two elements in the markup but then we would end up with the label underneath the input.

However, Flexbox gives us the ability to visually reverse the order of elements (read all about that in *Chapter 3, Fluid Layouts and Responsive Images*, if you haven't already) with ease. That allows us to use this markup:

```
<div class="form-Input_Wrapper">
  <input id="film" name="film" type="text" placeholder="e.g. King
Kong" required/>
  <label for="film">The film in question?</label>
</div>
```

And then simply apply `flex-direction: row-reverse` or `flex-direction: column-reverse` to the parent. These declarations reverse the visual order of their child elements, allowing the desired aesthetic of the label above (smaller viewports), or to the left (larger viewports) of the input. Now we can get on with actually providing some indication of required fields and when they have received input.

Thanks to our revised markup, the adjacent sibling selector now makes this possible.

```
input:required + label:after { }
```

This selector essentially says, for every label that follows an input with a `required` attribute, apply the enclosed rules. Here is the CSS for that section:

```
input:required + label:after {
  content: "*";
  font-size: 2.1em;
  position: relative;
  top: 6px;
  display: inline-flex;
  margin-left: .2ch;
  transition: color, 1s;
}
```

```
input:required:invalid + label:after {
  color: red;
}

input:required:valid + label:after {
  color: green;
}
```

Then, if you focus on a required input and enter a relevant value, the asterisk changes color to green. It's a subtle but helpful touch.

 There are more selectors (both implemented and being specified) alongside all the ones we have already looked at. For the most up to date list, take a look at the latest editors draft of the Selectors Level 4 specification: http://dev.w3.org/csswg/selectors-4/

Creating a background fill effect

Back in *Chapter 6, Stunning Aesthetics with CSS3*, we learned how to generate linear and radial gradients as background-images. Sadly, it isn't possible to transition between two background-images (which makes sense as the browser effectively rasterizes the declaration into an image). However, we can transition between values of associated properties like background-position and background-size. We'll use this factor to create a fill effect when an input or textarea receives focus.

Here are the properties and values added to the input:

```
input:not([type="range"]),
textarea {
  min-height: 30px;
  padding: 2px;
  font-size: 17px;
  border: 1px solid #ebebeb;
  outline: none;
  transition: transform .4s, box-shadow .4s, background-position .2s;
  background: radial-gradient(400px circle,  #fff 99%, transparent
99%), #f1f1f1;
  background-position: -400px 90px, 0 0;
  background-repeat: no-repeat, no-repeat;
  border-radius: 0;
  position: relative;
}
```

```
input:not([type="range"]):focus,
textarea:focus {
  background-position: 0 0, 0 0;
}
```

In the first rule, a solid white radial gradient is being generated but positioned offset out of view. The background color that sits behind (the HEX value after the `radial-gradient`) is not offset and so provides a default color. When the input gains focus, the background position on the `radial-gradient` is set back to the default and because we have a transition on the background-image set, we get a nice transition between the two. The result being the appearance that the input is 'filled' with a different color when it gains focus.

Different browsers each have their own proprietary selectors and capabilities when it comes to styling parts of the native UI. For a handy list of lots of the specific selectors, Aurelius Wendelken compiled an impressive list. I made my own copy of it (or 'fork' in Git version control speak) for prosperity, which you can find at `https://gist.github.com/benfrain/403d3d3a8e2b6198e395`

Summary

In this chapter, we have learned how to use a host of new HTML5 form attributes. They enable us to make forms more usable than ever before and the data they capture more relevant. Furthermore, we can future-proof this new markup when needed with JavaScript polyfill scripts so that all users experience similar form features, regardless of the capability of their browser.

We're nearing the end of our responsive HTML5 and CSS3 journey. While we have covered an enormous amount in our time together, I'm conscious I'll never manage to impart all the information for every eventuality you'll encounter. Therefore, in the last chapter I'd like to take a higher level look at approaching a responsive web design and try and relate some solid best practices for getting your next/first responsive project off on the right footing.

10
Approaching a Responsive Web Design

In my favorite stories and films, there's usually a scene where a mentor passes on valuable advice and some magical items to the hero. You know those items will prove useful; you just don't know when or how.

Well, I'd like to assume the role of the mentor in this final chapter (plus my hair has waned, and I don't have the looks for the hero role). I would like you, my fine apprentice, to spare me just a few more moments of your time while I offer up some final words of advice before you set forth on your responsive quest.

This chapter will be half philosophical musings and guidance, and half grab-bag of unrelated tips and techniques. I hope at some point in your responsive adventures, these tips will prove useful. Here's what we'll cover:

- Getting designs in the browser and on real devices as soon as possible
- Letting the design dictate the breakpoints
- Embracing progressive enhancement
- Defining a browser support matrix
- Progressive enhancement in practice
- Linking CSS breakpoints to JavaScript
- Avoiding CSS frameworks in production
- Developing pragmatic solutions
- Writing the simplest possible code
- Hiding, showing, and loading content across viewports
- Letting CSS do the (visual) heavy lifting

- Using validators and linting tools
- Analyzing and testing web page performance (`webpagetest.org`)
- Embracing faster and more effective techniques
- Keeping an eye out for the next 'big' things

Get designs in the browser as soon as possible

The more responsive design work I have done, the more important I have found it to get designs up and running in a browser environment as soon as possible. If you are a designer as well as a developer, that simplifies matters. As soon as you have enough of a feel, visually, for what you need, you can get it prototyped in a browser and develop the idea further in a browser environment. This approach can be embraced more fully by letting go of high-fidelity full-page mock-ups altogether. Instead, consider things like Style Tiles—positioned between a moodboard and full mockup. The introduction to Style Tiles (`http://styletil.es/`) describes them as:

> *"Style Tiles are a design deliverable consisting of fonts, colors and interface elements that communicate the essence of a visual brand for the web."*

I've found graphical deliverables of this nature can be useful for presenting and communicating look and feel between stakeholders without resorting to the endless rounds of composites.

Let the design dictate the breakpoints

I'd like to reiterate a point made in previous chapters. Let the design define where breakpoints should be set. With a design in the browser, it makes this process far easier. You should always start amending the design from the smallest screen sizes upwards, so as the viewport size increases, you can see how far your design works before you need to introduce a breakpoint.

You'll also find that coding the design will be easier this way. Write the CSS for the smallest viewport first and then add any changes to different elements within media queries afterwards. For example:

```
.rule {
  /* Smallest viewport size styles */
}

@media (min-width: 40em) {
  .rule {
    /* Medium viewport size changes */
  }
}

@media (min-width: 70em) {
  .rule {
    /* Larger viewport size changes */
  }
}
```

View and use the design on real devices

If you can, start to build up a 'device lab' of older devices (phones/tablets) to view your work on. Having a number of varied devices is hugely beneficial. Not only does it let you feel how a design actually works across different devices, it also exposes layout/rendering peculiarities earlier in the process. After all, no one enjoys believing they have finished on a project to be told it doesn't work properly in a certain environment. Test early, test often! It need not cost the earth. For example, you can pick up older phone and tablet models on eBay, or buy them from friends/relatives as they upgrade.

Use tools such as BrowserSync to synchronize your work

One of the biggest time-saving tools I've used lately is **BrowserSync**. Once configured, as you save your work, any changes to things like CSS are injected into the browser without you needing to constantly refresh your screen. If that wasn't good enough, any other browser windows on devices you have on the same WiFi refresh too. This saves having to pick up each of your testing devices and clicking refresh with each change. It even synchronizes scrolling and clicks too. Highly recommended: `http://browsersync.io/`

Embracing progressive enhancement

In previous chapters, we have considered briefly the notion of progressive enhancement. It's an approach to development that I have found so useful in practice I think it bears repeating. The fundamental idea with progressive enhancement is that you begin all your front-end code (HTML, CSS, JavaScript) with the lowest common denominator in mind. Then, you progressively enhance the code for more capable devices and browsers. That may seem simplistic and it is, but if you are used to working the other way around; designing the optimum experience and then figuring out a way of making that thing work on lesser devices/browsers, you'll find progressive enhancement an easier approach.

Imagine a low powered, poorly featured device. No JavaScript, no Flexbox support, no CSS3/CSS4 support. In that instance what can you do to provide a usable experience?

Most importantly, you should write meaningful HTML5 markup that accurately describes the content. This is an easier task if you're building text and content-based websites. In that instance, concentrate on using elements such as `main`, `header`, `footer`, `article`, `section`, and `aside` correctly. Not only will it help you discern different sections of your code, it will also provide greater accessibility for your users at no extra cost.

If you're building something like a web-based application or visual UI components (carousels, tabs, accordions, and the like) you'll need to think about how to distil the visual pattern down into accessible markup.

The reason good markup is so crucial is that it provides a base level experience for all users. The more you can achieve with HTML, the less you have to do in CSS and JavaScript to support older browsers. And nobody, and I really mean nobody, likes writing the code to support older browsers.

For further reading and great practical examples on the subject, I would recommend the following two articles. They provide great insight into how fairly complex interactions can be handled with the constructs of HTML and CSS:

- http://www.cssmojo.com/how-to-style-a-carousel/
- http://www.cssmojo.com/use-radio-buttons-for-single-option/

It's by no means a simple feat to start thinking in this manner. It is however, an approach that is likely to serve you well in your quest to do as little as possible to support ailing browsers.

Now, about those browsers.

Defining a browser support matrix

Knowing the browsers and devices a web project needs to support up front can be crucial to developing a successful responsive web design. We've already considered why progressive enhancement is so useful in this respect; if done correctly, it means that the vast majority of your site will be functional on even the oldest browsers.

However, there may also be times when you need to start your experience with a higher set of prerequisites. Perhaps you are working on a project where JavaScript is essential, not an uncommon scenario. In that instance, you can still progressively enhance. Instead, you are merely enhancing from a different start point.

Whatever your starting point, the key thing is establishing what it is. Then, and only then, can you define and agree upon what visual and functional experiences the different browsers and devices that you intend to support will get.

Functional parity, not aesthetic parity

It's both unrealistic and undesirable to try and get any website looking and working the same in every browser. Besides quirks specific to certain browsers, there are essential functional considerations. For example, we have to consider things like touch targets for buttons and links on touch screens that aren't relevant on mouse-based devices.

Therefore, some part of your role as a responsive web developer is educating whoever you are answerable to (boss, client, shareholders) that 'supporting older browsers' does not mean 'looks the same in older browsers'. The line I tend to run with is that all browsers in the support matrix will get task parity, not visual parity. This means that if you have a checkout to build, all users will be able to get through the checkout and purchase goods. There may visual and interaction flourishes afforded to the users of more modern browsers, but the core task will be achievable by all.

Choosing the browsers to support

Typically, when we talk about which browsers to support, we're talking about how far back we need to look. Here are a couple of possibilities to consider, depending upon the situation.

If it's an existing website, look at visitor statistics (Google Analytics or similar). Armed with some figures you can likely do some rough calculations. For example: if cost of supporting browser X is less than the value produced by supporting browser X, then support browser X!

Also, consider that if there are browsers in the statistics that represent less than 10% of users, look further back and consider trends. How has usage changed over the last 3, 6, and 12 months? If it's currently 6% and that value has halved over the last 12 months you have a more compelling argument to consider ruling that browser out for specific enhancements.

If it's a new project and statistics are unavailable, I usually opt for a 'previous two' policy. This would be the current version plus the previous two versions of each browser. For example, if Internet Explorer 12 was the current version, look to offer your enhancements for that version plus IE10 and IE11 (the previous two). This choice is easier with the 'evergreen' browsers, the term given to browsers that continually update on a rapid release cycle (Firefox and Chrome for example).

Tiering the user experience

At this point, let's assume shareholders are educated and on board. Let's also assume you have a clear set of browsers that you would like to add enhanced experiences for. We can now set about tiering the experience. I like to keep things simple, so where possible I opt to define a simple 'base' tier and a more 'enhanced' tier.

The base experience being the minimal viable version of the site and the enhanced version being the most fully-featured and aesthetically pleasing version. You might need to accommodate more granularity in your tiers, for example, forking the experience in relation to browser features; support for Flexbox or support for `translate3d` for example. Regardless of how the tiers are defined, ensure you define them and what you expect to deliver with each. Then you can actually go about coding those tiers.

Practically delivering experience tiers

Right now, Modernizr facilitates the most robust manner to enhance and fork experiences based upon device capabilities. While it means adding a JavaScript dependency to your project, I think it is worthwhile.

Remember, that when writing CSS, the code outside of media queries and without selectors that require classes added by Modernizr should make up our 'base' experience.

Then thanks to Modernizr, we can layer on ever more enhanced experiences based upon the browser capabilities. If you refer back to `example_08-07` you can see this mind-set and code pattern applied to an off-canvas menu pattern.

Linking CSS breakpoints to JavaScript

Typically, with something web-based involving any sort of interaction, JavaScript will be involved. When you're developing a responsive project, it's likely you will want to do different things at different viewport sizes. Not just in CSS but also in JavaScript.

Let's suppose we want to invoke a certain JavaScript function when we reach a certain breakpoint in the CSS (remember that 'breakpoint' is the term used to define the point in which a responsive design should change significantly). Let's suppose that breakpoint is 47.5rem (with a 16px root font size that would equate to 760px) and we only want to run the function at that size. The obvious solution would be to simply measure the screen width and invoke the function if the value matched the same value you had decided for your CSS breakpoint.

JavaScript will always return the value of widths as pixels rather than REM values so that's the first complication. However, even if we set the breakpoints in CSS as pixel values, it would still mean two places to update and change those values when we are changing viewport sizes.

Thankfully, there is a better way. I first came across this technique on Jeremy Keith's website: `http://adactio.com/journal/5429/`

You can find the full code for this at `example_10-01`. However, the basic idea is that in CSS we insert something that can be easily read and understood by JavaScript.

Consider this in the CSS:

```css
@media (min-width: 20rem) {
    body::after {
        content: "Splus";
        font-size: 0;
    }
}
@media (min-width: 47.5rem) {
    body::after {
        content: "Mplus";
        font-size: 0;
    }
}
@media (min-width: 62.5rem) {
    body::after {
        content: "Lplus";
        font-size: 0;
    }
}
```

For each breakpoint that we want to communicate to JavaScript, we use the `after` pseudo element (you could use before too, either is just as good) and set the content of that pseudo element to be the name of our breakpoint. In our preceding example, I am using `Splus` for small screens and above, `Mplus` for medium screens and above, and `Lplus` for large screens and above. You can use whatever name makes sense to you and change the value whenever it makes sense to you (different orientations, different heights, different widths, and so on).

> The `::before` and `::after` pseudo elements are inserted into the DOM as shadow DOM elements. The `::before` pseudo element is inserted as the first child of its parent, and `::after` gets inserted as the last child. You can confirm this point in the developer tools of your browser.

With that CSS set, we can browse the DOM tree and see our `::after` pseudo element.

Then in our JavaScript, we can read this value. Firstly, we assign the value to a variable:

```
var size = window.getComputedStyle(document.body,':after').
getPropertyValue('content');
```

And then once we have it we can do something with it. To prove this concept I have made a simple self-invoking function (self-invoking simply means it is executed as soon as the browser parses it) that alerts a different message on page load depending upon the viewport size:

```
;(function alertSize() {
    if (size.indexOf("Splus") !=-1) {
        alert('I will run functions for small screens');
    }
    if (size.indexOf("Mplus") !=-1) {
```

```
        alert('At medium sizes, a different function could run');
    }
    if (size.indexOf("Lplus") !=-1) {
        alert('Large screen here, different functions if needed');
    }
})();
```

I'd hope you do something a little more interesting than alert a message in your projects but I think you will find great benefit in approaching the problem this way. You'll never be in danger of your CSS media queries and your width dependent JavaScript functions getting out of sync again.

Avoid CSS frameworks in production

There are a plethora of free frameworks available that aim to aid in the rapid prototyping and building of responsive websites. The two most common examples being Bootstrap (`http://getbootstrap.com/`) and Foundation (`http://foundation.zurb.com/`). While they are great projects, particularly for learning how to build responsive visual patterns, I think they should be avoided in production.

I've spoken to plenty of developers who start all projects with one of these frameworks and then amend them to fit their needs. This approach can be incredibly advantageous for rapid prototyping (for example, to illustrate some interaction to clients) but I think it's the wrong thing to do for projects you intend to take through to production.

Firstly, from a technical perspective, it's likely that starting with a framework will result in your project having more code than it actually needs. Secondly, from an aesthetic perspective, due to the popularity of these frameworks, it's likely your project will end up looking very similar to countless others.

Finally, if you only copy and paste code into your project and tweak it to your needs, you'll be unlikely to fully appreciate what's going on 'under the hood'. It's only by defining and solving the problems you have that you can master the code you place into your projects.

Coding pragmatic solutions

When it comes to front-end web development, 'ivory towered idealism' is a particular bugbear of mine. While we should always endeavor try to do things 'the right way', pragmatism must always win out. Let me give you an example (the finished code is `example_10-02`). Suppose we have a button to style that opens an off-canvas menu. Our natural inclination might be to mark it up something like this:

```
<button class="menu-toggle js-activate-off-canvas-menu">
    <span aria-label="site navigation">&#9776;</span> menu
</button>
```

Nice and simple. It's a button so we have used the `button` element. We have used two different HTML classes on the button, one will be a hook for CSS styling (`menu-toggle`), and the other as a JavaScript hook (`js-activate-off-canvas-menu`). In addition, we are using the `aria-label` attribute (ARIA is covered in more detail in *Chapter 4*, *HTML5 for Responsive Web Designs*) to communicate to screen readers the meaning of the character inside the `span`. In this example, we have used the HTML entity `&#9776;` which is the Unicode character 'Trigram for Heaven'. It's used here merely because it looks like the 'Hamburger icon' often used to symbolize a menu.

 If you'd like some solid advice on when and how to use the `aria-label` attribute I thoroughly recommend the following post on the Opera developer site by Heydon Pickering: `https://dev.opera.com/articles/ux-accessibility-aria-label/`

At this point, we seem to be in good shape. Semantic, highly accessible markup and classes to separate concerns. Great. Let's add some styling:

```
.menu-toggle {
    appearance: none;
    display: inline-flex;
    padding: 0 10px;
    font-size: 17px;
    align-items: center;
    justify-content: center;
    border-radius: 8px;
    border: 1px solid #ebebeb;
    min-height: 44px;
    text-decoration: none;
    color: #777;
}
```

```
[aria-label="site navigation"] {
    margin-right: 1ch;
    font-size: 24px;
}
```

Open this up in Firefox and this is what we see:

Not exactly what we were hoping for. In this case, the browser has decided we've gone too far; Firefox simply won't allow us to use a button element as a Flex container. This is a very real conflict for a developer. Do we choose the right element or the right aesthetic? Given that ideally, we would like to have the menu 'hamburger icon' on the left and the word 'menu' on the right.

You can see in the prior code we have used the appearance property. It's used to remove the browsers default styling for form elements, and has had a potted history. It was specified by the W3C for some time and then later dropped, leaving behind vendor-prefixed versions of the property in both Mozilla and WebKit browsers. Thankfully, it's now back on the standards track: http://dev.w3.org/csswg/css-ui-4/#appearance-switching

When a link becomes a button

I won't lie. Given this conundrum, I usually opt for the latter. Then I try and make up for the fact I'll be using the wrong element by choosing the next best element and changing the ARIA role where possible. In this case, while our menu button is certainly not a link (after all, it doesn't take the user anywhere), it's an a tag that I will be using. I've decided it's the next best thing—more like a button than any other element. And by using a link we can achieve the desired aesthetic. Here's the markup I'd go with. Note the added ARIA role on the a tag to indicate its role as a button (and not a link which is the default) to assistive technology:

```
<a class="menu-toggle js-activate-off-canvas-menu" role="button">
    <span aria-label="site navigation">&#9776;</span> menu
</a>
```

It's not perfect but it's a pragmatic solution. Here's the two (button element on the left, a tag on the right) next to each other in Firefox (version 39.0a2 if you're curious):

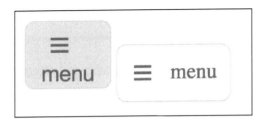

Of course, for this simplistic example, we could change the display from flex to block and play around with the padding until our desired aesthetic was achieved. Or, we could keep the button element and nest another semantically meaningless element (span) and make that a Flex container. There are trade-offs whichever approach you favor.

Ultimately, it's up to us to markup documents as sensibly as possible. At one end of the scale, there are developers that only markup with divs and spans to ensure no unwanted styles from the browser. The cost being no inherent meaning from their elements and in turn, no 'free' accessibility. At the other end of the scale are markup purists, who will only ever markup content in what they consider to be the correct element, regardless of how 'off' the visuals might end up as a result. There is a middle ground. I feel that's the sensible and most productive place to be.

Use the simplest code possible

It's easy to get drunk on the power that new techniques afford us. With this in mind, aim to solve your responsive problems in the simplest manner possible. For example, if you need to style the fifth item in a list of items and you have access to the markup, don't use an nth-child selector like this:

```
.list-item:nth-child(5) {
    /* Styles */
}
```

If you have access to the markup, make life easier by adding an HTML class to the item:

```
<li class="list-item specific-class">Item</li>
```

And then style the item with that simple class:

```
.specific-class {
    /* Styles */
}
```

Not only is this easier to understand, it gets you wider support for free (older versions of Internet Explorer don't support `nth-child` selectors).

Hiding, showing, and loading content across viewports

One of the commonly touted maxims regarding responsive web design is: if you don't have something on the screen at smaller viewports, you shouldn't have it there at larger ones either.

This means users should be able to accomplish all the same goals (buy a product, read an article, accomplish an interface task) at every viewport size. This is common sense. After all, as users ourselves, we've all felt the frustration of going to a website to accomplish a goal and being unable to, simply because we're using a smaller screen.

It also means that as screen real estate is more plentiful, we shouldn't feel compelled to add extra things just to fill the space (widgets, adverts, or links for example). If the user could live without those extras at smaller screen sizes, they'll manage just fine at bigger ones. Displaying extra content at larger viewport sizes also means that either the content was there at smaller viewports and was merely hidden (typically using `display: none;` in CSS) or it's being loaded in at a particular viewport size (with the help of JavaScript). Succinctly: either the content is loaded but not viewable, or it's viewable yet probably superfluous.

In broad terms I think the above maxim is sound advice. If nothing else, it makes designers and developers question more thoroughly the content they display on screen. However, as ever in web design, there are always going to be exceptions.

As far as possible, I resist loading in new markup for different viewports but occasionally it's a necessity. I've worked on complex user interfaces that rightfully required different markup and designs at wider viewports.

In this instance, JavaScript was used to replace one area of markup with another. It wasn't the ideal scenario but it was the most pragmatic. If, for whatever reason, the JavaScript failed, users got the smallest screen layout. They could accomplish all the same goals, just the layout was sub-optimal for achieving the task at hand.

These are the kind of choices you will likely face as you code more and more complex responsive web designs, and you'll need to use your own judgment as to what the best choice is in any given scenario. However, it's not a cardinal sin if you toggle the visibility of the odd bit of markup with `display: none` to achieve your goal.

Let CSS do the (visual) heavy lifting

It's a fact that JavaScript provides a level of interactivity on webpages that simply cannot be achieved with CSS alone. However, where possible, when it comes to visuals, we should still do all the heavy lifting with CSS. In practicality, this means not animating menus in, out, on and off, with JavaScript alone (I'm looking at you jQuery `show` and `hide` methods). Instead, use JavaScript to perform simple class changes on the relevant section of the markup. Then let that class change trigger the menu being shown/animated in CSS.

For the best performance, when toggling classes in the HTML, ensure you add a class as close as possible to the item you want to effect. For example, if you want a pop-up box to appear over another element, add the class on the closest shared parent element. This will ensure that, for the sake of optimal performance, only that particular section of the page is made 'dirty' and the browser shouldn't have to paint vast areas of the page again. For a great, free, course on performance, take a look at Paul Lewis's 'Browser Rendering Optimization' course: `https://www.udacity.com/course/browser-rendering-optimization--ud860`

Validators and linting tools

Generally speaking, writing HTML and CSS is pretty forgiving. You can nest the odd thing incorrectly, miss the occasional quotation mark or self-closing tag and not always notice a problem. Despite this, on an almost weekly basis I manage to befuddle myself with incorrect markup. Sometimes it's a slip-up like accidentally typing an errant character. Other times it's school-boy errors like nesting a `div` inside a `span` (invalid markup as a `span` is an inline element and a `div` is a block level element—leading to unpredictable results). Thankfully, there are great tools to help out. At worst, if you're encountering a weird issue, head over to `http://http/validator.w3.org/` and paste your markup in there. It will point out all errors along with line numbers, helping you to easily fix things up.

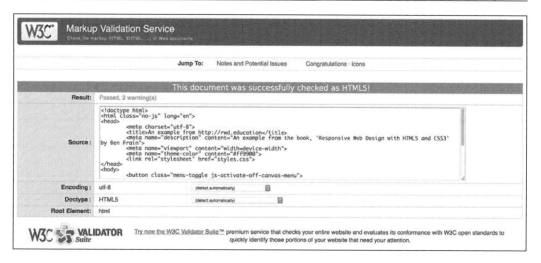

Better still, install and configure 'linting' tools for your HTML, CSS, and JavaScript. Or, choose a text editor with some degree of sanity-checking built in. Then problem areas are flagged up in your code as you go. Here's an example of a simple spelling error in CSS flagged up by Microsoft's 'Code' editor:

Like a clown, I've clumsily typed `widthh` instead of `width`. The editor has spotted this fact and pointed out the error of my ways and offered some sensible alternatives. Embrace these tools where possible. There are better uses of your time than tracking down simple syntax errors in your code.

Performance

Considering the performance of your responsive web designs is as important as the aesthetics. However, performance presents something of a moving target. For example, browsers update and improve the way they handle assets, new techniques are discovered that supersede existing 'best practices', technologies eventually get enough browser support that they become viable for widespread adoption. The list goes on.

There are however, some basic implementation details that are pretty solid (well, until HTTP2 is common place, more of which shortly). These are:

1. Minimize the number of assets (for example, don't load 15 JavaScript files if you concatenate them into one).

2. Minimize the page weight (if you can compress images to a fraction of their original size you should).

3. Defer non-essential assets (if you can put off loading CSS and JavaScript until the page has rendered it can greatly increase the perceived load time).

4. Ensure the page is usable as soon as possible (usually a by-product of doing all the preceding steps).

There are a number of great tools available to measure and optimize performance too. My personal favorite being `http://webpagetest.org/`. At its simplest, you pick a URL and click on **START TEST**. It will show you a complete analysis of the page but even more usefully, it shows a 'filmstrip' view of the page as it has loaded, allowing you to concentrate on getting the rendered page complete sooner. Here's an example of the filmstrip view of the BBC home page:

Whenever trying to optimize performance, ensure you take measurements before you begin (otherwise, you have no idea how effective your performance work has been). Then make amendments, test, and repeat.

The next big things

One of the things that make front-end web development interesting, is that things change rapidly. There is always something new to learn and the web community is always figuring out better, faster, and more effective ways of solving problems.

For example, three years before writing this edition of the book responsive images (`srcset` and the `picture` element that are detailed in *Chapter 3, Fluid Layouts and Responsive Images*) simply didn't exist. Back then, we had to use clever third party workarounds to serve up more appropriate images to different viewport sizes. Now that common need has been rationalized into a W3C standard we can all now use and enjoy.

Similarly, not long ago, Flexbox was just a twinkle in a specification writer's eyes. Even when the specification evolved it was still difficult to implement until Andrey Sitnik and those clever folks at Evil Martians (`https://evilmartians.com/`) created Autoprefixer and we are subsequently able to use it cross-browser with relative ease.

The future holds yet more exciting capabilities for us to understand and implement. We've already mentioned Service Workers in *Chapter 4, HTML5 for Responsive Web Designs*, for example (`http://www.w3.org/TR/service-workers/`); a better way to create offline capable web-based applications.

There is also 'Web Components' a collection of standards made up of Shadow DOM (`http://w3c.github.io/webcomponents/spec/shadow/`), Custom Elements (`http://w3c.github.io/webcomponents/spec/custom/`) and HTML Imports (`http://w3c.github.io/webcomponents/spec/imports/`) that will allow us to create entirely bespoke and re-usable components.

Then there are the other forthcoming enhancements such as CSS Level 4 Selectors (`http://dev.w3.org/csswg/selectors-4/`) and CSS Level 4 Media Queries, which we covered in some detail in *Chapter 2, Media Queries – Supporting Differing Viewports*.

Finally, another big change looming on the horizon is HTTP2. It promises to make many of our current best practices, bad practices. For a good in-depth primer I'd suggest reading *http2 explained* by Daniel Stenberg (it's a free PDF). Alternatively, for a lighter summary, read Matt Wilcox's excellent post, *HTTP2 for front-end web developers* (`https://mattwilcox.net/web-development/http2-for-front-end-web-developers`).

Summary

As we reach the end of our time together, your humble author hopes to have related all the techniques and tools you'll need to start building your next website or web application responsively.

It's my conviction that by approaching web projects with a little forethought and by making a few modifications to existing workflows, practices, and techniques, it's possible to create responsive web designs that provide fast, flexible, and maintainable websites that can look incredible regardless of the device used to visit them.

We've covered a wealth of information in our time together; techniques, technologies, performance optimizations, specifications, workflow, tooling, and more. I wouldn't expect anybody to take it all in in one read. Therefore, next time you need to remember this or that syntax, or refresh your mind about one of the responsive related subjects we've covered, I hope you'll dip back in to these pages. I'll be right here waiting for you.

Until then, I wish you good fortunes in your responsive web design quests.

See you again sometime.

Index

Symbols

\<address\> element
about 90
URL 90
::after pseudo-element 111
\<article\> element
about 86
URL 86
\<aside\> element
about 86
URL 86
\<a\> tag 83
::before pseudo-element 111
\<b\> element
about 91
URL 91
\<details\> element
about 87-89
URL 89
\<em\> element 91
\<figcaption\> element
about 87
URL 87
\<figure\> element
about 87
URL 87
:first-line pseudo-element 130
@font-face CSS rule
about 133
URL 133
used, for implementing web fonts 134-136
\<footer\> element
about 89
URL 89

:has pseudo class 132
\<header\> element
about 89
URL 89
\<i\> element 91
@import
used, for combining media queries 24
:last-child selector 121
\<main\> element
about 84
URL 84
\<nav\> element
about 85
URL 85
\<section\> element
about 85
URL 85
\<summary\> element 87-89

A

alignment properties, Flexbox
align-items property 57
align-self property 58, 59
justify-content property 59-61
possible alignment values 59
reference link 59
alpha channels 139
alpha transparency 137
alternate languages
specifying 80
Android Software Development Kit (SDK)
URL 33
animating, with CSS3
about 225-228
animation-fill-mode property 228

application programming interfaces (APIs) 77
audio
  adding, in HTML5 97, 98
audio tags 99
Autoprefixer
  about 48
  URL 48

B

backface-visibility property
  about 220
  URL 220
background fill effect
  creating 256, 257
background gradients
  'extent' keywords, for responsive sizing 150, 151
  about 146
  linear-gradient notation 147
  patterns 152, 153
  radial background gradients 149
Blink 247
Bootstrap
  URL 267
Box Alignment
  reference link 50
box shadows
  about 144
  inset shadow 144
  multiple shadows, adding 145
  spread 145, 146
  URL 146
breakpoint 12
browser support
  defining 263
  functional considerations 263
  selecting 263, 264
  setting 3, 4
  text editors 5
  tooling editors 5
browser support, Flexbox
  auto-prefixing solution, selecting 48
  prefixing issue 47
BrowserSync
  about 261
  URL 261

C

Candidate Recommendation (CR) 20
cascading style sheet. *See* CSS
Character Data (CDATA) marker 191
character encoding
  reference link 81
  specifying 81
combined media queries
  reference link 32
cross axis alignment, Flexbox
  baseline 59
  center 59
  flex-end 59
  flex-start 59
  stretch 59
CSS
  about 26
  conditional logic, for media queries 21
  feature forks, facilitating 112
  media queries, combining 24
  performance, optimizing 165
  SVG, animating 191-193
  SVG properties 191
  SVG values 191
  wrapping, in media queries 28
CSS3
  CSS multi-column layouts 105-107
  features 105
  forms, styling with 251-253
CSS3 2D transforms
  defining 210
  matrix 215, 216
  rotate 214
  scale 211
  skew 215
  transform-origin property 217
  translate 212
  URL 216
CSS3 3D transformations
  about 218-221
  transform3d property 221, 222
  URL 220
  using, with progressive enhancement 222-225

CSS3 color formats
about 137
alpha channels 139
color manipulation, with CSS Color
    Module Level 4 140
HSL color 138, 139
RGB color 137
CSS3 selectors
about 116
attribute selectors, for selecting classes 120
attribute selectors, for selecting IDs 120
CSS3 attribute selectors 117
CSS3 substring matching attribute
    selectors 117
gotchas, with attribute selection 119, 120
URL 128
CSS3 structural pseudo-classes
:first-line pseudo-element 130
:last-child selector 121
about 121
empty (:empty) selector 129
negation (:not) selector 128
nth-based selection, in responsive web
    designs 125-127
nth-based selectors 122, 123
nth-child selectors 122
CSS3 substring matching attribute selectors
'beginning with' 118
'contains an instance of' 118
'ends with' 119
about 117
CSS3 transitions
defining 204-206
fun transitions, for responsive websites 210
multiple properties, declaring 208
properties 206
timing functions, defining 208, 209
transition shorthand property 207
URL 204
using 204-206
CSS breakpoints
linking, to JavaScript 265, 266
CSS calc
about 131
URL 131

CSS clipping
about 166
URL 166
CSS Color Module Level 4
URL 140
used, for color manipulation 140
CSS Conditional Rules
URL 112
CSS custom properties 130, 131
CSS Extensions module
URL 131
CSS filters
about 158
available CSS filters 159-164
combining 164
URL 158
CSS frameworks
avoiding, in production 267
CSS Level 4 selectors
:has pseudo class 132
about 131
responsive viewport-percentage
    lengths 132, 133
URL 131
CSS masks
about 166
URL 166
CSS multi-column layouts
column divider, adding 107, 108
fixed columns 107
for responsive designs 105-107
gap, adding 107, 108
reference link 108
variable width 107
CSS rule 104
CSS Transforms Module Level 1
URL 221
CSS Transforms Module Level 3
URL 20
CSS variables
about 21, 130, 131
URL 21
Cufón
URL 133
custom @font-face typography 136

D

data URIs 180, 181
defs tag 175
desc tag 174
doctype 79, 80
dots per centimeter (dpcm) 157
dots per inch (dpi) 157
Draw SVG
  URL 176

E

easing function
  references 209
Embedded Content
  about 72
  reference link 72
  URL 75
empty (:empty) selector 129
Extensible Markup Language (XML) 172
external style sheet
  used, for styling SVG 190, 191

F

fallback capability
  for older browsers 99
feature forks
  conditionals, combining 114
  facilitating, in CSS 112
  feature queries 112, 113
  Modernizr 114, 115
  text ellipsis 116
fixed pixel design
  converting, to fluid proportional
    layout 40-44
Flexible Box (FlexBox)
  about 39, 46
  browser support 47
  characteristics 49
  different layouts, inside different media
    queries 53, 54
  features 46
  implementation 71
  iterations 47
  need for 45

reference link 47, 59, 71
Flexbox, characteristics
  alignment properties 55-57
  flex property 61-64
  footer, adding 64, 65
  inline-flex 54, 55
  items order, reversing 52
  offset items, listing 50, 51
  perfect vertically centered text 49, 50
  source order, modifying 65-70
flex property
  about 61-64
  flex-basis 62
  flex-grow 62
  flex-shrink 62
floats 46
Fluid Grids
  reference link 40
fluid layouts 39
fluid proportional layout
  fixed pixel design, converting 40-44
  floats 45
  inline-block 45
  table 46
  table-cell 46
  whitespace 45
  with Flexbox 45
Font Deck
  URL 134
Font Squirrel
  URL 134
forms
  about 232, 233
  autocomplete attribute 236, 237
  autofocus attribute 236
  background fill effect, creating 256, 257
  components 233
  datalist element 237, 238
  list attribute 237, 238
  placeholder attribute 234
  reference link 237, 250
  required attribute 234, 235
  styling, with CSS3 251-253
  styling, with required input fields 254, 255
Foundation
  URL 267

G

g element 175
Google web fonts
  URL 134
gotchas
  with attribute selection 119, 120
graceful degradation 4
graphical user interface (GUI) 176
GreenSock
  SVG, animating with 194, 195
  URL 193
Grid Layout Module Level 1
  about 71
  reference link 71
gzip
  about 30
  URL 30

H

h1-h6 elements
  about 90
  URL 90
HiDPI devices
  media queries, using 28
high-resolution background images 157
horizontal scrolling panels
  creating 110-112
HTML5
  <a> tag 83
  about 78, 79
  easy-going code 81, 82
  elements, selecting 94
  elements, using 93
  media, embedding 97
  obsolete features 92
  references 101
  semantic elements 83
  text-level semantics 91
  URL 77
HTML5 Boilerplate
  URL 82
HTML5 markup 82
HTML5 page
  about 79
  alternate languages, specifying 80

character encoding, specifying 81
doctype 79, 80
HTML tag 80
lang attribute 80
Hue, Saturation, and Lightness
    (HSL) color 138, 139

I

IcoMoon
  URL 183
Iconizr
  URL 181
icon services
  URL 176
  used, for creating SVG 176
iFrames 99, 100
image editing packages
  used, for creating SVG 176
image sprites
  generating 181
img tag 178
Inkscape
  URL 176
inline-block
  about 45
  reference link 45
inline-flex 54, 55
inline SVG
  colors, modifying 185
  dual-tone icons, creating 185, 186
  graphical objects, re-using 183, 184
  graphical objects, re-using from external
      sources 186
  inserting 182
input types
  about 239
  color 246
  date 246, 247
  email 239, 240
  month 248
  number 240, 241
  number, with max range 241
  number, with min range 241
  number, with step attribute 241
  pattern 245, 246
  range 249

search 244
tel 243
time 246-249
url 242
week 248
inset shadow
creating 144
internal styles
used, for styling SVG 191
items order, Flexbox
column reverse, performing 53
items, laying out vertically 53

J

JavaScript
CSS breakpoints, linking 265, 266
SVG, animating with 193
jQuery library
URL 251
justify-content property
about 59-61
reference link 56

L

lang attribute
about 80
URL 80
linear-gradient notation
about 147
color stops 148, 149
fallback, adding 149
gradient direction, specifying 147
reference link 149
link tags
media queries, implementing 22
linting tools 272, 273

M

matrix transformations
about 216
URL 216
media
audio, adding 97, 98
audio tags 99

embedding, in HTML5 97
fallback capability, for older browsers 99
video, adding 97, 98
video tags 99
media queries
about 20
benefits 20
capabilities, for test 25, 26
combining 23
combining, in CSS 24
combining, with @import 24
conditional logic, in CSS 21
considerations 29
considerations, for combining
or writing 31, 32
CSS, wrapping 28
implementation tips, for SVG 200
implementing, in link tags 22
inside SVGs 199, 200
linking, to different CSS files 29
nesting 30
reference link 20
separating, practicalities 30
syntax 21
used, for altering design 26-28
used, for HiDPI devices 28
Media Queries Level 4
about 35
deprecated features 26
environmental features 38
interacting, with media features 36, 37
media features, hovering 37
media features, scripting 35, 36
URL 35
Modernizr
about 79, 114, 115
URL 79
used, for feature detection 115, 116
multiple background images
about 154
background position, setting 155, 156
background shorthand 156
background size, setting 155
multiple shadows
creating 145

N

namespace 174
negation (:not) selector 128
non-supporting browsers
  dealing with 250, 251
non-visual desktop access (NVDA)
  about 96
  URL 96
nth-based selectors
  about 122, 123
  example 123-125
nth-child selectors 122

O

object tag
  about 178
  reference link 178

P

Perspective Page View Navigation
  URL 221
picture element
  fangled image formats, facilitating 75
  used, for art direction 74
pixels (px)
  about 23
  reference link 23
polyfill
  about 79
  handling 250
progressive enhancement
  about 4
  embracing 262
properties, CSS3 transitions
  transition-delay 206
  transition-duration 206
  transition-property 206
  transition-timing-function 206
Proposed Recommendation (PR) 20

R

radial background gradients
  about 149
  syntax 150

Red, Green, and Blue (RGB) color 137
regular expressions
  about 245
  URL 245
render blocking CSS
  reference link 29
repeating background gradients
  creating 151, 152
responsive HTML5 video
  about 99, 100
  reference link 100
responsive images
  about 40, 71
  advanced switching, with sizes 73, 74
  advanced switching, with srcset 73, 74
  art direction, with picture element 74
  intrinsic problem 71, 72
  resolution switching, with srcset 72, 73
responsive viewport-percentage lengths
  URL 132
  vh 132
  vmax 132
  vmin 132
  vw 132
responsive web design
  about 2
  breakpoints, setting 260
  custom @font-face typography 136
  defining 2
  enhancements 275
  in browser environment 260
  link, used as button 269
  nth-based selection 125-127
  performance 274
  pragmatic solutions, coding 268, 269
  references 275
  simplest code, using 270
  using, on real devices 261
  viewing 261
responsive web page
  amending, for larger screen 13-16
  building 5
  HTML file, creating 6-9
  images, taming 9-11
  media queries, entering 12, 13
  shortcomings 17

root SVG element
  about 173
  references 174

S

scalable vector graphics. *See* **SVG**
Selectors Level 4
  URL 256
semantic elements
  <address> element 90
  <article> element 86
  <aside> element 86
  <details> element 87-89
  <figcaption> element 86
  <figure> element 86
  <footer> element 89
  <header> element 89
  <main> element 84
  <nav> element 85
  <section> element 85
  <summary> element 87-89
  about 83
  h1-h6 elements 90
  URL 84
sIFR
  URL 133
sizes attribute
  browser support 74
  used, for advanced switching 73, 74
Sketch
  URL 176
SMIL animations
  about 189
  limitations 189, 190
  URL 188
Snap.svg
  URL 193
Spackling Paste 79
spinner controls 240
srcset
  used, for advanced switching 73, 74
  used, for switching resolution 72, 73
structural pseudo-classes
  about 128
  URL 128

Style Tiles
  URL 260
SVG
  about 17, 169
  animating, with CSS 191-193
  animating, with GreenSock 194, 195
  animating, with JavaScript 193
  capabilities 188
  creating, with icon services 176
  creating, with image editing packages 176
  history 171
  oddities 188
  optimizing 196
  references 201
  SMIL animations 188, 189
  styling, with external style sheet 190, 191
  styling, with internal styles 191
  URL 171
  used, as filters 196-199
  with media queries 199, 200
SVG document
  about 172, 173
  defs tag 174
  desc tag 174
  g element 175
  namespace 174
  paths 175
  root SVG element 173
  shapes 175
  title tag 174
SVG-edit
  URL 176
SVG For Everybody
  about 186
  URL 186
SVG, inserting
  as background image 179, 180
  browser implementation 188
  caveats 187
  data URIs 180, 181
  image sprites, generating 181
  into web pages 177
  methods 187
  with img tag 178
  with object tag 178
SVGO
  URL 196

SVGOMG
  URL 196
SVG paths 175
SVG properties
  about 191
  URL 191
SVG shapes 175

T

table 46
table-cell 46
text editors 5
text ellipsis 109-116
text-level semantics
  <b> element 91
  <em> element 91
  <i> element 91
  about 91
  URL 91, 92
text-overflow property
  URL 109
text shadows
  about 142, 143
  blur value, omitting 143
  multiple text shadows, adding 143
  reference link 144
title tag 174
tooling editors 5
transform-origin property
  URL 218
transforms
  matrix 211
  rotate 211
  scale 211
  skew 211
  translate 211
translate
  about 212
  used, for centering absolutely positioned
    elements 212-214
translate3d
  URL 222
tweening 189
Typekit
  URL 134

U

Ultimate CSS Gradient Editor
  URL 151
Uniform Resource Identifier (URI) 180
user experience
  delivering 264
  tiering 264

V

validators
  about 272, 273
  URL 272
Velocity.js
  URL 193
video
  adding, in HTML5 97, 98
video tags 99
viewport meta tag
  about 33, 34
  reference link 34
viewports
  about 8
  content, displaying 271
  content, hiding 271
  content, loading 271
  heavy lifting, with CSS 272

W

W3C validator
  URL 82
Web Accessibility Initiative-Accessible Rich
    Internet Applications (WAI-ARIA)
  about 78, 94, 95
  ARIA 96
  correct elements, using 96
  roles, avoiding for semantic elements 95
  URL 96
Web Content Accessibility Guidelines
    (WCAG)
  about 78, 94, 95
  URL 94, 95
WebP
  about 75
  URL 75

web pages
  SVG, inserting 177
WebPagetest
  URL 274
Webshims lib
  URL 250
web typography
  @font-face 134-136
  @font-face CSS rule 133
  about 133
  custom @font-face typography 136
whitespace 45
word wrapping
  about 108, 109
  horizontal scrolling panels,
      creating 110-112
  text ellipsis 109, 110
Working Draft (WD) 20

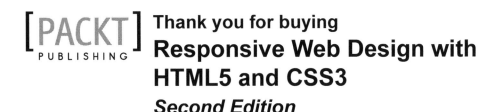

Thank you for buying
Responsive Web Design with HTML5 and CSS3
Second Edition

About Packt Publishing

Packt, pronounced 'packed', published its first book, *Mastering phpMyAdmin for Effective MySQL Management*, in April 2004, and subsequently continued to specialize in publishing highly focused books on specific technologies and solutions.

Our books and publications share the experiences of your fellow IT professionals in adapting and customizing today's systems, applications, and frameworks. Our solution-based books give you the knowledge and power to customize the software and technologies you're using to get the job done. Packt books are more specific and less general than the IT books you have seen in the past. Our unique business model allows us to bring you more focused information, giving you more of what you need to know, and less of what you don't.

Packt is a modern yet unique publishing company that focuses on producing quality, cutting-edge books for communities of developers, administrators, and newbies alike. For more information, please visit our website at www.packtpub.com.

Writing for Packt

We welcome all inquiries from people who are interested in authoring. Book proposals should be sent to author@packtpub.com. If your book idea is still at an early stage and you would like to discuss it first before writing a formal book proposal, then please contact us; one of our commissioning editors will get in touch with you.

We're not just looking for published authors; if you have strong technical skills but no writing experience, our experienced editors can help you develop a writing career, or simply get some additional reward for your expertise.

Sass and Compass for Designers

ISBN: 978-1-84969-454-4   Paperback: 274 pages

Produce and maintain cross-browser CSS files easier than ever before with the Sass CSS preprocessor and its companion authoring framework, Compass

1.   Simple, clear, and thorough. This book ensures you don't need to be a programming mastermind to wield the power of Sass and Compass!

2.   Previously tricky and time-consuming CSS tasks will become trivial. Easily produce cross-browser CSS3 gradients, shadows, and transformations along with image sprites, data URIs, and more.

3.   Follow along with installing, setting up, and working through an entire project, implementing the Sass and Compass techniques and tools as we go.

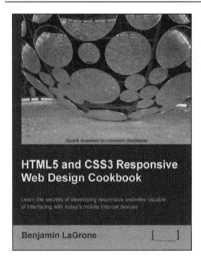

HTML5 and CSS3 Responsive Web Design Cookbook

ISBN: 978-1-84969-544-2   Paperback: 204 pages

Learn the secrets of developing responsive websites capable of interfacing with today's mobile Internet devices

1.   Learn the fundamental elements of writing responsive website code for all stages of the development life cycle.

2.   Create the ultimate code writer's resource using logical workflow layers.

3.   Full of usable code for immediate use in your website projects.

4.   Written in an easy-to-understand language giving knowledge without preaching.

Please check **www.PacktPub.com** for information on our titles

HTML5 and CSS3 Transition, Transformation, and Animation

ISBN: 978-1-84951-994-6   Paperback: 136 pages

A handy guide to understanding Microdata, the new JavaScript APIs, and the new form elements in HTML5 and CSS3 along with transition, transformation, and animation using lucid code samples

1. Discover the semantics of HTML5 and Microdata.

2. Understand the concept of the CSS3 Flexible Box model.

3. Explore the main features of HTML5 such as canvas, offline web application, geolocation, audio and video elements, and web storage.

4. Master the tools and utilities in HTML5 and CSS3.

Mastering CSS [Video]

ISBN: 978-1-78439-187-4   Duration: 03:00 hrs

Get to grips with CSS best practices to create modern, responsive, and retina-ready websites

1. Understand the role of CSS in responsive web design.

2. Write modular, reusable CSS for better management of style sheets.

3. Learn everything there is to know about creating a multi-column layout and menu using floats.

4. Explore web fonts, icon fonts, SVG, and techniques used to support HiDPI devices.

Please check **www.PacktPub.com** for information on our titles

Printed in Great
Britain
by Amazon